Feminists Reclaim Mentorship

SUNY series in Feminist Criticism and Theory

Michelle A. Massé, editor

Feminists Reclaim Mentorship
An Anthology

Edited by

Nancy K. Miller and Tahneer Oksman

Published by State University of New York Press, Albany

For information, contact State University of New York Press, Albany, NY
www.sunypress.edu

Library of Congress Cataloging-in-Publication Data

Names: Miller, Nancy K., 1941– editor. | Oksman, Tahneer, editor.
Title: Feminists reclaim mentorship : an anthology / edited by Nancy K. Miller and Tahneer Oksman.
Description: Nancy K. Miller and Tahneer Oksman, [2023] | Series: SUNY series in feminist criticism and theory | Includes bibliographical references.
Identifiers: LCCN 2022023973 | ISBN 9781438491851 (hardcover : alk. paper) | ISBN 9781438491868 (ebook) | ISBN 9781438491844 (pbk. : alk. paper)
Subjects: LCSH: Mentoring. | Feminism.
Classification: LCC BF637.M45 F46 2023 | DDC 158.3—dc23/eng/20221115
LC record available at https://lccn.loc.gov/2022023973

10 9 8 7 6 5 4 3 2 1

For those who came before,
and for those who will come after.

And where will such mentoring come from? whose power will validate it?

—Adrienne Rich, "Arts of the Possible"

Be the supervisor and mentor you wish you once had.

—Roxane Gay, Work Friend

Contents

Part II. Rearview Mirror: Mentoring at a Distance

Part III. The Traffic in Mentors: Horizontal Scripts

Acknowledgments

We began work on this book a few months before the COVID pandemic hit New York with spectacular force. This is also to say that in sync with the temporalities and frustrations of lockdown, the trajectory of our book has been a long and winding road. We are beyond grateful to the anthology's writers, whose patience made it possible for us to reach the promised land of publication. These are just the beginning of our debts.

Our thinking about the book, its shape and tone, benefited immensely from many conversations with friends, colleagues, journalists, and contributors. We thank: Victoria Rosner and Rachel Adams from our incipient writing group. Writer and activist Ellen Cassedy shared valuable insider information about the documentary *9 to 5*, and the movement. Nan Bauer-Maglin provided useful insights about the innovative mentoring process at Girls Write Now. We received important advice from Jacob Aplaca, Maurice Biriotti, Ari M. Brostoff, Sarah Burnes, Cecelia Cancellaro, Sara Jo Cohen, Jojo Karlin, Cindi Katz, Lynn Povich, and Ellen Sweet. Not to mention family members, Sandy Petrey and Jonathan Waldauer.

We also thank Allison Hughes and Daniel Drake for meticulous copyediting, and student assistants Sharifa Hampton and Sophia Yi Nian Yip for their timely and generous material support. Tahneer is grateful to Marymount Manhattan College's Faculty Development Committee, Division Chair Jennifer Brown, and President Kerry Walk for supporting this project with a course release.

At State University of New York Press, we are grateful to series editor Michelle A. Massé for welcoming the project, and to senior acquisitions editor Rebecca Colesworthy for shepherding the editorial process with deft and tact. This includes the choice of our anonymous readers, whose incisive critical gaze has moved our thinking beyond our original project.

Portions from "The Making of an Intellectual" by Michele Faith Wallace previously appeared on her personal blog (www.michelefwallace. com) and appears here by permission of the author.

"Ready" by Joy Ladin previously appeared in *Shekhinah Speaks*, published by Selva Oscura Press in 2022, and appears here by permission of the author. Joyladin@gmail.com.

Siri Hustvedt's "Mentor Ghosts" originally appeared in *Mothers, Fathers, Others*, published by Simon & Schuster in 2021 and appears here by permission of the author.

Introduction

Mutual Engagements

Nancy K. Miller and Tahneer Oksman

> The word itself, *mentor*, triggers a hunger from a time in my life that is now gone, the ache for an attachment to someone who recognized me as worthy of the life I had decided upon.
>
> —Siri Hustvedt, "Mentor Ghosts"

> My thought about mentoring is that it is hierarchical, and I want people to be engaged with me so I can engage with them and we're doing something collaboratively.
>
> —Daná-Ain Davis, "Widening the Way"

"It's like she wants to be my mentor!" Tess McGill, a go-getting temp from Staten Island with Farah Fawcett hair, gushes to her boyfriend early in the eighties' workplace comedy *Working Girl*. The would-be mentor is Katharine Parker, a sleek high-powered executive in corporate Manhattan. "Watch me. Learn from me," she instructs, assuring her new secretary that their office relationship will be "a two-way street" (*Working Girl*). Tess learns so well she ends up toppling Katharine, becoming a boss herself.

If *Working Girl* paints a portrait of female ambition in the universe of urban late twentieth-century capitalism, its crude version of women mentoring women parodies the classical model of mentorship. Mentoring takes its name from a character in Homer's *Odyssey*. An old companion of Odysseus, Mentor is asked to protect the great hero's son Telemachus. Endowed with the powers of the goddess Athena, who borrows the man's form to swoop down from Olympus, Mentor rescues the boy from dangerous situations and educates him for his future role as ruler.

From the start, mentoring was inscribed in the maw of power relations and as an affair between men. Paternal and patriarchal, it's a structure that, minus the goddess, has nevertheless been replicated in relationships between women as well as those involving other marginalized groups. The legacy of bonds between men, shaped by the vertical architecture of inherited privilege, is familiar to the two of us from our lives in academia. In the modern university, the cutthroat model of competition through individual striving is veiled only by the thin veneer of professionalism, which increasingly has adopted the values of top-down corporate organization.

Until affirmative action forced open the doors of privilege, and for decades after, Homer's legacy prevailed, and it still haunts professional worlds. The situation is yet more complicated for first-generation students as well as students and professors of color for whom, Ashna Ali writes in this volume, "the terms and structures of traditional mentorship in academia have been shaped by white masculinity." Adjuncts and part-time instructors in particular, who are hired on limited contracts and on whom the university more and more relies to staff its classes, typically find themselves like Tess stuck in the typing pool, doing the necessary labor that upholds the academic workforce.

Through comedy and exaggeration, hugely popular movies like *Working Girl* expose the underlying power flows that govern so much of American workplace culture, not least in and around the academy. Why, then, continue to evoke this hierarchical model when it's long been clear that whatever the gender dynamic, this arrangement is not advantageous for many women and minorities, including those who identify outside the traditional gender binary. We, a working mentoring pair, for whom mentorship has been a sustaining intellectual and emotional project, don't believe this history should limit our ideas of what mentorship can do and mean.

Twenty-first-century ethics requires a reset in how we think about the model, notably what happens when we shift the emphasis from the lock of a binary in isolation to a pair or group located within specific social and political contexts. Despite Audre Lorde's oft-cited warning, of using the master's tools to dismantle the master's house, we have chosen to repurpose old methods as we showcase the complexities of new ones.[1] In the first-person stories collected in *Feminists Reclaim Mentorship*, we explore the possibilities of mentorship from a variety of standpoints. Why, for instance, does the desire for mentorship persist—as it does, overwhelmingly—when there are so many mixed, even depressing messages circulating throughout media, the business world, and the halls of academe?[2]

Our book is an experiment in collaboration between two women of different generations. Although our relationship began with the conventional academic structure of PhD advisor and advisee, after several years of writing on our own we came together for this project to act as a team, sharing our networks and creating a joint style and rhythm. The journey entailed negotiating the boundaries between print and internet cultures (borderline boomer and borderline millennial), and the subway lines between Manhattan and Brooklyn. Online resources like Twitter seemed alien to one of us, familiar and welcoming to the other. Working in tandem was framed by restrictions of family (childcare) and work (heavy teaching load), or the velleities of old age and the anxieties of pandemic life. Somehow, we negotiated our time and timing, making it up as we went along.

As we prepared the book, we were surprised by how strong many people's reactions were to the idea of mentorship itself, whether because they had been well or poorly mentored, or because they had found themselves searching for something that remained elusive. We hope this collection of writing will inspire readers to reflect on their own histories, and to invest in old/ongoing relationships or imagine new ones. Conversations about mentoring are especially urgent now with attacks on vulnerable populations and rights, including the pernicious overturning of *Roe v. Wade*, making the need for channels of interdependence ever more pronounced.

At the same time, while we don't yet fully understand the complex ways in which COVID-19 will transform the idea of the workplace itself, we know that the pandemic disproportionately continues to threaten whatever job security women, LGBTQ+ people, and service workers have attained. Despite the uneven global effects of the pandemic, we still imagine opportunities for local, positive change.[3] We also hope that the stories in the book might catalyze rumination—perhaps even future collaboration—about the limitations and potentials of feminist mentorship as it operates within the institutions of teaching, writing, publishing, and other creative endeavors from which these stories emerge.

The history of feminism has taught us the importance of mutually reimagining our self-definitions, including gender identity itself. Second-wave feminism in large part emerged through, was even propelled into visibility by, anthologies. Best-selling collections like *Sisterhood Is Powerful*, *This Bridge Called My Back*, and *Home Girls* brought together voices of critique and calls for social justice. This was also the project of seventies consciousness-raising, thought, at least ideally, to be a site of building solidarity through the sharing of differences and commonalities within safe spaces.

In our anthology, we narrow in on the workplaces we both inhabit and know best. The stories focus on university and literary worlds, zones of publishing and editing, making art and fictions. While these are professions of relative privilege, they are equally dependent on scarce resources, precarious labor, and an inadequately addressed lack of accessibility.

But precisely because we are required to navigate modern versions of the epic universe we've inherited, we're not ready to give up on it. *Feminists Reclaim Mentorship* gathers a range of feminist voices to survey what the desire for mentoring has meant, stories of the good, the bad, and everything in between. Many among us still crave the relationship's best practices, while others have experimented with new forms that combine a push and pull between interdependence and autonomy. The model of two remains entangled with the many: a both/and of intimacy and collectivity. However much we debate the values of the one-on-one mentorship structure, those values persist, multiplied and diversified, within given communities.

In part because we've experimented with the project of intergenerational collaboration—our own two-way street—we've felt moved to figure out how this kind of relationship works for feminists who have been making changes in their lives. Over the years, this connection has expanded to the intersections of friends and colleagues we've introduced each other to and brought together, as we've done here. Our mutual engagement with the topic has also meant that we've continued to trade resources—from the intellectual to the intimate—a system of exchange that marked our relationship from the start. Collaboration, at its most enlivening, can lead to reversibility and renewal, while generative reciprocity thrives alongside a commitment to transparency and accountability. As the collective logic of these stories reflects, we've learned the necessity of moving in alignment with the changing structures of work and relationships within the zeitgeist, notably knowing when it's time to mentor the mentor.

In reclaiming mentorship in this book as a feminist project for new generations, we see possibilities for the emergence of more fluid and innovative interactions over time. Mentor or mentee, mentorship above all is a relationship.

&

Working Girl's gender and class politics mark a dramatic retreat from another hugely popular late twentieth-century comedy about women in the workplace, *9 to 5*, an earlier fictional film also set in a large city. Its version of female bonding moves from satire to farce. The (handsy) boss is white, male, and evil and the (mostly white) women act in solidarity, and in this case really do learn from each other. In anticipation of what we're calling collaborative mentorship, the women in the office bring each other along, at first through shared fantasy and storytelling, later, through tangible, conspiratorial interventions.

At the movie's end, the boss's superior—a six-foot-tall honcho complete with white suit and Stetson hat—turns up unexpectedly and approves the changes the women have made, unbeknownst to their boss: daycare center, job sharing, wellness programs. But the big guy draws the line at the bottom line: "That equal pay thing, though, that's got to go" (*9 to 5*). Equal pay along with equal rights were among the first demands of feminist strikes and movements throughout the seventies. Notably in New York, the context we know best, recent student strikes at Columbia and union demands across CUNY have continued the struggle for equity through collective action. What can feminist mentoring mean in this context?

Seen through these two cultural touchstones, styles of mentoring relationships, as they relate to women's and minorities' participation in the workplace, have transformed over time in tension with political change and the ever-shifting structures of work. In the documentary *9 to 5: The Story of a Movement*, Jane Fonda explains that the movie in which she starred, along with Lily Tomlin and Dolly Parton, emerged directly from the women's organization "9 to 5," which was committed to improving the conditions of secretaries (as they were then more commonly called) and clerical staff.

Fonda's conversations with the real-world "9 to 5" women, not least their "jaw dropping" fantasies about doing in their bosses, she says, "unlocked this idea for the movie," a send-up of course, but one "married to the movement." That vision of women acting together—for shared rights, in pleasure and in friendship—prefigures the kinds of horizontal mentorships that emerge within, and sometimes beyond, feminist circles. The organization "9 to 5" was one of many affirming the need for collaborative, goal-oriented feminist activism in the seventies, not limited to office culture and in fact still urgently needed in academia and the economy of scarcity that regulates its organization.

The women's liberation movement hoped to serve as an umbrella for gender-based injustices, but many were not addressed. Keeanga-Yamahtta Taylor's introduction to *How We Get Free: Black Feminism and the Combahee River Collective* underscores the role played by the women of the collective, formed in 1974, in organizing public protest and centering race, class, and sexuality as feminist issues. These women, Taylor writes, "were not only making a political intervention into the feminist movement, but by doing so, they were also creating new entry points into activism for Black and Brown women who would otherwise have been ignored" (6). Though Combahee was not the only radical offshoot, nor the only group of organizing Black women, it had an outsize effect on the movement, in part for its commitment to working "in a collective style, not in a hierarchical style" (Frazier 126).

In a similar instance of innovative feminist mentorship through collective action, in this case in the publishing world, Kitchen Table: Women of Color Press of New York, which emerged from the Combahee River Collective, republished *This Bridge Called My Back: Writings by Radical Women of Color* in 1983. Personal, often polemical, even, at times, righteously angry, taken together the essays in *This Bridge* created a more complicated and inclusive story of feminist politics. Gloria Anzaldúa wrote in the foreword to the second edition, a manifesto for a renewed feminist project, "We have come to realize that we are not alone in our struggles nor separate nor autonomous but that we—white black straight queer female male—are connected and interdependent" (iv).

Both Combahee and Kitchen Table were formed in urban settings, Boston and New York, which made collective action more possible and inherently plural. They exemplify feminist visions that connect the personal to the political in concrete and symbolic ways, a move that anticipates how feminist mentorship has been reimagined as relationships that move beyond the boundaries of the workplace to enact and respond to social change.

&.

In the years separating *9 to 5* from *Working Girl*, the scenario of women competing with each other, animated by a pseudo-mentorship plot, returned (had it ever really left?). The Hollywood clichés about women's rivalry, inherited from the ur-incarnation of female envy and ambition, the 1950s' *All About Eve*, also characterized popular feminist discourse in the 1980s. In the real-life contexts of work, as in the movies, it was difficult for some to resist the lure of ladder-of-success feminism. For example, in the media's invention of the postfeminist, have-it-all 1990s and 2000s, "Girl Power" (originally a feminist interventionist slogan that was co-opted by, among others, the Spice Girls) masqueraded as a positive collective solution for the problems facing women across all kinds of workspaces, and well into the 2010s Sophia Amoruso and other entrepreneurs popularized the figure of the #Girlboss. In *The Devil Wears Prada* (2006), the machinations of trickle-down-feminism captivated audiences with yet another plot about a beautiful, bitchy boss manipulating an ambitious young woman willing to pay the price of admission to her circle of power.

In *Late Night* (2019), however, Mindy Kaling attempted to reinvent the stereotypical models of hyper-ambitious women and their competitive relationships with other women. The conventional script represents intergenerational mentorship as simultaneously coveted and punitive: both boss and mentee suffer public and private, not to say sexual, humiliations as their narratives unfold. In the film, a young comedy fan, Molly Patel (played by Kaling), is an Indian American woman adrift in a sea of white male writers, suspecting correctly that she has been given this opportunity only as a "diversity hire." The show, one of the few hosted by a woman—Katherine Newbury—has fallen in the ratings. Katherine (played by Emma Thompson, for whom Kaling had written the part), known by her employees as a woman who "hates women," is desperate not to be replaced.

Late Night tries to counter the clichés of competition between powerful older women and untried younger women and moves cautiously past the template of traditional Hollywood scenarios. It no doubt took creator and producer Kaling to push that plot to its slightly redemptive ending: the brittle, narcissistic, middle-aged boss recognizes, in a moment of panic, that she needs her employee as much as her twenty-something, feisty employee might need her.

If the hint of dual reciprocity signals a more porous model, it remains all the same entrenched in that fundamental dynamic. While the drama circles around the two women, it's in fact the television moguls who call the shots. The film may aim to celebrate women's bonds, or at least the elevation of women in spaces otherwise hostile to their independence and success. But, as in academia, ultimately we're left with an unfinished amelioration of inherited workplace structures.

❧

In the culture at large, mentorship scenarios, often intergenerational, continue to take center stage, obscuring the broader picture. Examples of the classic male mentorship model crop up in mainstream media almost daily, from breaking political news to professional advice podcasts and celebrity profiles. These accounts portray mentorship both in its idealized form and at its most narcissistic and debased. In tributes to cultural icons Virgil Abloh and Stephen Sondheim after their deaths, the portraits of male-to-male mentorship emerge as artistic collaborations born out of supportive recognition and a desire to allow individuals to fully express themselves. On the other hand, what could felon Jeffrey Epstein have meant when he referred to financier Leslie Wexner as his mentor, or Donald Trump, when he longed in public for help from his early mentor, the infamous Roy Cohn? Indeed, the classic model of bonds between men accommodates a wide range of performances on a variety of platforms.

Men, of course, have always mentored women, though what mentoring means in these cases depends on one's perspective. Perhaps the gold standard in the matter of men mentoring women is that of the world-famous anthropologist Franz Boas. Boas mentored Zora Neale Hurston when she was a graduate student at Columbia in the early decades of the twentieth century. He failed to persuade the young scholar to write a dissertation (she had other plans) but helped launch her brilliant career as writer and anthropologist. This story of felicitous mentorship, however, was not typical at Columbia. In her memoir *When Men Were the Only Models We Had* (2002), feminist critic and detective story writer Carolyn Heilbrun describes her unfulfilled longing, when she was a junior faculty member of the English Department, to have the celebrated master of literary criticism, Lionel Trilling, as mentor. He distinctly preferred his male "disciples," she recalls, several of whom later became, as she thought of them, her "adversaries" (66–67).

As these two New York stories suggest, gender paradigms offer variations on a theme: when men mentor women, it's not a simple story.

For example, Supreme Court nominee Brett Kavanaugh touts himself as a supporter of women's careers. "Kavanaugh is a Mentor to Women," reads the title of an op-ed by Yale Law School professor Amy Chua in the *Wall Street Journal*, citing his many female law clerks. Her piece did not go without its own critique.[4] The presumed support of women through mentorship runs counter not only to the individual harm Kavanaugh was accused of by Christine Blasey Ford, who, during a Senate hearing for his confirmation, charged Kavanaugh with sexually assaulting her when they were young. But it also contradicts, one might even say potentially masks, the conservative positions that Kavanaugh upholds that unduly affect women and minorities. Whether concealing misogyny under the mantra of female empowerment or simply refusing to mentor women because it's too dangerous in the age of #MeToo (famously, former vice president Mike Pence refused even to have lunch in public with a woman alone, except for his wife), the mentorship formula is never as straightforward as it might appear.

Despite the attention paid to bad actors and the publicized abuses of one-to-one relationships, mentoring has become a rallying cry for social change. From Billie Jean King to Shonda Rhimes, Ruth Bader Ginsberg to Florynce ("Flo") Kennedy, Janet Mock to Margaret Cho, many of the most visible American feminist figures have publicly acknowledged the ways that active mentorship, particularly of people from marginalized communities, can help level the playing field. In a recent interview about her career, Kaling was asked to describe her approach as a boss. "When you're a woman of color, who is also an employer," she replied, "you can't just be someone who employs people, you also have to be a mentor. It's sort of your responsibility because there are so few of us" (Marchese). Or as writer and academic Roxane Gay puts it in *Bad Feminist*, describing the burnout associated with being a Black faculty member in a majority-white profession: "When it comes to mentoring and being there to support students, I feel it's everyone's job (regardless of ethnicity)" (7).

Questions of education and professional advancement and access to it by younger generations often dominate conversations about why and how mentorship matters. For instance, in *The Lived Experiences of African American Mentors*, Wyletta Gamble-Lomax underscores the importance for young African American women of being surrounded by "community pedagogues"—a group that includes mentors as well as coaches and other leadership figures outside of schools (xx). Gamble-Lomax argues that if young African American women are to succeed, they need "African American female mentors" and to be privy to "intellectual insights exclusive to the Black female experience" (xviii). In Gamble-Lomax's view, vulnerability ideally should characterize both sides of the pair, mentor and mentee, a relationship situated within the goals of collective action.

Mentee. The term dates from the twentieth century and lacks Mentor's legendary pedigree. Girls Write Now, for example, a pioneering arts organization based in New York City devoted to mentoring teens from underserved communities, embraces the language of the mentor/mentee model as the bedrock of their mission of preparing these young writers for college and after. The pairings are designed both to create reciprocal relations and build community.[5] Individual relationships flourish within the collective space of intergenerational bonding and shared creation, embodied by the publication of the GWN annual anthology.

But even the most well-intended pairing within ostensibly progressive communities can result in unintended consequences. Meg Wolitzer's best-selling novel *The Female Persuasion* (2018) tells the story of female mentorship between an eager young woman and a dazzling veteran feminist, Faith Frank, who runs a foundation devoted to helping women. The novel charts the ups and downs of their ambivalent mentor–mentee relationship but also sharply mocks the foundation's project to promote their brand by mentoring poor women in Ecuador while forgetting the women they set out to help.

Indexing that same toxic spirit of white saviorhood, American sociologist and writer Tressie McMillan Cottom tweeted in 2020: "Let me tell you about white women's incessant need to mentor black women who know more than they do: they are dangerous." (Introducing a longer thread, the tweet has received thousands of likes and hundreds of retweets.) Though lauded, at times, as a panacea, mentorship often comes at the price of an individual's sense of her own value and agency—forms of violence and erasure antithetical to what mentorship, in its best configurations, can do.

॰॰

Often the writers in our collection look back at the mentoring experiences that influenced them starting out, and, in many cases, their own subsequent experiences as mentors. From either position, the essays show, it's not easy to escape the effects of hierarchy that organize the academic and publishing worlds, even as card-carrying feminists. The so-called ivory tower tends to mistake itself for Olympus and mere mortals—the ever-increasing numbers of those who do not land the scarce and fetishized tenure-track positions—find themselves stuck at the bottom, ignored or punished by the would-be gods.

When these writers share their experiences of mentorship from within, a striking number of common themes emerge: a mentor's failure to recognize their achievements or their vulnerabilities, the thwarting of ambition, the sense of something missing, a lack of reciprocity, crossed signals, and, of course, rigid assumptions about identity positions. These anxieties punctuate the individual narratives, even when mentorship proves successful. For many of the positive models, what a great mentor does is what psychotherapist Esther Perel, in her paean to mentorship relationships, describes as opening "the door to a different world than the one we come from" ("How a Great Mentor").[6]

The stories here take us inside experiences that travel to new places, meld the intellectual and the affective, the confessional and the manifesto, worst- and best-case scenarios. They offer lessons for variations on these themes for the future, especially a recognition that the way forward for feminists rethinking mentorship requires establishing channels for transparency and inclusion.

We initially divided our book into two parts, a neat binary between vertical and horizontal mentorship scenarios. But as readers will find, stories that initially seem to fit easily into one category or the other often blur the lines. A few pieces introduce a question of temporality—the haunting of mentors, real or imagined. For these we designed a third interstitial section, a holding place but also an implicit invitation to put the three sections into dialogue.

Part I. Two-Way Streets: Finding Mentors/Becoming Mentors

This group of stories reflects the writers' one-on-one mentorship experiences. Finding the right mentor, if and when it happens, is a process. Sometimes it's a long journey to find a match. A number of our writers find themselves lovingly recalling mentors who supported them and offered what seem to be two key elements of positive outcomes: recognition and reciprocity. Others remember instead a feeling of not being seen, even at times disappointment and harm.[7] For some, being well mentored or even poorly mentored leads people to become mentors themselves, however reluctantly or imperfectly.

The section opens with essays focused on mentoring within academia. Many of these stories have a happy ending, one of mutual recognition between a pair, and a turn toward assuming the mentor position—but often only after a trial by fire and a redefinition of the terms of mentorship itself. Unsurprisingly, experienced mentors tend to view themselves in a rather different light from that of their students; often the mentees rewrite history in a way that reminds us just how difficult it is to gauge the degree of reciprocity the relationship entails from one position or the other. For the lucky few, looking back inspires gratitude toward the individuals who recognized their abilities and potential, and helped them navigate the gender and racialized hierarchies inherent to academia.

From these stories, we turn to narratives of professional trajectories in the no less white- and male-dominated industries such as publishing, journalism, and creative writing that operate alongside and often overlap with academia. Without the structural arrangement of the PhD-to-tenure-track progression, which relies on a conventional mentorship model, these contributors had to hustle. Some found role models—people they aspired to be like who did not necessarily offer concrete forms of mentorship. Others were accidentally mentored by those within their orbit, whether family members or those from their cohorts.

For individuals bridging not just the usual professional obstacles but also the changes that flow from immigration and geographical inflections—Australia, India, Ireland, and Israel—the mentorship process is still more complicated. These stories expose the innovations and resistances unique to specific locations. Composed almost (in one case explicitly) as love letters, these contributions mark the ways in which mentorship, at its best a form of inspiration, offers not guidance or advice so much as permission, Aoibheann Sweeney suggests, permission to trust in oneself.

Part II. Rearview Mirror: Mentoring at a Distance

Three pieces—two essays and a poem—in this section describe a posthumous or otherworldly expression of the one-to-one mentorship experience. They recall a relationship that continues in a form difficult to define, almost, as two of the titles suggest, ghostly, or reconstructed in belated, loving, distant, sometimes readerly homage.

We want to recognize the engagements with mentors who have died but with whom, in some sense, we continue to live.

Part III. The Traffic in Mentors: Horizontal Scripts

Many contributors in this third section expose the problems in two-way mentoring that led them to seek alternate paths. They focus on more complicated structures of mentorship, what we have come to think of as horizontal modes, which describe communal ways of connecting even if they begin with one-to-one relationships. The work here, mostly essays but also an interview, deploys a range of rich metaphors to describe new, nonhierarchical ways of relating, from Melissa Coss Aquino's "the mentoring mirror" to Daná-Ain Davis's "widening the way." These alternative forms of supportive mentorship typically emerge in response to problems of situational miscommunication and differences in background and identity. The mentors self-described in these pieces are committed to engaging with all the possibilities their mentees bring to the table.

Two essays consider mentorship in the time of #MeToo, showing how a single abusive mentor and the lack of a community of care undermine individual agency. These stories fall on a spectrum of abuse and point to the ways in which mentorship can be used as a screen for extremes of negative behavior, including sexual assault and violence. From poster boy Harvey Weinstein to former governor Andrew Cuomo and Harvard anthropologist John Comaroff, men (and sometimes women) in power have finally been exposed, too often to disappointing outcomes, thanks to those who have gone public with their stories in order to create new outlets for solidarity and justice.

Some, not liking its connotations of hierarchy and whiteness, resist the word *mentor* itself. They have turned, instead, to relationships that emphasize collaboration, commonality, and a move to plural arrangements. While horizontal mentorship can happen at the individual level—with those in positions of power ethically minding their status and working to support rather than lead—some of our contributors have found it more comfortable to dwell instead in community. Their discomfort with conventional mentorship paradigms, including the personal/professional divide, prompts a turn instead to other, communal supports. From backyard gatherings of intimate friendships to running clubs and group texts, these writers prefer to collapse binaries, choosing instead connection and acknowledging that work problems and successes are just two of many important components of a fulfilling life.

At the same time, we give full recognition to the reality that instances of bad or inadequate mentorship are entrenched in macro-level inequities and injustices that cannot be solved by reshaping the model. As Angela Veronica Wong argues, echoing Audre Lorde on the master's tools, "Too often, professional mentorship replicates the logic of investment, not the logic of dismantling." Wong underlines the importance of moving beyond individual stories to establish sites of collective creativity and action. This means acknowledging the economies of racial capitalism underlying our social interactions in the workplace—and beyond.

The mentorship model continues to loom large in stories about work and personal lives, in unexpected settings, with unanticipated transformations, including bitter disappointment. Taken together, the essays, interviews, and poem in *Feminists Reclaim Mentorship* challenge the foundational assumptions that drive tried-and-true patterns, the obstacles that make it so hard to connect meaningfully and ethically. Will the practice of mentoring, even in a creative or collaborative form, fully serve those it's aimed at helping? Does affinity—often assumed to be the ground for creating mentorship pairs or cohorts—require sameness? How might we find different ways to connect with one another?

What has worked for the two of us—intense professional collaboration interspersed with breakdowns and rescue missions—is not meant as a model or prescription. The writers offer a range of novel solutions to effects of disparities and other potential obstacles to reciprocity. At best, they strive for relationships that acknowledge the full recognition of differences and interdependence alongside the necessity of forging common bonds.

Mentorship is complicated. Nonetheless, for many of us it's impossible to imagine the shapes of our lives without the mentors who've inspired us.

Nancy K. Miller—memoirist and feminist critic—is author and editor of more than a dozen books, including the feminist classic anthology *The Poetics of Gender* and autocritical essays *Getting Personal*. With Cindi Katz, she coedited and transformed the journal *WSQ: Women's Studies Quarterly*, which won the CELJ award in 2007 for Significant Editorial Achievement, and with Victoria Rosner, she is coeditor of the Gender and Culture series at Columbia University Press, founded by Heilbrun and Miller in 1983. Her most recent book is the memoir *My Brilliant Friends: Our Lives in Feminism*. She teaches life writing and cultural criticism at the Graduate

Center, City University of New York, where she is distinguished professor of English and comparative literature. Having enjoyed the support and protection of feminist mentorship throughout her career, she has gone on to mentor several generations of students and writers, including her coeditor for this volume, who was once her doctoral advisee. Website: Nancykmiller.com.

Tahneer Oksman, scholar, teacher, and writer, is author of *"How Come Boys Get to Keep Their Noses?" Women and Jewish American Identity in Contemporary Graphic Memoirs*, and coeditor of *The Comics of Julie Doucet and Gabrielle Bell: A Place Inside Yourself*, winner of the Comics Studies Society Edited Book Prize for 2019. Her cultural criticism has appeared in *The Believer*, *The Comics Journal*, *The Forward*, *The Guardian*, *Los Angeles Review of Books*, *Public Books*, and *Women's Review of Books*, and her academic writing can be found in journals and collections including *A/B: Auto/Biography Studies*, *Keywords for Comics Studies*, *Life Writing*, *Literature and Medicine*, *Pathographics*, *Shofar*, *Studies in American Jewish Literature*, *Visualizing Jewish Narrative*, and *Women's Studies Quarterly*, among others. She is associate professor in the Department of Writing, Literature, and Language at Marymount Manhattan College. Her interest in mentorship comes from experiencing the benefits and pleasures of being mentored, including by her coeditor for this volume, and she has continued the practice alongside students and colleagues. Website: tahneeroksman.com.

Notes

1. At the 1979 "Second Sex" conference, Lorde protested the absence of "poor women, Black and Third World women, and lesbians" in the program. Her talk, "The Master's Tools Will Never Dismantle the Master's House," was eventually collected in the literary anthology *This Bridge Called My Back*.

2. In the business world, Sylvia Ann Hewlett's 2013 book on the subject, published by Harvard Business Review Press, announces its thesis in the title: *Forget a Mentor, Find a Sponsor: The New Way to Fast-Track Your Career*.

3. In her 2021 *Work Won't Love You Back*, Sarah Jaffe addresses labor activism, past and present, and discusses a variety of related movements, including in academia. See chapter 8, "Proletarian Professionals: Academia," pp. 231–62.

4. A follow-up article in *The Guardian* described the practice of Yale Law professors—including Chua—vetting clerks who wanted to work for him and suggesting

that Kavanaugh hires women with a certain "look." See https://www.theguardian.com/us-news/2018/sep/20/brett-kavanaugh-supreme-court-yale-amy-chua.

5. Many mentorship organizations for young people exist, like the Posse Foundation (https://www.possefoundation.org/) and Scholarship Plus (https://www.scholarshipplus.org/).

6. Perel, best known as a relationship guru, recently turned to the subject of workplace relations in her podcast, *How's Work*. Roxane Gay has written about the subject, too, in her *New York Times* column, Work Friend.

7. On the complex feelings mentorship can elicit, see Bonnie D. Oglensky's *Ambivalence in Mentorship: An Exploration of Emotional Complexities*.

Works Cited

9 to 5. Directed by Colin Higgins, 20th Century Studios, 1980.

9 to 5: The Story of a Movement. Directed by Julia Reichert and Steven Bognar, PBS Distribution, 2020.

Anzaldúa, Gloria. "Foreword to the Second Edition." *This Bridge Called My Back: Writings by Radical Women of Color*, edited by Cherríe Moraga and Gloria Anzaldúa, Kitchen Table: Women of Color Press, 1983, pp. iv–v.

Cottom, Tressie McMillan (@tressiemcphd). "Let Me Tell You about White Women's Incessant Need to Mentor Black Women Who Know More than They Do: It's Dangerous." *Twitter*, 18 Jan. 2020, twitter.com/tressiemcphd/status/1218551730490740736?s=20. Accessed 8 Dec. 2021.

Frazier, Demita. "Demita Frazier" (interview with Keeanga-Yamahtta Taylor). *How We Get Free: Black Feminism and the Combahee River Collective*, edited by Keeanga-Yamahtta Taylor, Haymarket Books, 2017, pp. 111–43.

Gamble-Lomax, Wyletta. *The Lived Experience of African American Women Mentors: What It Means to Guide as Community Pedagogues*. Lexington Books, 2016.

Gay, Roxane. *Bad Feminist: Essays*. HarperCollins, 2014.

Heilbrun, Carolyn. *When Men Were the Only Models We Had: My Teachers Fadiman, Barzun, Trilling*. U of Pennsylvania P, 2002.

Hewlett, Sylvia Ann. *Forget a Mentor, Find a Sponsor: The New Way to Fast-Track Your Career*. Harvard Business Review Press, 2021.

Jaffe, Sarah. *Work Won't Love You Back: How Devotion to Our Jobs Keeps Us Exploited, Exhausted, and Alone*. Bold Type Books, 2021.

Late Night. Directed by Nisha Ganatra, FilmNation Entertainment, 2019.

Lorde, Audre. "The Master's Tools Will Never Dismantle the Master's House." *This Bridge Called My Back: Writings by Radical Women of Color*, edited by Cherríe Moraga and Gloria Anzaldúa. Kitchen Table: Women of Color Press, 1983, pp. 98–101.

Marchese, David. "Mindy Kaling on Not Being the Long-Suffering Indian Woman." *New York Times*, 10 June 2019, nytimes.com/interactive/2019/06/10/magazine/mindy-kaling-late-night-diversity-comedy.html. Accessed 8 Dec. 2021.

Moraga, Cherríe, and Gloria Anzaldúa, editors. *This Bridge Called My Back: Writings by Radical Women of Color*. Kitchen Table: Women of Color Press, 1983.

Oglensky, Bonnie D. *Ambivalence in Mentorship: An Exploration of Emotional Complexities*. Routledge, 2018.

Perel, Esther. "How a Great Mentor Makes All the Difference: Letters from Esther Perel." *YouTube*, 16 Dec. 2020, youtube.com/watch?v=92LVhslvEwU. Accessed 8 Dec. 2021.

Taylor, Keeanga-Yamahtta. *How We Get Free: Black Feminism and the Combahee River Collective*. Haymarket Books, 2017.

Wolitzer, Meg. *The Female Persuasion*. Riverhead Books, 2018.

Working Girl. Directed by Mike Nichols, Twentieth Century Fox, 1988.

Further Reading

Bauer-Maglin, Nan. "Mentoring at Girls Write Now." *Radical Teacher*, vol. 109, Fall 2017, http://radicalteacher.library.pitt.edu/ojs/index.php/radicalteacher/article/view/387/301.

Brown, Nadia E. "Mentoring, Sexual Harassment, and Black Women Academics." *Journal of Women, Politics and Policy*, vol. 40, no. 1, 2019, pp. 166–73.

Clark, Anna E. "Twilight of the Mentors: Or How I Learned to Stop Worrying and Love My Gatekeeper." *New Inquiry* 19 May 2020, https://thenewinquiry.com/twilight-of-the-mentors/.

Gay, Roxane. "It's My Idea. She's Taking Credit." Work Friend. *New York Times*, 19 March 2021, https://www.nytimes.com/2021/03/19/business/roxane-gay-work-friend-managing-interns.html.

Johnson, W. Brad, and Davis Smith. *Athena Rising: How and Why Men Should Mentor Women*. Bibliomotion, 2016.

LeFevre, William. "Mentoring in the Age of #MeToo." *Information Management*, vol. 52, no. 3, May/June 2018, pp. 32–35.

"Mentoring Event Offers Fresh Perspectives." *MLA Newsletter*, vol. 51, no. 3, Fall 2019, p. 5. https://www.mla.org/content/download/112061/2418334/NL_51-3_web.pdf.

Miller, Nancy K. "Mentoring the Mentor." *Avidly*, 7 Jan. 2020, https://avidly.lareviewofbooks.org/2020/01/07/mentoring-the-mentor/.

———. "When Your Friend Is Also a Mentor: The Mentrix Identity." *Tulsa Studies in Women's Literature*, vol. 38, no. 2, Fall 2019, pp. 435–41.

Rich, Adrienne. "Arts of the Possible." *Arts of the Possible: Essays and Conversations.* Norton, 2001, pp. 146–67.

Soklaridis, Sophie, et al. "Men's Fear of Mentoring in the #MeToo Era—What's at Stake for Academic Medicine?" *New England Journal of Medicine*, vol. 379, no. 23, 6 Dec. 2018, pp. 2270–74.

Part I

Two-Way Streets

Finding Mentors / Becoming Mentors

Rosemarie's Hands

RACHEL ADAMS

Dear Rachel,

I will write this letter, but in the future you should ask your new colleagues for recommendations.

Good luck with the fellowship application.

A.

I know the message went something like this, although my email files don't go back far enough to preserve a copy. The gist of it is seared in memory: because I had a job, my former teachers were no longer obligated to write me letters of recommendation, and this one was unceremoniously vacating our relationship. The author is my dissertation director. It was the first semester of my first job as an assistant professor, and I was applying for a fellowship to spend a month doing archival research on my book project. I remember the small blue screen of my 1990s-era computer, the screechy noise of the dial-in modem, and A.'s message like a punch in the stomach.

The rejection came as a shock because I thought my relationship with A. was just getting started. She was a model in so many ways. On a campus where professors lectured in sandals and T-shirts, she wore dark tailored suits, imposing glasses, and dramatic scarves. She was young and stylish, with a European accent and a cloud of black hair. She didn't

21

claim to specialize in any particular literary field, instead listing as areas of expertise "the body," "theories of subjectivity," and "new materialism." I took every course she offered. I loved her syllabi, a salad of films, works of art, and written narratives paired with dense theoretical readings by Marx, Foucault, and Irigaray; Hardt and Negri, Deleuze and Guattari, Klaus Theweleit, and Kaja Silverman. I loved her poise, her complexity and mystique. She didn't return my work promptly, but it eventually came back covered with comments in her elegant, looping script. She challenged my ideas and asked hard questions, but always with an underlayer of affirmation.

Things with A. weren't perfect. She could be cold and moody, complaining of migraines and toothaches. Sometimes, despite our years of work together, it seemed she didn't know me at all. When I was invited for a campus visit, she warned me, in a scolding voice, to dress appropriately. At the time, I bought most of my clothes in vintage stores, looking for garments that announced—with a fur collar, wasp waist, or calf-length pencil skirt—what I believed to be an idiosyncratic but stylish professionalism. I was affronted by the suggestion that I couldn't be trusted to pick the right outfit for my job visit. Once I landed the job, A. cautioned me to sit quietly during faculty meetings in my new department to avoid drawing attention to myself. I considered myself a shy and cautious person. Did she really think I might act otherwise in my professional life?

But in the whirlwind of accepting a job, filing my dissertation, and moving across the country, I shrugged off these incidents. A. was an eccentric European theorist, preoccupied with lofty and complex ideas. Was it any wonder she didn't pay attention to the mundane details of my clothes and behavior?

But then that email, just a few months into my semester. I thought the role of dissertation advisor would segue neatly into that of professional mentor, just as I had transitioned from graduate student to assistant professor. Instead, A.'s coldness continued. I heard she had a baby and sent a gift that was never acknowledged. I mailed her a copy of my first book, having thanked her copiously in the acknowledgments, and heard nothing. When I got tenure, I wrote again, telling her I would be in town for a weekend. Did she want to get together and could I meet her children? This response was recent enough to be saved in my files:

Dear Rachel, what a wonderful surprise! And congratulations on your tenure, this is truly great news. I think, though, that

we will have to wait for seeing each other again, perhaps in
the fall?

All the best to you,

A.

She didn't want to see me. Her written congratulations rang hollow, as
did her offer to meet in the future. We lived on opposite sides of the
country and by fall I would be thoroughly caught up in the semester's
work, thousands of miles away.

During the years that A. kept me at arm's length, I had been swept up
by a different kind of mentor. Although my new department had no official
system of faculty mentoring, a dynamic senior colleague had appointed
herself to this role even before I arrived on the job. Of all my colleagues,
she was the person I most feared and idolized. In graduate school, I had
been dazzled by the brilliance and audacity of her research, and riveted by
stories of her notorious eccentricities. B. seemed to know everything and
everyone, to have read every book, and seen every important film. When
I arrived for my job interview at the MLA convention hotel, she opened
the door in a teal faux-fur coat that would be her trademark for years
after. It accentuated the spiky hair that was sometimes white-blonde and
sometimes closer to red, adding at least an inch to her already magisterial
height. I never worried about saying inappropriate things, since B. would
talk in long monologues without stopping for a breath. When she asked
me a question, she also answered it. I didn't mind because I felt so lucky
to have B. as my advocate, not to mention a source of amusing stories,
like the one about the time she strode into my apartment, wiped a finger
across a dusty radiator, and announced, "At home, I use Pledge." I thrived
on B.'s affirmation, as well as her honest and sometimes blunt criticism
of my work. She wrote letters when I needed them, and supported me
vigorously at every step toward promotion.

All wasn't perfect with B., of course. I was assigned a faculty apartment
in her building, so she literally lived on top of me for almost ten years.
When she wanted to talk, she would peer into my ground-floor apartment
to see if the lights were on, before ringing my doorbell insistently. Once
I opened the door, she would sweep in, commenting on my clothes, the
arrangement of furniture, the program on TV. When she didn't want to
see me, she would pass by on the street with her eyes fixed somewhere

over my head. With time, her inability to listen became more grating than charming. I disliked the turmoil she created by sparring with our male colleagues and urging me to take sides. And while she was always enthusiastic about my work, I sometimes got the feeling she didn't like me. Once we left a dinner party together in the early hours of the morning and she insisted on taking the subway instead of sharing a cab. Another time, she told me I was the happiest person she knew. I was stunned at how little she seemed to know me, having spent my untenured years smiling through a haze of anxiety and depression. Worse yet, B.'s tone suggested she couldn't abide happy people.

None of this seemed to matter when I got tenure. My predominant feeling was gratitude for B.'s support. I looked forward to being her colleague, free from the constant threat of losing my job. But instead of evolving, my relationship with B. simply vanished. I moved to a different building and had children who demanded my time and energy. B. could no longer just drop by my apartment on her way home. As she prepared to retire, she reduced her hours on campus and stopped participating in department life. When we passed on the street, increasingly she swept by as if I were too short to be seen. Sometimes I catch sight of her, shoulders slightly rounded with age but still imposingly tall and thin. She never acknowledges me. I'm filled with appreciation for her support when I needed it, but find it hard to believe we ever ate a meal together, sat on the same couch, or had what she would call "a conversation."

When I decided to have children, it was clear that neither A. nor B. would be a mentor. Like many successful women intellectuals of her generation, B. had never committed to a life partner or parenthood. Once while I was in her apartment our visit was interrupted by a loud bang. B. leapt up, suddenly remembering the egg she had left boiling on the stove until it exploded. It was a scene of near allegorical significance: there simply was no room in the brilliant and preoccupied coils of B.'s imagination to care for the everyday world in front of her, let alone a child. But I also refused to take the path of A., who seemed to have vanished into motherhood, abandoning not only her writing but all professional ties and obligations beyond the bare minimum to keep her job.

This is where the essay gets stuck. In draft after draft, I elaborate the disappointments of A. and B. and then come up short, uncertain about where to go next. By all accounts, I've had a remarkably successful professional life. As a scholar of American literature, I'm skeptical of the classic narrative about a rugged individual who triumphs through her own hard work and perseverance. Nobody becomes a tenured professor without a wide and supportive network of teachers, colleagues, and advocates. But I also want to write honestly about how those networks fall short, especially when powerful women speak the language of feminist solidarity while failing to sustain women coming up behind.

While struggling with this impasse I went to hear a panel that included Rosemarie Garland-Thomson, whom I've known as a colleague and friend for over twenty years. We've never lived in the same place or had an institutional connection, but I try to see her when she gives a lecture or we attend the same conference. On this night, I arrived late and only just managed to find a seat in the packed auditorium. I hadn't seen Rosemarie in at least a year and there was no time to say hello, but she caught my eye from the stage, smiled warmly, and waved.

In Rosemarie's gesture, I realized I had found my ending.

Throughout my difficulties with A. and B., Rosemarie was always waving in welcome. Rosemarie is a founding figure in the field of literary disability studies, which is one of my favorite intellectual communities. When I was a graduate student, she accepted the first essay I ever wrote for publication. Later, we met in person over dinner at a conference. Even through the fog of severe imposter syndrome that clouded my first years as an assistant professor, I felt her treating me as a respected colleague. Rosemarie introduced me to many of the colleagues I love and admire most. She even had a name for this process. "Recruitment" was her strategy for enfolding promising newcomers into the field of disability studies. Rosemarie wrote letters for me. She mentioned my name to editors and hiring committees. When I disagreed with her, she took criticism as an opportunity for discussion rather than fighting. And even as she became an academic celebrity surrounded by friends and admirers, I never felt forgotten or overlooked. Waving from the stage was a gesture of recognition and inclusivity that is vintage Rosemarie.

Rosemarie's wave also had other meanings. She used her arm, which is the most visible aspect of her identity as a person with disabilities. Rosemarie describes her arms as "asymmetrical," ending in hands that have a total of six fingers, rather than the conventional ten. I find them beautiful because they are such a powerful and unique expression of who she is. In my favorite portrait, Rosemarie stands with one three-fingered hand on her hip, her shorter arm curled at her other side. Sunglasses make it hard to tell exactly where her gaze is directed, but I think she's looking invitingly at an approaching friend. When we first met, Rosemarie didn't speak openly about her disability but over time she has claimed disability as an identity, as well as an academic pursuit. "I have learned to be disabled," she writes, "what has been transformed is not my body, but my consciousness" ("Becoming Disabled"). I admire her optimism about how embodied difference can be a prompt for creativity and resourcefulness.

It seems obvious now, but until she waved from the stage it never occurred to me to write about Rosemarie. Maybe her affirmation has been given so generously and continuously it became transparent somewhere along the way. Maybe it's because we never had an institutional connection, or because it was such a part of my professional identity to understand myself as neglected and abandoned. Maybe it was because I imagined a mentor as someone who earned my admiration via an enchanted combination of intimidation, mystery, and self-absorption. I think of my own mentoring as shaped by a powerful imperative not to be like A. or B. Thanks to their negative examples, I believe myself to be a warmer, more responsive, and consistent mentor to my own students. I also discourage the cult of personality that led me to them in the first place. Sometimes, I'm exhausted by the effort of trying not to be them.

It is much less exhausting to imagine myself passing along the steady supply of warmth and affirmation Rosemarie continues to offer. In contrast to the limited resources of A. and B., Rosemarie's are freely given, with no expiration date. I don't think I have her charisma or tireless energy. But I like to believe that, like Rosemarie, I'm the person who waves in recognition rather than gazing coolly off into the distance; that there is continuity between the way I live in the world and the ideas I value; and that I encourage students to become the best versions of themselves rather than mini-versions of me. I had imagined a mentor to be a woman whom I respected, at least in part, because she held me at arm's length, hovering at a remove that I could aspire to but never truly match. Rosemarie, whose arms are shorter and less symmetrical, modeled a form of mentorship that recognizes and bolsters up what others bring to a relationship. Rosemarie has given me my ending. A mentor so sustainable, low-impact, carbon-neutral, that I almost looked right past her. That is, until she caught my eye and waved.

Rachel Adams teaches in the English Department at Columbia University where, for the first time, a junior colleague she mentored has recently received tenure. May he wear it well.

Works Cited

Garland-Thomson, Rosemarie. "Becoming Disabled." *New York Times*, 19 Aug. 2016, https://www.nytimes.com/2016/08/21/opinion/sunday/becoming-disabled.html. Accessed 8 Oct. 2021.

Tears, Idle Tears

Mentoring English Graduate Students from 1973 to 2010

SUSAN GUBAR

In 2017, seven years after I had to retire because of cancer treatments, I received a grimly titled collection of essays, *The Guardians of Mediocrity: How Universities Use Tenure Denial to Thwart Change, Creativity, and Intellectual Innovation,* with a loving inscription inside from one of its contributors, a former graduate student of mine. Though I knew Kathleen Davies had not received tenure in the English Department at a branch campus of a major state university in the nineties, I was astonished to learn from her essay that the fault was not in the stars but in ourselves.

Kathleen had extended some of the arguments in *The Madwoman in the Attic* to produce the book required for her tenure decision, but it had not yet found a publisher deemed "good enough" by the university's standards. And by that time, she explained in her essay, "*Madwoman* had been trashed . . . by other feminist critics . . . who had climbed aboard the post-structuralist bandwagon" (95). In her department, which was attempting to build its reputation on sophisticated "theory," one female colleague argued that "Gilbert and Gubar's thesis" had been "disproven" (96). Kathleen went on to lament, "With the annihilation of *Madwoman,* my foundation had been yanked out from under me" (96), and then to confess, "I didn't feel comfortable consulting Gubar about the criticism of her approach" (96). Although I was all too familiar with critiques of *The Madwoman*'s "essentialism," the book had continued to be reissued and translated, so the idea that it had been "disproven" and thereby wrecked Kathleen's argument and career flummoxed me.

By 2019, Kathleen Davies had turned this essay into a memoir about her transition from the contempt she encountered in the secular groves of academe to the exultation she found in the sacred groves of a cemetery. Reading *Sacred Groves: Or, How a Cemetery Saved My Soul* (2019), I once again found myself surprised, this time by a portrait of my teaching that was embedded in an affectionate panegyric: "When someone came up with a particularly clever idea in seminar, she'd moan a paroxysm of orgasmic delight (intoned in a strong Brooklyn accent), 'O-O-O-O!'" (84). Worse, "in class, she was utterly charming, but one-on-one, Susan wasn't always so congenial. She was known to yell 'Go away!' if a student happened to knock on her closed office door when she was busy" (85). No worst, there is none: "Brutally frank, she made every woman graduate student who wanted to work with her cry at some point" (85).

Now I don't remember making *any* student cry—okay, maybe one or two, but those were undergraduate plagiarism cases. Yet I do remember chain-smoking under "NO SMOKING" signs in classrooms, urging dissertators to pare down gargantuan projects, and yelling "Go away!" when I hid out not only from my students but also from my kids in a closed (and often unlit) office within Ballantine Hall. So I probably did moan in orgasmic delight during seminars and make my graduate students weep. Maybe, like Kathleen, they held off until they left my presence.

I start with Kathleen Davies's story because it encapsulates both the psychological and the institutional constraints that I continually encountered in my almost half century of teaching at Indiana University. Consider the understandable reticence: Kathleen never told me at the time that attacks on my work were affecting her tenure decision, just as earlier she had not told me about her tears. Consider the professional tensions: the shadows cast by a tenure system at a branch campus (where tenure is awarded by branch as well as central campus committees) and by the requisite of publishing a book at just the moment when the publishing industry was downsizing.

Overriding all of this: tenure-track positions in the humanities were disappearing, being replaced by adjunct positions, which meant that graduate students rarely ended up at the sort of large research campuses on which we trained them. They often found no academic jobs at all. If they did land tenure-track jobs, the pressure to produce a book in a handful of years was enormous; and not receiving tenure probably meant leaving the academic life altogether. As I look back on these fetters on mentoring, it startles me that my students and I managed to bring it off at all.

When I arrived in Bloomington in 1973, I was still reeling from a miserable dissertation experience at the University of Iowa. The professor who had inspired my thesis, Robert Scholes, had accepted a position at Brown University, and I was left with an uncongenial committee. Needless to say, all of its members were white men. (I never had a female professor.) They neglected to read and critique my chapters—I would mail them from Chicago where I had a Newberry Dissertation Fellowship—until the date of the defense arrived. Their objections and caveats at the defense meant that I had to rent a place for a week in Iowa City so I could retype large chunks of the thesis. (This was in the days before the invention of the computer, when we would store our drafts in the freezer in case the house burned down.) Never would I do to a doctoral student what had been done to me, I vowed.

By the early seventies, the job market had already begun to tank; however, research institutions of higher education continued to admit big graduate classes. In an English Department consisting of seventy-three colleagues, an entering graduate class could be as large as seventy-three, or indeed larger, because of the necessity of using teaching assistants—at Indiana University they are called assistant instructors or AIs—to staff required freshmen composition classes. (Today, by way of comparison, the department consists of about forty colleagues with an entering graduate class of ten or twelve.) It quickly became apparent that I would have many opportunities to mentor. Over forty years, I participated in forty-one undergraduate honors, MA, and MFA theses committees; I directed forty-five doctoral candidates; and I served on the committees of thirty-nine others: for a grand total of 125 students.

Once I was embarked with Sandra Gilbert on a feminist project, it became politically imperative that our generation—the first to integrate the humanities faculty—mentor young, aspiring scholars. We needed to train the next generation, the first to study women's literature and history in the classroom, who could then go off to educate others. I did not want future female professors encountering what had happened to me when I walked into the English Department to pick up my mail: I was handed a syllabus to type by a senior colleague who assumed that I was a secretary. I have no doubt that I therefore set high standards.

I had only learned to write while composing books with Sandra. Never had any teacher in graduate school worked with me on my prose.

I was poised to read and comment on chapters in a timely manner; to work one-on-one on critical thinking as well as organizational, stylistic, and even grammatical glitches; to stage dress rehearsals for oral exams, defenses, and job talks; to churn out endless letters of recommendation, and so on. But mostly I was determined that my students would not suffer from the imposter syndrome that had me in its grip throughout my graduate training. Because I was ashamed of how little I knew, I had counterfeited knowledge repeatedly, and that process inhibited real learning. I wanted my students to ask not the questions they thought would make them look smart but the questions they needed answered, even if such queries exhibited their ignorance. Yet this sort of honesty is not easy when students want your approbation and when your own scholarly reputation is rising (despite the assumption of some that your work had been "disproven").

Such were my lofty goals, but what had been my students' experiences? Kathleen had taught me that their perspective might not accord with my own. Since I have an email list containing many (though not all) of my former graduate students, I emailed them, telling them about Kathleen's account and asking them if they wanted "to recall incidents (not asking for laudatory rhetoric here) that were especially telling about the dynamics of mentoring." And, sure enough, quite a few respondents admitted that I had made them cry!

To my shock, one of my first dissertators informed me that my response to a chapter I had mailed back to her triggered a five-year-long writer's block. Elizabeth opened the envelope to find "one sentence from you, scrawled at the top of page 1: 'If this is the quality of the work you are going to do, I cannot be your advisor.' Tears. Frustration. Desperation." Heather is a bit more upbeat about my being "gently unforgiving of failure," but just as clear: "By unforgiving of failure, I mean that you showed that you had no patience for people (myself included at times) who had not done the challenging work of trying to struggle through a complicated text or the time-consuming work of additional research when that text was not going to unravel (no matter how many times I re-read it). You seemed unconcerned about stopping someone mid-sentence if they took us off track in discussion."

Especially with dissertators, my goal was to get them to address interpretive puzzles not yet solved by already published criticism so they could produce innovative scholarship; they needed to move beyond the known to the unknown. Rod's account indicates that I did intuit how profoundly unnerving this process might be. He recalls my warning him at a meeting before his doctoral exam that I was "going to keep asking you hard questions aggressively until you can't answer them. Don't get upset, and don't cry. Just do your best and be ready for it." After he wondered what determined whether or not he would pass, I apparently replied, "It all depends on how fast we get to the point where you can't answer me properly." When that moment did arrive, Rod explains, he "felt a hint of panic"; then, he noted, "I recalled your words, relaxed, and said, 'I'm sorry, Susan, but I don't know the answer to that,' and then I looked at my watch and crossed my fingers . . ."

Johanna, who served as my research assistant while she was writing her dissertation, summarizes: "As to your grad students and tears, yes, that was common. What was also common was the current research assistant always met with said student and tempered their reaction. I'm not sure why that was, but it was an unspoken role of the RA; 'send them to Johanna' or whoever was in that role, was the line friends would say to the tearful person. I comforted many students." Renata attributes the trepidation of my graduate students to the fact that young women saw me "not only as an advisor but also a role model: the sort of faculty we wanted to become." She goes on to speculate that "the mirroring involved in such a relationship makes a comment from a role model far more weighty than one from a mentor whom you do not aspire to be like."

In an email that threatened to make *me* weep (because it was written by a dissertator who informed me that she had found wisps of my hair in her manuscript when I was editing during chemo), Jamie speculates that perhaps fear has to play a part in the mentoring process:

> You were never once unkind (although I used to sweat a little when you looked at me over the top of your glasses and raised your eyebrows), so I don't know why we were always a bit scared. . . . And actually, that fear of disappointing you was a central motivating factor; we worked hard because we didn't want to give you something subpar. I think that anxiety has got to be there, somewhat, in a mentoring relationship, right? Can anyone mentor a student without some intimidation, however deliberately uncultivated?

To be sure, all of these emailed comments on my severity—Kelly and Rod both call me "tough" in their letters—came peppered with compliments, gratitude, and statements thanking me for supplying the tools necessary to produce the books, articles, or skills their authors had gone on to develop. And some of them are funny. Here is Tamara:

> When I told you I was pregnant and leaving IU for a time, I appreciated your no bullshit response. . . . "Well, you have to finish the PhD." That's what I needed to hear at that time. That you believed in me. I could work with that. And then later, when I was really struggling to move beyond the lit review stage of my dissertation, you told me you already knew I was a good student and could analyze and summarize the things others were saying . . . but it was time to write my own stuff. I said something like "But I feel like I am just making shit up." You said (and this is a quote I remember), "Well, that's what makes a theorist, dear."

The softening of my tone might be an index of my changing relationship to graduate students as I aged. While I was ambitious to establish a reputation of my own and dealing with graduate students close to my own age, I was a hard-ass; however, in the blink of an eye, it seems, I was not only professionally secure but also old enough to be the mother of my dissertators. John's email explains my reputation and trajectory: "I braced myself for the man-eater I had been warned about, and what I found was this gentle woman who ushered me into an easy chair and asked me to talk about myself. And laughed." Once, John reminds me, during a reception or get-together that I periodically hosted at home, he got stuck in my bathroom and dwindled into "a terrified twenty-something graduate student who feared he might melt into the floor from the sheer mortification of it all": "The doorknob came off in my hand and the spindle, with the other doorknob still attached, fell onto the kitchen floor, if I recall. You were able to free me rather quickly . . . once you stopped laughing."

When I consider all the years, of course, more difficult events predominate. In the heady days of student strikes, one of my treasured dissertators joined a joint action suit against the department—some teaching jobs were at stake—and I was named in the suit. Another brilliant student was so terrified by the prospect of an oral exam that we devised secret hand signals so I could coach her throughout it. I needed to advise one teaching assistant to wear a vest or a jacket over her T-shirt or the freshmen in her class would never stop gawking at the trace of her nipples. A job had to be conjured for a fine student afraid to return home to a country coming under fundamentalist Islamic rule. I accepted another dissertator whose topic I knew nothing about because her previous advisor had sexually harassed her.

The worst was the murder of one of my most prized students and having to comfort her family at the memorial. Two others were killed too young by cancer. Easier times came later, often when the mentoring was over: inscribed publications, news of teaching awards and new job opportunities, pictures emailed or posted on Facebook, and return visits with or without partners and children.

But as I got older and the graduate students seemingly got younger, the knowledge/authority gap between us widened. Because anxieties threatened to inhibit my students, I needed to find strategies to subvert the power imbalance, to sponsor reciprocity between me and them. I devised two ways to even the playing field . . . at least a bit. First, I found team-teaching with my graduate students in large lecture halls, but also in smaller forums, helped us become collaborative together, especially if they chose some of the texts we were studying. For one participant, Matt, team-teaching "was where we got a chance to discuss pedagogies that take emotions into account." The give-and-take of orchestrating discussions or constructing a syllabus or an exam made for more equitable conversations in which I could learn from them as they did from me.

Second, as the sheer number of dissertators became burdensome, I got the genius idea of grouping them together in The Dissertation Factory (TDF). When we met around a table once a month to critique a draft-in-progress of one participant's thesis, the discussions were enlightening for them but for me as well. Our model was the writing workshop; Jamie called it "peer review": getting group feedback or giving it. According to Matt, "It was really a model of what a writing group can be and do (tough, dedicated to each other, and best of all, productive). I can draw a direct line from that experience of mentorship to becoming a mentor and now academic director of . . . a faculty writing group program, with groups of six untenured faculty members mentored by a tenured faculty member."

There was a third way that undercut my own authority, but it was quirky and often occurred after the granting of degrees: friendship. For how can such intellectual intimacy not foster the formations of close emotional bonds? One former graduate student taught me hand quilting; one was hired by one of my publishers and worked as the cherished copy editor of my last three books; one allowed me to serve as a hospice volunteer while she was dying; one demonstrated relaxation techniques when I sorely needed them. Quite a few invited me to visit their home institutions as a visiting lecturer. To this day, some read my drafts-in-progress and suggest revisions. Others provide me reading lists whenever I try to get up to date on an emerging aspect of women's literature, feminist criticism, or queer theory.

Yet it still remains suggestive that there is no word for the mentee that circumvents the powerfully overarching influence of the mentor. The word *ephebe* does not work since it has always referred to an adolescent boy. *Disciple, protégé, follower*: if anything, these terms are even more suppliant and subordinated. *Apprentice* or *intern* comes closer, but belies the fact that the guild is not hiring many new members and that quite a few of my students found their way to excellent nonacademic jobs. Nor do we have a term for mentee mates, although Nancy K. Miller and I became close friends while we were both being mentored by Carolyn Heilbrun.

Today a colleague confides that she worries about mentoring mentally ill students who might be carrying guns. In my day, we fretted about the erotics of pedagogy, a happier topic, despite the abuse potentials. Even though I remain clueless about how eroticism operated for my mentored students, one emailed response furnishes a hint. At the risk of seeming self-congratulatory, I will quote part of Helene's comments:

> I remember you taking copious notes during my dissertation defense and giving them to me afterwards. That was an incredibly useful, practical act of mentorship. However, it was also a profoundly important symbolic act. You communicated to me that you expected that dissertation to go beyond the dissertation—that you expected me to continue to write and to send [my work] out into the world. I returned to that moment many times during my early years at an institution that did not encourage me (and sometimes actively discouraged me) to see myself as a writer and a scholar. (I should note that many of my male peers were rewarded rather than punished for their writerly and scholarly ambitions.)

Helene quite rightly sensed my desire at her defense: I wanted her to publish her thesis and to keep on writing (which is precisely what she did). Kathleen Davies explains in her memoir that when she got stuck in her writing, she asked herself the question, "What Would Susan Do? (WWSD)" (85), praying that it would not tempt her to start smoking. I suspect that what attracted my graduate students was my ambition for their ambition. The phrase "my ambition for their ambition" sounds odd to my ear: generally, one has an ambition to do or achieve something. But my ambition as a mentor was to cultivate their ambition . . . as writers or as teachers or as thinkers bringing their proficiencies into other ventures. Maybe my orgasmic moaning in seminars attested to my delight in witnessing young women and men committing themselves to their own intellectual and professional aspirations, my pleasure in hearing them say, in effect, "I'll have what she's having." Still, needless to say, the dynamics of mentoring remain mysterious and I am only guessing.

I know that being mentored enthralled me. A dinner out with Carolyn Heilbrun was always a thrilling prospect that would, I believed, somehow change my thinking, my next project, my life. Throughout my decades at Indiana, my mentor was Don Gray, who read every word I wrote and responded with single-spaced commentaries that helped me understand what I was trying to say. And, yes reader, I did marry him. But we were colleagues, not enmeshed in the teacher/student hierarchy, and he never made me cry.

Why did some of my students cry? They were crying, I suspect, because they were young and they felt baffled and frightened at not being able to discern how the future in front of them would unfurl. They were crying because they realized (as I did) that our profession was deteriorating, and with it their prospects. They were crying because they wanted to become the person I wanted them to be and it was not clear that this could happen, given a thicket of health- and family-related constraints. Maybe they were crying because learning is often painful as one stumbles and startles in bewilderment before the lightbulb goes on. Then factor in exhaustion: most were being taught by me while they were teaching undergraduates and trying to make ends meet by taking on other part-time jobs.

But they were not only crying. They were formulating ideas to express their insights into a variety of cultural quandaries as they graduated and moved forward into all sorts of environments—public and private high schools, community colleges, colleges and universities, nonprofits, businesses of their own, churches, community centers, communications facilities, newspaper offices, libraries—that I would never inhabit but that (they kindly told me) I had somehow seeded. Even those who lost contact with me, I believe, managed to use and reinvent what they got from me in ways I cannot imagine.

My former graduate students are not my adopted children. Yet as I enter old age and as a few of them start to retire, they are my beloveds. I touch base with some of them only sporadically now. Yet they all remain vivid as I remember them back then, in all their vulnerability. For while I didn't know at the time that I was making them cry, I certainly realized that I was making them anxious, fearful of failing, wary because we came from different religious, racial, regional, and sometimes national backgrounds. And I remain proud of them for finding unique techniques to emblazon the complicated dialogues in which we engaged. They will not attend my funeral, but they will make my memory a blessing . . . each and every one of them. Amid the ups and downs of my personal life—my kids' achievements, divorce, remarriage, illness—we shared passionate convictions about how language and literature and the arts of reading, writing, and teaching can advance equality and justice.

This fact is a consolation when I am fearful about surviving in a society that seems at times to be hurtling us back to prefeminist days, despite all the hard, though "disproven," work of my generation. Do you get the impression that this particular remark rankled? Conceded. But I'm grateful that it sparked an investigation that has crowded my head with memories of throngs of vibrant younger people who have enriched my life enormously. Learning was so absorbing, disquieting, exhilarating in "the days that are no more" for me, but must (oh! how I hope so) must be ongoing for those now "fresh as the first beam glittering on the sail" (Tennyson).

Acknowledgments

With thanks (in the order of their appearance here) to Kathleen Davies, Elizabeth Baer, Heather May, Rod Taylor, Johanna Frank, Renata Kobetts Miller, Jamie Horrocks, Kelly Hanson, Tamara Berg, John Laudun, Matt Brim, and Helene Myers as well as to Alice Falk and Tricia Lootens, who read a draft, and to all the unnamed former students who keep on teaching me. A completely different essay would be needed to explore the dynamics of mentoring within the collaborative partnership I share with Sandra M. Gilbert, who has kept me honest from *The Madwoman in the Attic* to *Feminist Literary Theory and Criticism: A Norton Reader* to *Still Mad: American Women Writers and the Feminist Imagination, 1950–2020*.

At home in Bloomington, Indiana, **Susan Gubar** has most recently published *Late-Life Love* and, with Sandra Gilbert, *Still Mad: American Women Writers and the Feminist Imagination, 1950–2020*. She is currently at work on a book titled *How She Aged: The Inventive Endgames of Women Artists*.

Works Cited

Davies, Kathleen. *Sacred Groves: Or, How a Cemetery Saved My Soul*. Bink Books, 2019.

———. "Stop Clock, Cover Mirror." *The Guardians of Mediocrity: How Universities Use Tenure Denial to Thwart Change, Creativity, and Intellectual Innovation*. Foiled Crown Books, 2017, pp. 83–98.

Tennyson, Alfred. "Tears, Idle Tears." Poetry Foundation, www.poetryfoundation. org/poems/45384/the-princess-tears-idle-tears. Accessed 10 Dec. 2021.

The Making of an Intellectual

Mentoring, Mothering, and a Black Feminist Journey

MICHELE FAITH WALLACE

Black Macho and the Myth of the Superwoman was published in December of 1978, accompanied by a large excerpt in *Ms. Magazine* with my not-so-bad-looking face on the cover and thus on many newsstands where black faces were then a rarity. The book immediately generated controversy and outrage among its mostly black audience even before anyone had actually seen a single book. I was twenty-seven years old and I had my fifteen minutes of fame. I was not grateful. I was not surprised. I felt entitled.

At the time, I confidently anticipated that such furor would be my life from then on, but I was wrong. Although I was mistaken about how things would go, about some things I was right. The topics I touched upon and the way in which I raised them would continue to be of importance more or less exactly as I raised them at the time. My perspective was skewed by innocence and naïveté, even ignorance of the very things that obsessed me, but one thing I never would have guessed is how much things would change and yet remain the same.

After the first publication of *Black Macho* in 1979, I went back to school to do a PhD in American studies at Yale University. At the time I wrote *Black Macho*, I had only a bachelors in English from the City College of New York. I yearned deeply for more knowledge, which made Yale the perfect place for me for a time. Unfortunately, the flood of new knowledge was overwhelming and knocked me to my knees, resulting in my first nervous breakdown at the age of twenty-nine in 1981.

Of course, there were other factors in my illness, some of which would take me decades to discern, but what I remember most clearly about this time is the mind-blowing experience of the revelation that there were places like Yale where scholarship in the humanities was earnestly pursued. What really floored me was the manner in which Yale altered my perception of the potential compass of scholarship. First, given how intimidated I was by the newly fashionable approaches to English studies of deconstruction (Yale was then the home of this methodology of literary analysis, which included regular visits from its reigning star, Jacques Derrida), and poststructuralism, I chose rather to focus on my new and actually first scholarly love, American history, which was also a field strenuously represented by scholars in residence at Yale. Also, at the same time and quite accidentally, I found myself in the very place that was set to pioneer the new field of African American studies.

For the entire time I was in New Haven, even before I began to attend Yale, I yearned to explore thoroughly the conceptual universe that was opening before me, with an ache that could only come from a lifetime of having been headed in an entirely different direction. I had no idea who I was or would subsequently become intellectually. Indeed, I had no idea that mine was the temperament of an intellectual, and that until I felt comfortable in that world, I would never feel comfortable in the world at all.

My ambition until then had been to be a novelist. I was, in fact, at that very time working on the third or fourth draft of a novel for which I had a contract. My education at CCNY, which had been largely focused on literature and creative writing, had done fairly well by me, but it hadn't given me that sense of the place of the analysis of intellectual and cultural history, which was from that day to this the most important key to my future life of the mind that I would ever obtain.

I can still remember the excitement of the discussions that ensued with my CCNY mentor Mark Mirsky and his artist wife Inger at their loft on the Bowery on my visits to New York. Indeed, it had been Mirsky as my teacher as an undergraduate who use to say to me again and again, whenever we would inevitably encounter that lacuna in my endless questions about the nature of things literary and philosophical, "You should be at Harvard." He would tell me this on a weekly basis in 1970 when I was eighteen years old, "You shouldn't be here." The one thing I will say about CCNY is that it was the first place where anybody ever began to talk about me having intellectual capacities and the idea that I was smart.

At that time I decided to become a writer, but what I really wanted to be and always wanted to be was an intellectual. People ask me today, What do you do? and I always say I am an intellectual, which invariably elicits an uncomfortable laugh, followed by a stare to see how and when I plan to turn it into a joke.

Mark couldn't explain what he was trying to tell me or how he even knew that I could go to Harvard without any money and without being a straight-A student (he himself was a graduate of Harvard who had grown up in Boston's Jewish community), but I had missed out on my generation's (I think Gates said the entering class of black students at Yale in 1969 went from three to almost one hundred) entry into the Ivy League, because I had been sabotaged by people who knew nothing about the Ivy League or about the opportunities or possibilities that could be offered to someone who was under the tutelage of a Harvard University or really any decent private college in the United States then. I had been sabotaged by people who thought the only really significant career in the world was to be either a musician or an artist in the black tradition. Otherwise you were what my dad (Earl) used to call an "air inspector." In fact I think that's what they thought an intellectual was, an air inspector.

I was so clueless as to what such an education in the humanities might constitute (as are most Americans still, especially those who are black) that it never occurred to me to take Mirsky's suggestion seriously. We black folk hadn't yet entirely absorbed the national obsession with business, law, and medicine, but the humanities and the arts at any university were definitely not on the agenda either. But Mirsky was Jewish, only about ten years older than me, had come from the inner city of Boston and gone to Harvard as an undergrad himself, and he knew what such an opportunity to be exposed to world-class minds might do for one such as me. It wasn't a matter of just continuing the elite education I had begun at New Lincoln, the private school my sister and I attended. For my mother, though, New Lincoln was supposed to have been sufficient to open all the doors I might need. It made no difference, she thought, where you went to college. In fact, you should send yourself to college as she had done in going to City College. At that time it was still absolutely free.

For me, however, like Mirsky, it was more a matter of being some place where challenging intellectual discourse was the norm. Yale was such a place. And as I would subsequently discover on my lecture tours to promote *Black Macho*, there were many schools in the United States capable of providing this level of intellectual rigor. But when I finally found myself surrounded by such folk at Yale, I was caught short. And these students really were the best and brightest those very same American colleges had produced because, remember, no one who was trying to be rich or financially successful would be pursuing a PhD in history or literature or philosophy, or most especially American studies, which was kind of the new kid on the political block in academia. They didn't have any money and they had made financial sacrifices to pursue their PhDs at such an early age. They were the children of the New Left. In that sense, paradoxically, I was very much in the right place because that was what my mother had been and still was: a political progressive.

I was often quiet in class because I was simply flabbergasted by the depth of my ignorance of writings and concepts my classmates regarded as indispensable. Moreover, I quite simply did not know what to regard as important. I didn't know, for instance, what the lampposts of such a discussion were, the ebb and flow, the beginning, middle, and end. It seemed a kind of complicated rhetorical game in which actual knowledge was not the prize or even the measure. It had more to do with the production of knowledge. There was a gamesmanship about it. I knew when it was happening, but I could not yet identify or name its parts, much less describe it. I had read the book we were all assigned to read (we read at least a book a week for each class). Presumably everybody in the room had read some portion of the book, and yet the ensuing discussion seemed to have nothing at all to do with the book I had read.

Since I have taught so much myself since then, I can now look back on what happened in these classes with a good deal more analytical distance. Pretty soon I began to notice a few things that were entirely unspoken. First, certain students were the most vocal and exerted considerable leadership in the discussions. Second, often these students had quite apparently not done all or even most of the reading. Invariably, such a student would make a claim for an alternate reading or set of ideas as more important to the topic than the reading we had been assigned. I don't think I need to point out that this student was almost always male, or that I was invariably the only black student in any of my classes.

But every time I watched and heard this occur, I was so intimidated, it rendered me speechless. It went against my most basic assumptions about academic performance. I had never been a particularly proficient performer in an educational environment. I had become comfortable with the idea that I wasn't smart enough. But being smart seemed to have little to do with whether or not you had done the homework. From this I learned that it was the more relaxed mind, the familiarity with one's own intellectual disposition and what one thought about a variety of related matters that was much more important to holding one's own in discussion, or in any environment in which words provided the substance.

Meanwhile, I had my first encounter with the essays that made up W. E. B. Du Bois's *The Souls of Black Folk* (1903). He had been the first black man to complete a PhD at Harvard. His dissertation, which became *The Suppression of the African Slave Trade* (1899), was his first important book in a truly stellar career. Moreover, that you could still read such books and make discoveries you had not previously fathomed was a revelation, the power of which has never left me. As I, myself, was grappling with the difficulty of what I would do with the rest of my life, Yale helped me to begin to grasp the fruits of longevity and intellectual productivity, which were the daily preoccupation of everyone's study there.

It was with great and lasting regret that I was forced to leave Yale because of my illness in the fall of 1981. I was given the opportunity to return, but I had lost my nerve and all of my confidence that I could complete such a PhD. But what I did do—because I never really gave up on the life of the mind that Yale opened up to my examination—is that I kept all of the materials related to my education there, my papers, my study materials, my books (and I bought every book I could find). I took them with me everywhere and studied it all until I had mastered every page, every author, every word, every sentence. You could perhaps say that I took Yale on the road with me. And as I shifted my career from being a would-be novelist to being an academic and intellectual, I continued to study the ideas to which I had first been introduced at Yale on my own. Whenever I saw an opportunity to follow up on a set of ideas that I had had to abandon at Yale, I did so. For one day, I returned to Yale after the psychiatrist at the health center had okayed me for return to school. That first day, I had a class with David Brion Davis, all of whose books I have subsequently read, and he distributed photocopies of the manuscript of Orlando Patterson's *Slavery and Social Death*, which had not yet been published. I had it with me when I left New Haven for the last time. And a close study of this text, further pursued to the notes and supplementary materials when the actual book came out, began my education in my own Yale without walls.

I was a black woman, groomed and encouraged in my politics by my mother, the artist Faith Ringgold, who was also a black feminist. Still, black feminism wasn't any better received in those days in black communities than it is today. Nonetheless, I have come to see that I was destined to occupy this marginal position in relationship to the black status quo by a lifetime of unusual experiences, a lifetime of being in Harlem but not really of it. It took my mother a while to read *Black Macho*, but when she realized there wasn't really a word in it about her art or even about her contribution to my feminist consciousness, she was livid. She regarded my failure to recognize her importance in my development as a feminist as unforgiveable. Over the years as I reread the book, I often hear her voice in the narrative much more than my own. I think now that she was right. My mother's greatest concern was not that I would grow up never knowing that the world was a dangerous place but rather that my sister and I would grow up not rooted in African American culture and the Harlem community. My stepdad would have simply been unable to imagine anything else. To the two of them, Harlem—especially on the hill for Dad and anywhere hill or valley for Mom, who was born in the valley—was "safe" in a way that few other communities could possibly be for African American girls. It is very difficult for me to talk about or to remember these experiences, particularly the aspect of it that involved accepting the helplessness of most women in this environment. It was surely this kind of pressure in which young and old men openly hunted young women in the black community that made me take so readily to feminism.

So was my mother my mentor after all? Despite Mark Mirsky's constant encouragement, there was always something missing for me. Perhaps this is this why the term *mentor* turns me off so much, the mentors I have had, the job I have done at mentoring. Of course, mentoring is easier than mothering. The bar is lower, it seems to me, in comparison. The differences between mothering and mentoring and the mutual insufficiencies of the two I think may help to explain why my relationship with my mother has turned out pretty well after all. She really likes mentoring people and is good at it.

For now, while my mother is quite old, though still an actively producing artist, I attend to the details of her career, curating the Faith Ringgold Society, organizing her exhibits and interviews. Perhaps this is also, if belatedly for me, and enjoyably, another form of mentoring: mentoring in reverse.

Much to her astonishment, **Michele Faith Wallace** will be seventy in January and provides more services under more headings (director, Anyone Can Fly Foundation; president, the Faith Ringgold Society; and chief operating officer, Faith Ringgold Inc.) than she can comfortably conceive or fulfill. She is as well, for which no title can do justice, her famous mother's principal caretaker—Faith Ringgold, the artist, who turned ninety-one October 8, 2021, with much celebration both before, during, and after. She is a feminist writer, also an African American, contemplating a memoir from which this piece is taken. Finally, Wallace is professor emeritus in English, the City College of New York and the CUNY Graduate Center.

When Am I Supposed to Stop Asking You for Advice?

HILLARY CHUTE

In college, at Oberlin, things started really clicking for me intellectually once I became a research assistant to the professor who had taught my Feminist Theory class—the class that changed my life, in about 1993. In this class I remember writing two papers—one on *Jane Eyre*, still one of my favorite novels of all time—and a less-successful one on Riot Grrrl, the punk feminist movement of the 1990s that had affected me profoundly. This range shows, I think, what was so captivating to me about the class: it was a class in which my mind could be blown by reading established criticism and novels, opening all sorts of new vistas, and also one in which I could understand the contemporary cultural production I cared about in a direct, personal way as generative too, and part of a trajectory of feminist forms of expression. I was also captivated by my professor, who became my mentor. She was authoritative and calm; measured and deliberate in a way that inspired confidence.

Sandy Zagarell lived in a beautiful house with her partner and clearly beloved cats—a space I was thrilled to be invited to, where we would sometimes have meetings when I started working for her. She is a nineteenth-century Americanist, and the book of hers on which I worked, drafting annotations and background research reports, helped me understand what scholarly research is. Sandy once mentioned to me that a colleague had seen one of my reports and assumed it was written by another faculty member. I took compliments from her very, very

49

seriously, and they provoked me to conceive of myself as someone who might be talented. To put it another way, even small asides like this, from people I respected as thinkers, generated new forms of ideation for me. If someone articulated an aptitude in me, maybe it really was there, even if I hadn't thought that thought about myself; horizons seemed a little, or a lot, wider, like a modeling of the possible. And yet by the time I was a graduating senior, when, knowing I wanted to pursue a PhD, she took me out to a Mexican restaurant the week of graduation to give me an ethically humane, tough love speech about graduate degrees and my sure-to-be-dismal job prospects, I was by that point confident enough to tell her I wanted to pursue it anyway.

I have always loved mentors—particularly the mentorship of strong women. In graduate school—which I got into because of Sandy Zagarell's recommendation letter, as was reported to me directly from a professor who had served on the admissions committee—things clicked for me in my second term, when I took a 60s and Postmodernism class taught by the professor, Marianne DeKoven, who would later become my dissertation director and mentor. I was never consciously searching out mentorship—just ambling/bumbling along—but I felt keenly aware of a mix of admiration and comfort around certain faculty, whereas for many others I felt purely admiration. I gravitated to the former.

To note: I did study with some men; I had a brilliant professor, John McClure, on my oral exams committee, and I have deep respect for him and his ideas. I loved his classes; I still think about his seminars, probably way more than anyone would suspect. And I had an intense intellectual friendship with another male professor whose class I had taken, which included both discussions of work and also the shape of our lives. Both, I could tell, would be problematic for me for finishing a dissertation. During the process of studying for my oral exams, I had a vivid dream that I was in a motel room, cuddling in bed with John McClure while discussing the novel *White Noise*. (Our orals list was on the works of Don DeLillo.) It was a great dream was the problem. And I had developed a full-blown crush on the other professor; I truly liked, too much, having hours-long discussions with him in his office. I had made him a mixtape (now that I'm on the other side, as faculty, I cringe thinking about some of these details and how obviously weird it would feel to me if a student of mine acted in the same way). Clearly he could not be on my dissertation committee. I think I knew, even in my early twenties, that a dissertation would be hard enough to write without that kind of erotic static and attendant self-consciousness.

I was lucky to have so many brilliant professors in my PhD program (at Rutgers, the State University of New Jersey). And what happened to me is a story about three mentors who encouraged me to pursue, and help to create, a field without obvious roadmaps. In the past fifteen years or so I have been heavily involved in building the field of comics studies—especially in a literary and art-historical context, both inside and outside the academy. (I'm an English professor and a comics and graphic novels columnist for the *New York Times Book Review*.) No one in my department had devoted a dissertation to comics. It is a thriving field now, but during the years I was a graduate student it was not. It was unusual; nascent. As I opened a recent essay in the journal *Feminist Studies*, "Over a decade ago, as a graduate student in English, mentored by three inspiring feminist advisors on my dissertation committee, I longed to write the kind of analysis that I found largely missing in academic studies of comics and graphic novels" (153). My mentors modeled the kind of open intellectual thinking that gave me the confidence to be expansive and help build this field where it hadn't flourished before. And none of them was an expert in comics, per se.

I dedicated my first book, *Graphic Women: Life Narrative and Contemporary Comics*, to them. It reads, simply, "This book is dedicated to Marianne, Carolyn, and Harriet." I remember that the book designer at Columbia University Press added a little flower icon below the dedication, and I asked her to remove it and felt very strongly about it. Perhaps because I study images, and don't like to deploy them unnecessarily, the inclusion of this one felt like it struck the wrong note: sweet, sentimental. What I felt was: serious gratitude. I didn't need decoration to make this point more forcefully—just the words, in a hopefully elegant sans serif and this-is-vital all caps. Marianne, Carolyn, and Harriet were significant mentors to me on an intellectual and a personal level. To put it simply, their confidence in me helped me to be confident in myself. I absorbed that confidence and energy and sense of possibility they saw in me and ran with it; it enabled me to take risks.

From an intellectual point of view, how they mentored me meant modeling ways of thinking, not providing me with a body of knowledge (although they did this too). I wrote a dissertation, *Contemporary Graphic Narratives: History, Aesthetics, Ethics*, about nonfiction comics: works about history, both personal and world-historical. No person on my committee, as I mentioned, had scholarly expertise in comics—and they didn't need it to give me the intellectual grounding and confidence to write an analysis of an emerging form. I often talk to my own graduate students—I explained it to a student this morning—about how my dissertation committee was made up of professors whose own research didn't *match* mine, but whose distinct perspectives, especially in combination, showed me how to approach my own topic.

All of my mentors helped me understand the thing about contemporary comics that fascinated me through their only-seemingly different foci. Harriet Davidson is a scholar of poetry who thinks about feminism and critical theory and experimental form. I still remember how one of her offhand comments in an early dissertation meeting—"Trauma breaks the boundaries of form," she said as we were chatting in her office—rearranged my brain permanently and launched so much of my academic inquiry into comics. Carolyn Williams, a Victorianist, encouraged me to take a long view of popular culture, helping me to think about form historically (her recent book is *Gilbert and Sullivan: Gender, Genre, Parody*), and especially how to think about form and autobiography—she is a prominent voice on *Jane Eyre*, whose central fictive conceit is its first-person form and address to the (dear) reader. Marianne DeKoven is a theorist of modernism and postmodernism, known for being, among other things, a Gertrude Stein scholar (*A Different Language: Gertrude Stein's Experimental Writing*). Her exploration of the politics of form and profound literary experiment gave me a way to think about comics, with their repetitions, narrative inversion, extra-semantic marks, and ambiguous desires.

It felt like a confirmation of what I had been trying to conceptualize of the comics form's dynamism and avant-garde lineage when I read the following quote in an interview with cartoonist Art Spiegelman, in which he describes the influence of Stein on his work: "She is pushing as hard as she can *against* narrative content, and against clear exposition, and is getting drunk on the language and on the rhythm and on the sound of the words she's using, but she's still somehow saying something." I was able to connect the dots for a subject about which little had been written in the academy because of the breadth and depth my mentors gave me. It felt like putting puzzle pieces together in the most exciting way to work with them.

I first read Spiegelman's *Maus*, the book that inspired my interest in comics, in Marianne's Contemporary Literature class, in the year 2000 (I will always remember that year because I was writing my paper on *Maus* the night of the Bush v. Gore presidential election). Just the inclusion of that book on a syllabus next to Rushdie and DeLillo and Morrison and Pynchon fascinated me. For my oral exams, at the end of which I received my MA degree, I still wasn't clear on my dissertation topic, and I had a wacky-sounding exams category called "cross-discursive media," a helpful term another professor had suggested, which included comics and other hybrid forms. Marianne took me out to lunch at the art museum next to the English Department after I passed my exams and listened patiently to me launch a few ideas before stating, "I had always thought you would write a dissertation about comics." I responded, with honesty, "I can do that?" I didn't think that possible until that moment in which she exhibited confidence in me to make it work and confidence in me to be making it work as her student. Again and again, she suggested to me as a graduate student that I could take on things I wouldn't have thought possible. She encouraged me to submit to the biggest journal in literary studies, *PMLA*, which I thought was insane (when my essay was rejected, and I felt upset by the criticism, she had me write my responses to the reader's reports, to her—a very useful exercise). A few years later, I published an essay there, "Comics as Literature? Reading Graphic Narrative." She suggested we pitch a special issue of a journal on comics, which never would have occurred to me and led to Graphic Narrative, a special issue of *MFS: Fiction Studies*, and which I am proud to say was the first special issue of a journal in my field, literary studies, on comics (and a chance to actually collaborate with Marianne).

I admired my mentors deeply and felt devoted to them. At times, I probably parroted them too closely, as when I think I embarrassed Marianne in my oral exam by reciting one of her central arguments from her book *Rich and Strange: Gender, History, Modernism* in an answer to a question. But it was a good argument and I believed in it, I think back . . . She convinced me on the substance. It wasn't for show. It felt good to have women in my life to whom I wanted to hew so closely. I never minded being an apprentice; I was happy to be able to look up to them. I am reminded of a line from Chris Ware's graphic novel *Jimmy Corrigan*, in which a son recollects following his father, as a child, up to the top of a tall building: "I followed him like a loyal animal right up to the edge of the largest building in the world" (n.p.). In the book, the father abandons his son there—the book's central trauma. I was a loyal animal as a graduate student—but in my case, that trust didn't do me any harm; and unlike as is often the case with filial relationships, it was purely elective, and informed. And my mentors were gentle in teaching me how to write, and even separate from them—I will always remember Marianne very gently suggesting I was "too dutiful" in my citations of others, which was a diplomatic way of encouraging me to let my own ideas assume space. I also remember asking her in an email about the Spiegelman–Stein connection, as if she could verify it, and being disappointed when she redirected the question back at me. In retrospect, it was an important moment, in which she wasn't going to answer my query for me but rather show me without stating it explicitly that I had the skills to generate the account on my own.

Within this past year, I had a dream about Marianne: I was supposed to be on an academic panel with her, but somehow I was running late and was going to miss it, and was beside myself. How could this have happened—I was not only late for a panel, but late for a panel with *my advisor*! I defended my dissertation in 2006, and I still, on occasion, have dreams like this. I prefer the clarity (if not the affect) of this kind of transparent anxiety dream—letting down someone you revere—to the cuddling in a hotel dream. (In a real-life version of the letting-your-mentor-down logistical fail, I recently returned to Oberlin to celebrate cartoonist and alumna Alison Bechdel's honorary degree, stayed with Sandy at the beautiful house I had admired for twenty years, and lost her house key, forcing her to change all her locks—ugh!) Perhaps Marianne and my other mentors remain so active in my unconscious dreaming—and conscious thinking!—because the central reward of their mentorship is their continuing role in my life. At my dissertation defense—to which Carolyn, ever classy, brought a bottle of Veuve Clicquot, something I now do for my own students—I asked them, at the close, my most significant question: When am I supposed to stop asking you for advice? The response: "Never."

Hillary Chute is distinguished professor of English and Art + Design at Northeastern University, and a comics and graphic novels columnist for the *New York Times Book Review*. She is the author or editor of seven books, including *Why Comics? From Underground to Everywhere* (2017), and the edited collection *Maus Now: Selected Writing* (2022).

Works Cited

Chute, Hillary. "Feminist Graphic Art." *Feminist Studies*, vol. 44, no. 1, 2018, pp. 153–70.

Ware, Chris. *Jimmy Corrigan: The Smartest Kid on Earth*. Pantheon, 2000.

Mentorship

By Any Means Necessary

SHARIFA HAMPTON

Introduction

I still have the now-dog-eared note a woman with a wide smile handed to me as she thanked me for the words I had just delivered at the English Department's commencement ceremony. The sprawling script covered the entire length of stiff blue cardstock she had torn from the program the day I graduated with my master's degree. I remember feeling amazed that my ideas meant something to someone—a teacher and administrator who was endeavoring to teach (reach) her students across their racial differences.

Like this woman's students, my schooling was in classroom settings with mentors and teachers who were always racially different from me. From a very young age, I rode a school bus that shuttled me from my predominantly Black neighborhood, to an elementary school, then to a junior high, and later a high school where the majority of the students and teachers were white. I quickly developed strategic code-switching and toggled my identity between my two competing, and very valued, communities—one Black and one white. Keith Gilyard's interwoven autobiography as/and academic text, *Voices of the Self*, describes this intellectual phenomenon for Black students in predominantly white settings as a trifecta of "survival, race consciousness and communicative skill" and raises disquieting concerns about the "psychic costs" Black students pay in these scenarios—another Black tax (11). In high school, steeped in whiteness, I began to sense that if I wanted help negotiating the unfamiliar terrain of what I would later come to know as Gilyard's conceptual triangle, it was available to me.

My high school dean was the first woman to avail herself to me as a mentor, and thankfully there were many others to follow. I noticed that the women in authority around me, mostly white women, were not always averse to helping me navigate my way from one job to the next, or from one career to another. They recognized that I was genuinely open to friendship, mentorship, and direction. At some point in my early twenties I began to unconsciously seek out mentors in every setting, and they were always there—in my places of employment, houses of worship, in schools. Most were able to read the sign that must have been—and still is—affixed to my forehead that announced I was a willing, honest and open-minded young person who would appreciate all their coaching efforts had to offer.

My high school dean understood my lack of financial stability and made sure I had a clear-cut path to employment after I graduated. "Don't worry. College will be there when you're ready," she said, and it was. My mentor from corporate America nudged me forward in my career in banking by opening doors and pathways for advancement. When she hired me she told me it was okay if I couldn't fathom the numbers in the billions (way too many zeros for me) that represented the money in our clients' accounts; just use the calculator and "fake it 'til you make it—it will come," and it did. As I transitioned from college student to instructor, my mentor in higher education recommended me for programs and opportunities that have led me to the PhD program I am presently completing. She also held space for me as I cried, as a fairly new Adjunct instructor, when a student I thought I liked called me the N-word in his final paper. She told me to report it and hold the college accountable until they acted on my behalf, and I did. My relationships with all these powerful and intelligent women have been invaluable, and I still gratefully call most of them friends, colleagues, and mentors today.

My graduation speech was both autobiographical and critical. I journeyed successfully through years of schooling in predominantly white institutions but, as Gilyard cautioned, I paid deep psychic costs. I went to college as a first-generation African American woman with pitifully inadequate knowledge of why Black people in the 1960s needed (and still need) a civil rights movement. My mentors, especially those I turned to in higher education, gave me the tools to assess and understand my positionality within our culture and the academy. As they created their syllabi they determinedly decentered whiteness and inserted "blackness and being." They encouraged me to choose areas of research and subjects that inevitably helped shape my identity and my writing. I discovered that these research areas—theories of linguistic discrimination; free and enslaved Black women's writings and their efforts of resistance; Black feminist theory and literature regarding motherhood and constructions of the Black family and Black studies in general—placed me in subject position; they were about me and they strengthened my *authentic* voice.

Now, I think I finally consider myself an academic; I've taught Black feminist and African/African American literature classes and classes on racism and language diversity. I also feel I've found a home teaching in a Black and Latino Studies Department whose chairperson is also a Black woman. I am honored to be a part of a community of powerful Black feminist and Black studies scholars who offer friendship, coaching and mentorship. Black women scholars and their labor may be invisible to others in the academy, but we see and care for each other. I can now generously pay something forward to my students, especially other Black women—that same friendship, coaching, and mentoring that has so long been offered to me. I can now offer others what that woman at my graduation heard in my words, what my teachers and mentors provided for me: a widened and lightened path through mentorship. I still have work to do, and I am prepared to do it, especially in what has become for me the most important place/space any and everywhere—the classroom.

Graduation Speech, May 31, 2016

English department graduates! We will run the world! Celebrate yourselves!

I would like to thank all of the English literature and composition professors here today, as well as those who are not, and especially those whose courses I've taken because those professors all helped me to understand why I needed to be here at the College of Staten Island. Cheers!

Professor Sarah Benesch, who introduced me to sociolinguistics and helped me uncover and reconcile my own experiences with linguistic discrimination, and whose classes came to be my most self-actualizing and intellectually affirming. She introduced me personally to Keith Gilyard at a conference, the then president of the National Council of Teachers of English, who was from a neighborhood just like mine. And then she introduced me to Gilyard's book, *Voices of the Self*, which told his story of linguistic discrimination, code-switching, and bidialectalism. I was completely blown away because as Gilyard told his story he also told mine, uncannily, page after page. This led me to search for and seek out my own voice, which in turn has led me to this space today. Professor Benesch helped me understand why I *needed* to be here.

Professor Maryann Feola discussed with me at length Aphra Behn's novel, *Oroonoko: Or the Royal Slave*, to help me better understand that Africans were very much complicit in the African Maafa, more commonly known as the Transatlantic Slave Trade. I was in stunned disbelief for quite some time. This was a complete aberration from the television series *Roots* that I watched as a youth. Professor Feola helped me better understand why I, again, *needed* to be here.

Professor Dalia Kandiyoti, on the first night of her class, screened James Allen's traveling photo exhibit, *Without Sanctuary*. I've never sat so rooted to my chair in a classroom with such mixed emotions. It's an exhibit that exposes the spectacle that the lynching of African Americans became in the Jim Crow South. Allen exposes the horror of lynching as he juxtaposes photograph after photograph, postcard after postcard depicting the lynchings that white spectators kept as souvenirs and were passed down to their children and their children's children. That was the South that my father, who died last year at ninety-four, had to flee. When I pulled up the images on my laptop to show him, he remembered that time and that place, so he also reminded me why I needed to be here.

Professor Hildegard Hoeller, whose nineteenth-century literature class was themed around American women's writing and its connection to women's rights and slavery, informed me that I rightfully and necessarily needed to be here. I had never read a slave narrative before, and we read slave narratives written by various women writers but most important several narratives written by formerly enslaved women, who were my ancestors. As a descendent of enslaved Africans, I found these narratives about as close to a far-gone family tree as I could get. Thank you, Professor Hoeller.

Professor Ellen Goldner's class gave me the works of Zora Neale Hurston, of whom I had heard but never read. But I knew Alice Walker, had fallen in love with her, and decided she was her muse—so I made Zora mine for a time as well. Walker and Hurston, both celebrated African American women writers, reminded me that I had a space here at the

College of Staten Island in which to write, create, dream. A space where I could belong.

I had no idea that coming to CSI, the school around the corner, would have such a profound impact on my life and my family's life. Let me also thank my family, especially my husband, life partner, and mentor, for allowing me the space in our lives to complete what I started here. They all made space for me to do this. Even when it got really tough, and my dad was diagnosed with cancer, and we knew he was going to die, even he would say, "Sharifa, don't you have some schoolwork you need to go do?" Thank you, Professor Katie Goodland, our MA coordinator, for giving me permission to grieve the loss of my father the way I needed and put this moment off for a season or two.

In retrospect, I didn't know that what I started here would be much more than just "going back to school." I didn't know it would answer my oldest daughter, Whitney's call, "Ma, go get your life." And that was exactly what I did, but it was a very long journey for me to get to this point, and I needed and was blessed with many mentors along the way. Neither of my parents attended college, nor their parents before them; they couldn't help me navigate those academic waters after high school, so I didn't go straight to college. Instead, I did what they had done; I went straight to work. My high school dean, my first mentor, sent me on interview after interview as I neared graduation—I even interviewed with her mother's employer, Cushman Wakefield Realtors, one of the largest realtors in New York City at the time—but to no avail. My dean finally advised me to take the school secretarial exam for the Board of Education—which she knew I would pass—and they would have no choice but to hire a young Black girl. She was right. I was with the New York City Board of Education for the next fourteen years. However, it didn't take me long to remember that I liked school, I missed it, and I thrived there.

I started by taking just one class at a local college in downtown Brooklyn, and three schools and sixteen years later, as a single parent, I received my bachelor's degree—and believe me sometimes it got really crazy. I had transferred to New York University and, at one point, I would leave my job in downtown Brooklyn, hop on the train to school—which was thankfully a short ride away in downtown Manhattan—take a class, hop back on the express train all the way out to Sheepshead Bay, Brooklyn, to pick my daughter up from afterschool, get back on the train with her, drop her off at her grandmother's house, then get back on the train to school and take another class. And that went on until she was in junior high school and could travel a little bit better on her own. However hectic it was, my example of "education by any means necessary" paid off, as she is a college graduate today.

As I look back over sixteen years of college-level schooling, I believe my real education did not begin until I came to CSI and was mentored by the faculty here—faculty that understood the difference between an education and schooling. I recently heard an analogy that likened the difference between schooling and education to trees. Schooling has broad trunks, soaring branches, and abundant foliage that can hide in plain sight what might really need to be exposed. Schooling also has shallow roots, which makes it more vulnerable in a storm. Education, however, has deep roots that better anchor, support, and sustain it and is therefore more trustworthy and stable in a storm. An education answers fundamental questions: *Who am I?* and *Why am I here?* The answers to those questions, at least for me, lie in the honest and accurate knowledge of culture, but it needed to be my culture—my African American, descended-from enslaved-people-but-We-Shall-Overcome-singing culture. That kind of *critical education* builds a student's knowledge of self; it necessarily builds student self-esteem. Most important, for me, it built a *critical hope* inside that helped me navigate the stress of balancing a family, caring for and losing a sick father, while simultaneously struggling to do research, teach class, and get an A on my final exams. Critical education, critical pedagogy, and critical hope interrupt stereotype threat, the situations where students of color might find themselves at risk of conforming to and confirming the images that have been inscribed by popular culture about the group or intersectional groups to which they may belong. Critical education increases the Pygmalion effect, which proposes that when one internalizes positive labels, one succeeds accordingly. I lived this. This type of education, not schooling, ultimately gives us a critical growth mindset that makes us comfortable questioning information that just doesn't make sense anymore. This was the critical education offered to me by my professors/mentors that told me I needed to be here, and I deserved to be here. They made me believe I could be successful and give back here.

The lesson that has loomed largest in my thinking through these mentoring and educational experiences is the difference between equity and equality. We know that many have fought and are still fighting for equal educational conditions in the United States, where equal equates to all having access to the same standard of education—and yes, as we should. However, if I may use a simplified analogy by scholar Dr. Jeff Duncan-Andrade, if we look at the matter critically, we can liken it to quenching the thirst of different groups of people. One approach is to hand them all the same bottles/amounts of water. That is equal treatment. Equity, however, causes one to pause and pose questions before the water is distributed. Questions such as: What exactly is this group thirsty for? Equity uses information to determine what type of liquid and how much of it might need to be given to a particular group, because every group thirsts for something different.

My high school dean knew I needed something different from what some other students needed, and she responded according to my need. So, before we just hand everyone the same bottles of water, or the same books with the same stories, for the sake of equality, let's try to determine what student groups are thirsty for and give them what they need to succeed. That is equity. People, students, especially those that find their group way out on the fringes of the margins, need a critical cultural education so they are better able to determine and define for themselves who they are in the face of all the varied, often negative voices, perceptions, and images they are commonly assaulted with on a daily basis. They are then enabled to succeed as they build upon a stable, self-affirming foundation.

The teachers/mentors I had here in the English Department attempted to understand me and others around me, individually as well as within our intersectional groups, and offered us what they considered an equitable education. In order to genuinely consider equity, one must have a capacity for empathy. Empathy is attempting to place oneself in another person's shoes. Empathy allows teachers to acknowledge the hard and complicated issues embedded in our lived experiences. Issues such as discrimination, racism, police brutality, microaggressions, privilege, Standard English, cis-heteronormativity, toxic masculinity, slavery, which students make up the majority of special education classes and also why, why the Confederate flag is still flying in South Carolina, and why Black Lives Matter (and I could go on ad infinitum). Critically empathetic teachers and mentors understand that 40 percent of schools in the US do not have a single teacher of color on staff, and that only 7 to 20 percent of current teacher education students nationwide are of color; that fewer than 10 percent of full-time college faculty in the United States are professors of color (National Center for Educational Statistics). That said, critically empathetic teachers and mentors understand that most of them do not come to the profession predisposed to think about what the roles of equity, diversity, inclusion, and justice have to do with teaching. Therefore, they are willing to learn to engage differently: by forming caring relationships, including culturally relevant material on their syllabi, and cultivating empathetic responsiveness in their pedagogy. I found that type of teacher/mentor here in this graduate program, right around the corner, at CSI.

Professor Kelly Bradbury, who has left CSI to pursue other endeavors, introduced me to educational researcher and author Lisa Delpit, who stated in her book, *Other People's Children: Cultural Conflict in the Classroom*:

> We do not really see through our eyes or hear through our ears, but through our beliefs. To put our beliefs on hold [my dear teacher and mentor] is to cease to exist as ourselves for a moment—and that is not easy. It is painful as well, because it means turning yourself inside out, giving up your own sense of who you are, and being willing to see yourself in the unflattering light of another's angry gaze. . . . It is the only way to learn what it might feel like to be someone else and the only way to start the dialogue. (46–47)

I am thankful for the professors and mentors that I have had here who were willing to take the time not only to begin the dialogue but to remind me again and again—and then again—why I needed to be here and to stay here.

Sharifa Hampton: Wife. Mother. Teacher. Student. Juggler extraordinaire. Writer. Abolitionist. Generous with care.

Works Cited

Delpit, Lisa. *Other People's Children: Cultural Conflict in the Classroom*. New Press, 1995.

Gilyard, Keith. *Voices of the Self: A Study of Language Competence*. Wayne State UP, 1991.

National Center for Educational Statistics. 2016, https://nces.ed.gov. Accessed 10 Dec. 2021.

The Accidental Mentor

JENNIFER CREWE

In the academic world, the advisor–advisee role is typically routine and sanctified. Student and teacher *choose* to work with one other. If you are a PhD advisor you are a mentor, and if you are a graduate student you are a mentee (even though, to be sure, the relationship can be replete with complications). The roles are institutional requirements. Although I work in the general sphere of academia, and have the unusual title—for someone in my position as director of a university press—of associate provost, I am a publisher; those particular roles are not so clearly defined in my industry. Early on in a career one usually has no choice about one's supervisor, who may or may not serve as a mentor.

I must confess that at first I drew a blank when asked to write about the topic of mentorship—no one had been a satisfactory mentor to me, I thought, and it seemed that I had been an accidental mentor myself, at best. When I thought more I realized: If you are an older sister, you inhabit the role of mentor. If you are a mother, you are a mentor. If you are a boss, you are a mentor. I am all those things. In fact I started early—just before I turned five my sister was born and after that I was to be my mother's "important helper." Three years later there was another sister and then, when I was nine, a brother. I accepted my role willingly—it never occurred to me to rebel. I gave generously of the wisdom of my years. As an adult I realized that I had learned to expertly squash my own needs, and felt proud that I was able to do so. I had been given an important role and I lived up to it. Later, when I had my own children and a husband whose very intelligent head was usually somewhere in the clouds, I did the same.

I completed high school a year early and left for college—eager to start my own life. I wanted to be a poet, and I studied with several writers in college, and then at my MFA program, whom I considered to be mentors. I felt awkward and needy in the role of mentee—asking for advice seemed intrusive. But I soaked up everything they had to offer. I was therefore thrilled when my favorite of these writers—a leading American poet—pulled me aside one day. I was eager and hopeful for his advice. But to my great disappointment it emerged that instead of focusing on my writing or my future career he wanted to discuss a new freshman classmate, and he asked whether I knew anything about her. I had seen her in class—she seemed very young and naïve—but I didn't know her and was relieved when I couldn't supply any information. Later I learned that this poet was considered something of a philanderer. A mentor was what I sought, but he had other things on his mind.

My pragmatic nature told me that poetry wouldn't pay the rent, and so I went into publishing, which only barely could. For some years I continued to write but soon enough the demands of the job, not to mention childrearing, took over. Like many in the book publishing world I was promoted into a managerial position without having had any experience or training in managing people. I tried to mentor—I am certain I wouldn't have used that term—by example, and to model the behavior I expected of my staff. I tried to listen, which was harder than I expected, especially when I disagreed with someone or when they had a complaint. Though I ran a fairly large department and I knew some people looked to me as a role model, I didn't really think of myself that way. I just wanted everyone to work together and get the job done, and to create an atmosphere where people could succeed and thrive.

In retrospect, especially as during this period most managers were men, I am sure I must have been afraid of my own power. I tried to tread lightly, to suggest rather than demand, to avoid direct criticism of others. I was able, to a fault, to see other points of view. I was occasionally accused by male bosses over the years of being "too nice." One, who was hell-bent on firing someone on my team, responded to my defense of the editor by saying, "I guess you just see the glass as half-full and I see it as half-empty." I silently agreed. I *do* tend to see the good in people and encourage them to work to their strengths.

So it was unwelcome news when I once received a clear message that my expectations could cause stress in others. One editor, in her mid-forties, had a mild heart attack. I was shocked—she was active and seemingly healthy. I was even more shocked later when someone told me this editor thought *I* had been the cause of the heart attack! After much soul-searching and self-doubt, in the end I concluded that this purported perception of hers was absurd. I had, I thought, treated her with understanding and advice rather than reprimands. I'd supported her, and I'd given praise when it was due. Years later, though—long after she had left the company—I ran into her on the street and greeted her heartily. But when I perceived that she was noticeably backing away from me I remembered that colleague's comment—she really *did* think I'd caused her heart attack. She couldn't get away from me fast enough that day. I have tried, unsuccessfully, to erase this unsettling encounter from my conscious mind. I learned from it, though. Whatever I think I have conveyed to someone, either verbally or by example, is not necessarily the way they perceive the message. In other words, it's always a good idea to check in and try to ascertain how you've been heard.

Fortunately, no one else who ever worked for me demonstrated signs of stress-induced ill health. All in all, I think I have at best been an unwitting mentor to my staff. I am proud of them, particularly proud of the young women who charge ahead, seemingly unafraid, unselfconscious, and who strive to do a good job and be noticed for it. It took me years to feel this self-confident. How much time and psychic energy did I waste trying to please an older male boss? Too many years and too much angst to quantify. I usually didn't have the gumption to assert myself and make my views known. And when I finally mustered the courage I occasionally got slapped down or, more often, was ignored or talked over. Sometimes I *was* heard—but that was usually after allowing my boss to think my idea was his to begin with. Maybe what I'm describing is true of everyone, female or not, my particular era or not. But I think women of my age, children of second-wave feminism, were caught between being told, and believing, that we could indeed "have it all"—achieve what men could achieve, be respected professionally, *and* be a "good mother"—and realizing the near-impossibility of that goal because we weren't thought of as leaders at work. But most of us moved ahead anyway, in one direction or another, however tentatively. One publisher friend, when our children were small, told me she was going to abandon her career to focus on the kids. When I questioned her decision she said, "[Her husband's name] can do only one thing, and that's concentrate on work." Obviously it was up to her to handle everything else.

I had mentors in my early career, even if they were not my direct managers. One of them, about twenty years my senior, was in our production department. She was the only Black person in our office at the time—indeed she was one of very few in the profession. She was highly competent, professional, strongly principled, and respectful of colleagues, expecting to be treated the same way. We talked a lot, often on weekends when we'd both come into the office to finish something we couldn't get done during the week. In fact, we often spent more time talking than catching up on work. She gave me advice about getting ahead, and what I should or should not do or say to my (often our) superiors. She kept much of her personal life close to the vest. One day I was astonished to learn that she had *two* full-time jobs. She left our office at 5 p.m. to go to a midtown law office where she supervised a pool of paralegals until midnight. She was single and without children and claimed she needed only five hours of sleep, but still it must have been a grueling schedule. When, after a team of consultants told him she was the best qualified candidate at the press, the director finally made her head of the department and put her on the management team, she quit the other job in order to devote herself to the new position. I knew that if she hadn't been promoted she would have quit the press on principle and kept the job at the law firm. Some years later, when a new director came in (via the old boy network) whom she didn't respect, she retired early after having taught herself various skills she could use to take on freelance work during her retirement. She simply could not work for someone she didn't look up to. I am more than sorry to report that I was too afraid for my own career to follow her example. Moreover, I didn't realize how much she had taught me until long after she left. I didn't think enough about it at the time, but she must have faced huge discrimination, conscious or not, and stoically forged her career in a notoriously white industry at a time when recognition of the importance of diversity did not exist.

As the years went on I realized that some younger women in the office *did* clearly consider me a mentor. I noticed that assistants and junior editors were watching me in meetings—imitating me, even. Sometimes this made me uncomfortable, especially when I thought they were just trying to please me as I had wanted to please my own managers. But usually I felt encouraged to know I was able to provide them with something I had not experienced myself. Except in the very beginning of my career, all my bosses were men. They taught me much, but truth to tell they were usually negative examples for me. I learned from them behavior I knew I would not want to imitate. Can one teach by negative example and still be a mentor of sorts? I sound to myself churlish and ungrateful as I write this. I liked them all—well, almost all—and got along well with them. I keep in touch. But I think I've learned more from men who are younger and junior to me, who didn't come to the workplace equipped with the same armor and assumption of privilege.

The book publishing business, which otherwise has a serious problem with lack of diversity, is now comprised of 74 percent cis women, and at the executive level 60 percent are cis women, according to a survey conducted in 2019 by Lee and Low. But for much of my career this was not the case, and even now most of the top jobs are occupied by men. And the profession remains far too white. I always wanted a top job but in my era this was considered surprising—if it was considered at all. In fact, at my own company the old boy network prevailed the first two times I tried for the position of director, but the third time, years later, was the charm. I became the first woman director of an Ivy League university press, and now there are several others. Today 43 percent of the press directors in the Association of University Presses are female. The year I was completing my presidency of the Association of University Presses, I held a party in my hotel suite and invited them all—it was delightfully crowded. I do try consciously to help these and other women in the field—I try to make time, to talk, to give advice if asked, to share; I try to be a supportive colleague. I want them to succeed. We are nourished by each other's success. In our university press world we share information and support each other in formal and informal gatherings. That's one of the things I love about it. And I regularly meet with young people who want to "go into publishing"—they are legion. They want to work with serious books despite perennial challenges to the industry, low entry-level salaries, and the paucity of job openings. I am happy to encourage them and give advice I would have been intimidated to ask for at their age.

Mentorship *can* happen, at any age or stage in life. I have a number of female friends and acquaintances in their eighties and beyond. Some are mothers of friends, some are authors of books I've published, some are retired publishers or scholars. These women seem to me to be thoroughly admirable, active, and relevant. And they faced far greater obstacles in their careers than I ever did. I find myself watching them for signs of how I might ensure that I become like them. They are my current role models. They are mentors by virtue of their experience and how they continue to engage with the world. I want my life to be what I imagine theirs to be—intellectually stimulated and stimulating, confident, vibrant, involved.

Jennifer Crewe is associate provost and director of Columbia University Press, where she has also served as editorial director and, before that, as an acquisitions editor, learning mentorship all the while. She has served as president of the Association of University Presses and on the executive council of the Modern Language Association. She has an MFA in poetry from Columbia's School of the Arts, where she searched desperately for mentors.

Can a Therapist Be a Mentor?

Kamy Wicoff

In considering this question myself I have posed it to others, and it often elicits a visceral response, especially from those who have been in therapy and benefited from it. *No!*

A mentor's realm is the workplace, and the relationship between mentor and mentee is a mutually beneficial—and sometimes mutually calculated—one, carried out in the public sphere and focused on the public-facing selves of each participant. The currency exchanged is social capital, whereas with a therapist the currency is, to put it plainly, currency, and in exchange for the clarity produced by paying for her time, a patient secures unconditional attention and care, often directed precisely at the parts of herself that are least likely to make an appearance when presenting one's "mentor-able" self. "Wounded child," "traumatized survivor," "aggressive protector," or "rageful narcissist" are not parts of ourselves we would feature on a résumé. They do not attract patronage or promotions. They are parts of ourselves we hide, and while many of us enter therapy with the aim of exorcising them, in a successful treatment they are the parts that most need to be heard, healed, validated, and even loved. Therapists, as the British psychoanalyst Donald Winnicott famously observed, create a holding environment. If they were to assume the position of mentors, we might feel, rather than held, pushed.

But what if the patient becomes a therapist? What is her therapist to her then?

I don't remember the first time I mentioned to my therapist, whom I had been seeing for more than a decade by then, that I was considering becoming a therapist myself—not giving up my career as a writer but, as I saw it, adding another way of being in the world. I do, however, recall the feeling I got, of being met with enthusiasm, curiosity, acceptance, and love. In this room, it didn't matter if I acted on this aspiration, or if I turned out to be a "success." It was simply another expression of self, a possible path, and whether or not I pursued it was far less important than the knowledge that I was worthy, loveable, and okay whether I pursued it or not.

I was worthy no matter what. This was, at any rate, what my therapist had been telling me—and showing me, as important to do in therapy as in writing—for years. It was a message I had received with longing and hope, but also, and more often, with resistance and contempt. This is perhaps best explained by the reactions of my parents when, a year later, I told them I'd enrolled in a master's of social work program. From my father, who was himself a therapist, there was a quick moistening of the eyes, a warm smile, and affirming, unconditional words of support. (I remember the feeling I got, more than the words.) From my mother, there was a tight-lipped grimace, raised eyebrows, and the words, "Well . . . you tried the writing thing." (I remember the feeling and the words in that unfailing way our minds grip the things that hurt us.) I was forty-five years old. I had worked as a television writer and producer, published two books, started a community and publishing company for women writers, gotten an MFA . . . if this sounds like a defensive accounting for myself vis-à-vis my accomplishments, it is. In fact, it is a habit of accounting for my worth ingrained in me since childhood. From the day I won a poetry contest in San Antonio, Texas, at age eight, and was featured on the local PBS station, my mother hammered into me the message that I was to be *"a writer!"*—which meant I could not rest until I had achieved fame and fortune as such, and she could go to the National Book Awards on my arm. There were tears in my mother's eyes when, upon the publication of my novel, we posed for a picture under the marquee of the Austin bookstore Book People, which featured my name for a reading that night.

"Finally!" she sighed. "You don't know how long I have waited for this!"

My mother's particular reasons for attaching her love to achievements of mine she could advertise, and for withdrawing it when I failed to measure up, are their own story. But her fixation with my public-facing self was one of the primary wounds I went to therapy to heal.

I didn't know this, of course. I went to therapy to turn failure into success, to stop whipping myself without getting anywhere and start whipping myself into shape instead. In order to achieve this, it was first necessary to establish the scope of my failure. I delivered self-loathing monologues about my mediocrity, my laziness, my revolting hesitancy in the face of adversity. I compared myself to Salieri, doomed to recognize greatness but never to achieve it. Why couldn't I be different? I asked, again and again. *What was wrong with me?*

Until one day my therapist looked at me and said, "So what?"

The part of me whose job it was to wake me up to the tune of "you're not enough" and put me to sleep at night (or, more often, to keep me awake at night) with "what have you done with your life?" shot back.

"So what?"

My therapist nodded. "So what?"

I was angry, startled, and scared. "So I will never accomplish anything at all and I'm just not supposed to care?"

Silence.

My inner critic wanted to scream, "What are you trying to do, kill me?" But something else stirred. Hope. Recognition of a truth. Which I immediately buried.

It took many years for me to trust that my being was not bound up in my doing. It took many more years to believe I did not have to do anything to be loved, listened to, or okay.

Then I started my training. Almost immediately, something began to change.

Some days I came in with thoughts on a text I'd read in class. My therapist responded, and occasionally asked if I had read other things, many of which I hadn't, causing my "not enough" alarm bells to distantly but distinctly sound. Another week I'd come in with my mind racing about a new treatment modality and ask her about it. As I listened to her reply, the depth of her knowledge and the extent of her training split me in two. My insecure, frightened parts felt incompetent and judged, cringing with embarrassment at my ignorance. My public-facing, striving, mentor-able self, however, shoved the wounded worriers aside, leaning in to soak up what the wise, experienced, skilled therapist before her had to say. When I started seeing patients, I began discussing cases during my sessions. My therapist consistently redirected me to explore my countertransference, the things not related to theory but to self. But I could not shake the feeling of being evaluated or the sharp shame of falling short.

I wanted my therapist to be my mentor. I did not want my therapist to be my mentor. I wanted to impress my therapist. I did not want to impress my therapist. And so began our dance. Arriving for my session, I would be unable to resist my compulsion to perform my newly emerging "therapist" self, while my unlovable, ugly, resistant, and angry selves sat crumpled and sulking on the far end of the couch, watching the clock and wondering when this try-hard, ass-kissing show-off would shut up and let them have a turn. I had enough awareness to disrupt this dynamic myself, at times, and of course my therapist did too.

"I think I need to stop talking about this with you," I finally said one day.

"Okay," my therapist replied.

"I want you to be proud of me," I said. "And I hate that."

She nodded. "The old battle." I noticed she used the word "old." Something stirred. Hope. A recognition of a truth. This was old. It was familiar. I could hold it.

"I may be a terrible therapist," I said. "I may quit."

She looked at me for a minute and smiled.

"So what?"

So what.

Who would you be, the Buddhist psychologist and author Tara Brach asks her patients, *what would you do, if you didn't believe that something was wrong with you?*

Letting go of the belief that something is wrong allows me to seek help with what is difficult. I was starting a new career. I could use a mentor! There is a name for the mentor of a therapist: a supervisor. That week I contacted a former teacher and asked if she would be mine. When we meet, I am frequently overwhelmed by feelings of inadequacy, plagued by imposter syndrome, and filled with fears of failing. In supervision, as in therapy, it is important that I name these feelings, but the focus is on understanding how they show up in my work. As it turns out, one of the most powerful forces they exert on me is an urge to *do*—to advise, to instruct, to project authority, to collude with my patients' inner critics' obsession with "self-improvement," to push, rather than to hold. But my patients don't need a mentor. They need a therapist. And so do I. Luckily, I'm still in therapy.

Kamy Wicoff is a writer and psychotherapist living in Brooklyn, New York. She is the founder of She Writes and She Writes Press, and the author of *I Do but I Don't: Why the Way We Marry Matters* (2006) and *Wishful Thinking* (2015).

The Reluctant Writer

Looking Back on My Mentors

SARAH GLAZER

I grew up with two fathers—a biological father and a stepfather—who were more mentors than parent figures. My father did not live with me most of my childhood. My stepfather, a professor of history and a writer, never really knew how to take on the parental role. But he was a great teacher.

Although I grew up in a family of writers (my mother was one too), I never wanted to be a writer—at least an academic one. I had heard too many stories at the kitchen table about my stepfather's favorite graduate students—brilliant but blocked—who spent years trying to write that promising PhD thesis.

And I knew the feeling. Many were the evenings when I would sit at my desk staring at a white sheet of paper in the typewriter trying to figure out how to start a thirty-page term paper. (I went to a demanding private high school.) I would frequently set the alarm for 3 a.m. or even 1 a.m. so I could finish a paper by the next school day.

On the evenings when I managed to finish a draft before bedtime, I would take it to my stepfather in his study. The study was a quiet book-lined haven adorned with a bust of Voltaire, my stepfather's own idol, whom he admired for his rationalism and anticlericalism and who figured centrally in my stepfather's books about the French Enlightenment. It was while sitting alone with me, with the sheets of paper in front of us, that my stepfather showed his most generous side. Today I recognize that he was an elegant writer although I'm not sure I realized it at the time. He would pick out a sentence and show me how I could make it better. I can't remember any of those specific tips now. But I do remember that he would often say, "I learned this from Richard Hofstadter," the historian who had been his own mentor when he was a graduate student. It made me feel that I was part of a much larger enterprise—of writers struggling to figure out the best way to say things and sharing their knowledge with one another.

I would become a writer for reasons that had nothing to do with crafting perfect sentences. At one party at my parents' apartment, a voluble Englishman showed up. I was fascinated by the dramatic and sardonic way he told stories of politicians and their adversaries in some faraway country (England? India?). He was in the thick of it, and I realized I wanted to be in the thick of it too. "What does that man do?" I asked my parents. He was a journalist.

I would spend the rest of my life using journalism as a ticket to explore the world, whether that meant walking into strange neighborhoods or asking questions about society that intrigued me. For that wide-ranging curiosity, I think back to my father.

Since my parents had a typical 1950s divorce, my father got me and my two younger sisters just on Saturdays. Every Saturday he would take us to a different part of New York City—to admire the architecture of some Beaux Arts building, to appreciate the design brilliance of Olmsted's Central Park, or to see a film he thought important to our understanding of the world. I have a vague memory of seeing the black-and-white footage of the McCarthy hearings in a darkened theater, although it was very unclear to me as a child whether it was McCarthy who was the bad guy or the witness he was grilling.

My father was a sociologist whose passion was exploring urban problems and trying to solve them. I could spend an entire dinner with him discussing just one of New York City's problems and the pitfalls of all the solutions—the failed remedy, for example, of replacing slums with sterile high-rise projects, destroying neighborhoods in their wake.

Although my father was also a professor, he had started out in something more akin to journalism, writing a column for *Commentary* magazine in the 1940s and 1950s about new sociological studies that interested him. But he and his friends felt just as confident writing about a new avant-garde novel from Europe.

I once heard my father explain this expansiveness to an interviewer: His group of fellow New York intellectuals, who started out as socialists from poor New York Jewish families, had a certain arrogance as young men about their capacity to analyze anything that interested them, which he said emanated from their left-wing roots performing Marxist analysis.

In some ways, it doesn't feel like a close fit to place my father in the role of "mentor." Our discussions felt more like that of one intellectual to another; I don't think he ever dumbed down his analysis of a situation in talking to me. And he conveyed his first love, architecture, through passionate expressions of appreciation rather than instruction. Yet through his own questing he inspired mine, and somehow passed on the confidence that I could pose any question, no matter how complicated.

Here I should pause to mention another mentor by example—my mother. She, too, had started out life as a journalist. Her most famous article from her early career was an appreciative feature on the Jewish delicatessen for *Commentary*. During my growing up, however, I didn't think of her as a working person since she toiled alone in her study working mainly on a book about a nineteenth-century English explorer that she never finished.

One day I returned home from school to find her sitting on the floor next to her desk surrounded by files and papers containing her published and never-published writing. She announced shortly afterward that she was giving up writing. Essentially, she said, she had failed to make this a career. *Commentary* was no longer interested in the kinds of pieces she wrote, affectionate and analytical, about the nature of Jewish life. She had decided to go to library school to become an archivist, an occupation my stepfather made clear he thought was far below her intellectual capabilities.

The pain and disappointment I heard in my mother's voice when she told me of this decision had a lot to do with my ambivalence about becoming a writer. From watching her face when she emerged from a day of writing in her study, pale and drawn, I understood the writer's life as difficult and lonely. But more frightening, I now saw it could be ultimately demoralizing, destroying a life's worth of desires and ambitions.

Happily, my mother began to publish articles and books again in her seventies, writing about the subject nearest to her heart—the lives of Jews, past and present, in Europe and the United States. She published three books before her death. A fourth, which she finished writing with pen and paper from her hospital bed, was published the year after she died.

When I first read the manuscript of her memoir, about how her parents' generation of Jewish immigrants adapted to America, *Unfinished People*, I finally saw her as a "real" writer—one who could make another world come alive and move me as much as my favorite novelists.

Throughout my growing up, my mother had an ability to engage any person who came to the house, whether a student or a famous scholar, with her intense curiosity and affection. Her follow-up questions indicated that she was interested in pursuing whatever they told her—where they came from or the subject they were working on.

At the time, I didn't think of her as either a great writer or a model for myself to follow. She didn't present herself with the brio of the two men she married—as either a public intellectual or an elegant stylist. She was a product of the 1950s, not the age of feminism. Yet with her book *Unfinished People*, she recaptured her personal voice—warm and sardonic at the same time—conveying what was to be treasured in the customs and attitudes of her parents' generation. Through her vignettes about hats and food, one understood her immigrant Jewish parents' longing for their old country's ways even as they tried to adapt to the strange traditions of a new land. With her usual penetrating gaze on the culture, she explained how the old Jewish joke of the anxious Jewish mother stemmed from the genuine anxiety her parents and their generation felt as "unfinished people." They had arrived alone in America as such young teenagers that they were forced to become adults and parents without the benefit of their own parents' guidance through their adolescence.

While writing this essay, I didn't immediately think of my mother as a writing mentor, not just because of her own interrupted career but also because she was never critical of my work. If I sent her a published piece, she would always send an enthusiastic and warm reply—picking out a particular quote or sentence she liked. By contrast, during my high school days, my stepfather could detect when my writing reflected a feeling of tedium with my subject—the times when I couldn't seem to rise above a stilted paraphrase of the *Encyclopedia Britannica*.

What I probably yearned for more than anything was recognition from my physically absent and often absent-minded father. I got that, briefly, many years later when I showed him an essay I had written for a book, looking critically at the way the American nursing establishment had embraced alternative medicine and the strange roots of this relationship in theosophy and postmodern philosophy. "I want that," my father said, for a magazine he coedited, "but you need to make it more of a magazine article." He took a pencil and scrawled in several subheadings to break up the piece—and suddenly the article came alive on the page. It was the first time he had edited something I'd written.

Once I started writing for newspapers, my writer's block disappeared. I found that sitting in a noisy newsroom in the morning knowing I had an 11 a.m. copy deadline gave me a shot of adrenaline. It sent my fingers speeding over the typewriter keys to get my story out.

Later, I had a series of what I would call negative mentors. After I left college to become a reporter for newspapers and later magazines, I accepted that editors had a right to change my copy in the hierarchical system that existed in the newsroom, especially since their main job was to root out errors or inconsistencies.

But over time, it seemed that some editors were trying to remake my writing in their own image: if they liked hard numbers, the article became a blizzard of statistics; if they liked "lively" writing, sentences and quotes were reshaped to reflect a reality that didn't exist but sounded good. As I look back, I realize that my younger writer self didn't protest changes that I now see undermined my voice and my respect for my interview subjects.

One example continues to haunt me. In a magazine interview with a former drug addict about the depths to which addiction had driven her, I wrote that, during that time, "she lied; she stole." My editor changed that to "she was a liar and a thief."

From the person I was trying to portray sympathetically, the editor had rendered someone completely different—"a liar and a thief." But it was something I could only articulate years later: the new sentence wasn't factually wrong, but it wasn't *right* either.

Along the way I've had some great editors, along with the negative mentors. At my first newspaper job in Alabama in the early 1970s, an editor sent me out to interview men and women in their eighties who had worked in the local textile mills as children—before child labor laws. I discovered that I could knock on a stranger's door, get invited in for a glass of iced tea, then hear stories told in quaint turns of phrase, still unpolluted by TV or radio. Surprised by their fond memories of a community of families working together, I wrote a long story told mainly in their own words.

While learning on the job at newspapers in the 1970s, I was schooled in the standard reporting tone of those days—what news editors considered an "objective" voice. A reporter would only refer to himself or herself as "a visitor" or "an observer"—always in the third person.

For me, that started to change in 1990 when I found myself without a full-time job, having quit my magazine to deal with a childcare crisis. With two children under eight at home, I started freelancing for the *Washington Post*'s health magazine, writing about dilemmas I was encountering—childcare pros and cons, the overdiagnosis of learning disabilities in boys, and misguided health recommendations aimed at women and children. In my first article for the *Post*, I used the word "I" for the first time in a lead sentence. Although an editor who came on the scene after me questioned whether *Post* reporters could really do that—a no-no in the news section—I was allowed to continue doing so in the somewhat more squishy, personally oriented health section.

A few years later, I would encounter a group of female mentors who guided me as I started to write in what, for me, was a novel genre—a blog. At "She Writes," a website and online community for women writers, the organizers, editors, and tech people were all women, mostly younger than me. They generously shared their knowledge about how to use what seemed like intimidating new technology. It was also a revelation to be helped along so easily, after having relied on my own home-based technical staff—my overbearing male family members, who usually approached my technological naïveté with disdain.

Although I had been asked to write a blog about books and publishing, a beat I had been covering for the *New York Times Book Review*, I found that my blogs became increasingly personal as I explored this more informal form. It allowed me to write entirely in my own voice. In one blog, written as the sexual assault charges against French politician Dominique Strauss-Kahn had just exploded, I wrote that the incident had brought back the memory of a dark Chicago street where a stranger had pushed me to the ground and attempted to rape me. I had never written about this event, which occurred while I was in college, or talked about it much. The blog spurred an outpouring of comments from other women writers, with some sharing their own experiences of sexual assault for the first time, and it made me realize the potential power of my own personal voice.

In recent years, I've increasingly chafed at the old-school editors who still insist on the "objective" tone, removing any colorful or insightful word that reflects my perspective. In an article I wrote on the presidency describing President Donald Trump's governing style as "idiosyncratic," an editor insisted on removing the adjective as too "biased," leaving behind a bland mush in its place. I once thought the writer's voice was a luxury that belonged only to novelists; I now understand that my voice is something I want to reclaim in my writing.

Today I'm teaching journalism. When I was first asked to teach a feature writing course, I couldn't imagine that I had enough knowledge to convey instruction for two hours every week—I had no stack of rules or tips at hand, no written guidebook. But these days when I receive a piece of writing from a student, I find that I do know more than I realized about this craft. As I improve a student's sentence, I can say, "This is something I learned from someone else along the way."

Sarah Glazer has worked as a journalist for over thirty years, starting out on small newspapers in the South and publishing articles in the *Washington Post*, the *New York Times Book Review*, and *Congressional Quarterly*. She teaches feature writing at New York University's School of Professional Studies, where she enjoys mentoring new and aspiring writers. She is still trying to figure out what kind of writer she wants to be.

"That was where I felt most myself"

A Conversation with Sarah Burnes about Books, Mentors, Feminism, and Mothers

Tahneer Oksman

If you follow Sarah Burnes, literary agent extraordinaire, on social media, you'll know that her passion for politics runs as deep as her passion for books. (See, for instance, her current Twitter tagline: "Sarah Ban the Filibuster Burnes.") Perhaps what is more accurate is to say that Burnes's passion for politics runs through her passion for books, and vice versa. In other words, she believes in the power of books to shape people into forces that can go out into the world and enact change. This is not the status quo for people in the thick of the business of books, at least not as far as I can tell.

In a recent podcast conversation (with one of her authors, YA fiction writer Sarah Enni), Burnes was asked what her goals are as an agent. Her answer, in keeping with the preceding, was simple but to the point: "Well, I'm a gatekeeper, and I want to use that privilege for people who don't have it." Burnes is currently a literary agent at the Gernert Company, which she joined in 2005, and she represents adult fiction and nonfiction writers as well as children's and young adult authors. Most recently, you can find her cheering on her author Honorée Fanonne Jeffers, whose debut novel, *The Love Songs of W. E. B. Du Bois*, was longlisted for the National Book Award for fiction and is also the latest Oprah's Book Club pick.

In early fall, Nancy and I managed to squeeze in a one-hour Zoom interview with Sarah, who, as you might imagine, has a very busy schedule. For this collection on feminism and mentorship, with essays mainly from the points of view of writers, including academics, we wanted her perspective. What does the writing industry look like from an insider's standpoint? How does mentorship apply to the process of getting important work out into the world?

Our conversation came just close to a month after Sarah's beloved mother, Nonnie Burnes, a social justice advocate in her own right, had died. Talking about these topics in the wake of her mother's passing was a tribute, as much as anything else, and a testament, too, to the complicated connections and disjunctions between mothering and mentorship.

Tahneer Oksman (TO): I want to begin with your early career in publishing. You started out as an intern, then an editor, and eventually you became an agent. What attracted you to the book business in the first place?

Sarah Burnes (SB): When I graduated from college, I didn't know what I wanted to do at all. A friend had a friend who needed a roommate in New York, and I had been thinking about moving to New York and going into books. The truth is, I felt the only thing I was good at was reading. That was where I felt most myself.

And so when I moved, the first thing I did was get a job at a bookstore. At the time, some of my friends couldn't imagine why I wanted to do that. But to me it seemed almost magic that it was possible to work with books. And it was where the book people were.

TO: What store was it?

SB: It was the Shakespeare and Company on the Upper West Side. *When Harry Met Sally* had just been filmed there—it was the fall of 1989—and there was this train of young people coming through. I started out at $4.75 an hour and got a raise to $5.25.

It's hard to imagine, but it was a great place to work. We could take books out of the hardcover room and return them if we hadn't damaged them. That was when I got a crash course in American literature, the contemporary American literature that I hadn't read until then.

TO: In an interview up on *Kirkus*, you describe how, when you began your work of agenting, Henry Dunow (cofounder of Dunow, Carlson &

Lerner Literary Agency) said to you, "Welcome to the side of light." Could you explain what he meant by this—and what it meant for you to move from editing to agenting?

SB: I think what Henry meant was that as agents, we're on the side of making things happen for writers.

At the time he would have said that, in the fall of 2000, literary agents were seen as these rapacious moneymakers, people who were driving advances up. The most famous literary agent at the time was Andrew Wiley, who was nicknamed "the jackal."

My experience of the publishing industry led me to want to be on the side of writers—to advocate for them in a direct way. Of course, we need editors who can advocate for writers in the publishing system as well.

TO: Given the implicit hierarchy in the publishing business, what are the biggest gaps? Do you feel that you were well mentored?

SB: One of the reasons I left the publishing side was that I had not found a mentor—I had not felt mentored, even though I worked with some pretty extraordinary people. But they weren't the right match for my skills. And possibly, I just wanted to do my own thing anyway. I'm much more suited to being an agent.

Publishing is a bit like academia in that people care about things in inverse proportion to what's at stake. Somebody once said that to me about academia: because there's so little money, there's cultural capital instead.

It's a hit business. When you have a hit, people tend to feel that there's not enough to go around. That was my experience with my first jobs in publishing. Everyone was competing with each other for perceived scarce resources when in fact there's plenty to go around. It just happens that sometimes other people have something that you don't, and you just have to sit and wait for your turn. This book right there—can you see it? It's Honorée Jeffers's *The Love Songs of W. E. B. Du Bois*. It came out this fall, and she's a writer I've worked with for sixteen years. It's her first novel—she's written five works of poetry—and I'm very conscious of the fact that I have the thing that people want right now. But it's actually about the work.

TO: I want to prod you a bit more about your early experiences in the publishing industry. Could you expand on those early circumstances that led to feeling, or not feeling, mentored?

SB: In my first jobs it was explicitly understood: young people aren't going to get promoted because the higher ups don't want you coming up and taking their stuff. And I was not going to stand for that one way or the other. I worked with a woman I really loved and admired, and one day she said, "You know, you're so like the character in *All About Eve*." I thanked her, and then I saw the movie and was completely horrified. I thought, "I don't want your job!"

Then, in my next job, I had a colleague who was a mentor to the degree to which he was able to be. He said I was straight out of *The Best of Everything*, the Rona Jaffe novel. But I just wanted to work!

Nancy K. Miller (NKM): I'm amazed he would bring that book up. It's set in the world of the fifties. I guess you're saying that not too much had changed in publishing.

SB: I mean, it had, and it hadn't. One of the stories I like to tell about my publishing career is about when I was Sonny Mehta's assistant at Knopf, which was a very glamorous, high-profile job. I understand that now—at the time, I was just keeping my head down and trying to get my work done.

But Sonny was a strong personality. He was supportive of me, but only to a degree. We got along well, but I felt everything was on his terms, which, by the way, it was.

Soon I talked my way into becoming an associate editor at Vintage, Knopf's paperback imprint. I was probably twenty-eight. I'd been an editorial assistant for five and a half years. When I left, Sonny said to me, "You need to read more, and you need to be more patient." And I accepted that.

But then I left, and I realized two things about what he had said to me: (a) I read women writers and he didn't, which is why he thought I hadn't read anything; and (b) when he was twenty-eight, he was already the publisher of a paperback imprint!

This wasn't just about me. There wasn't a lot of elasticity in the system because people in power wanted to preserve their power. That has loosened up somewhat, I think, in publishing. But it was just so incredibly male.

NKM: I was just going to ask about that, the gender balance or imbalance.

SB: Even though I then went to work at Little, Brown, where the publisher was a woman, everything was still very male-dominated in setting the tone and things to do with women. In the case of women's fiction, nobody thought that feminist books would work, which maybe, frankly, they wouldn't have at that time.

I told the publisher there that I wanted to start publishing feminist books. She came into my office the following day and said, "There really isn't anything going on in that world because there really isn't an enemy anymore."

TO: Would you say you have a philosophy of agenting? Do you see mentorship as part of the work, or is it something else?

SB: My agenting has changed as I've gotten older. I have a different kind of relationship, probably, with my younger writers than I do with my peers, same-age peers, even though it's the same job.

I just got off a Zoom with a younger writer of mine. We're working on her stories. I've been an agent for twenty years now and I've seen that path lay out, so I can advise her in a different way than I could when I was younger and less experienced.

But I think mentorship comes in more with the people I work with, my assistants. I'm conscious now of trying to help people to the degree that I can, and I'm sure I have assistants who think that I do and assistants who think that I don't.

TO: In a series of *Paris Review* blog posts from 2010, you walk readers through a week in your life. Your days then—as now, I suppose—were full of reading (magazines and books, old and new), parenting, work, and various social engagements. You're clearly someone who is always reading, who has a deep investment in what books can do. Would you talk a bit about how books affected you over the course of your life? What are the books that had the greatest influence, especially early on?

SB: Carolyn Heilbrun's *Writing a Woman's Life* continues to be, as you know, important to me and has guided the kinds of books I take on. I was reading it again recently, after my mother died.

I think about it in relation to the biographies I work on but also in relation to feminist fiction, especially historical fiction, which I think of as kind of stand-ins for biography.

Historical fiction is doing very well now. *The Love Songs of W. E. B. Du Bois* is stratospheric at the moment, but even other books like Kate Manning's *My Notorious Life*, or Rachel Kadish's *The Weight of Ink*, are feminist historical fiction that recast women's lives in a kind of Heilbrun-esque way. So certainly, that book has been one I have carried all the way through my career.

The other book I think about often, although I haven't reread it in a couple of years, is Carol Gilligan's *In a Different Voice*. I think a lot about her notion of the ethic of care. There's a movement now in politics toward communities and communitarianism that you can think about in relation to Gilligan. I also think about the end of Zora Neale Hurston's *Their Eyes Were Watching God* where Janie talks about her net of memory coming in, casting a net, gathering stories from her past. ["She pulled in her horizon like a great fish-net. Pulled it from around the waist of the world and draped it over her shoulder. So much of life in its meshes!" (193).]

It's all this stuff that I read when I was in my twenties.

I should also say that on the night of the 2016 presidential election, I listened to Madeleine L'Engle's *A Wrinkle in Time*, which is my absolute go-to comfort book. It grounds me and brings me back to my nine-year-old self. I know [L'Engle] was a problematic character in some ways, but the vision in that book is pretty unimpeachable.

TO: In those same blog posts, you describe various engagements with others, many women—college friends, colleagues—people with whom you share both professional and personal interests and investments. It sounds as though your life, and work, is buoyed by those relationships. In many of our essays, we also see how important the sense of horizontal relationships can be over the course of a career.

But we tend to think of agents as lone figures. Would you say a bit about the role of what we've been thinking of as this kind of horizontal, collective mentorship—the role it has played in your life?

SB: It's very much how The Gernert Company is set up, and why I've been so happy there. We each have our own lists. But we're also a network, a community. We advise each other, and we support each other.

It was different with the generation and a half before me. Binky Urban, for example, was Toni Morrison's agent and Jay McInerney's. I saw her at an event shortly after I had left Knopf. I had become an agent by then, and she was with her husband Ken Auletta, and she said to him, "Oh, this is Sarah Burnes. She used to be Sonny's assistant." And then she apologized and said, "I'm so sorry; you know, for decades people would introduce me by saying, 'This is Binky Urban, and she used to be Clay Felker's assistant.'" [Clay Felker had been the editor of *New York*.]

One of the things I realized then about that generation is that they had come through these corporate systems as assistants. Women like Binky had gone into publishing, hadn't been able to succeed because they weren't allowed to succeed in the publishing houses, and so became agents. Those women ultimately formed their own companies, which was kind of amazing if you think about it. Maybe there wasn't room for them to be part of a network then, but there was enough change by the time I had become an agent, and I knew that I wanted to be part of a team. And I knew there were people out there that I could do that with.

I'm in two book clubs, and a cooking club, and an agent's group. I like to create those communities around me.

TO: I'm very curious about book clubs, because I assume it would be a bit contentious, what books to choose. Is it hard to agree?

SB: One of the clubs I'm in was started by my friend Gretchen Rubin, who wrote *The Happiness Project*. She started a young adult book club because she wanted to create a group for people who like to read kids' books, and I love it.

And then there is my grown-up book club, as I call it. There are five of us, all in publishing, and we read only books by dead people. Right now we're reading detective novels—writers I'd never heard of. I once had them read Zora Neale Hurston, and they didn't like the novel, which shocked me. We read Toni Morrison when she passed. And Nella Larsen.

TO: There's a lot of reading happening in your life, in different genres.

SB: I do read a lot. In 2016, I had surgery and started listening to audiobooks while I was recovering.

The truth is I listen to many more books these days. After the election and during COVID, when it became hard to concentrate, I started always listening to something. I fell down a rabbit hole and listened to all the classics by women, "reread" them all. Jane Austen, Edith Wharton. Which I would recommend.

TO: Even as an agent, you continue to be an involved editor. We've been editing many essays for this collection lately, thinking together about what makes for a good editor. We've talked about the differences between commenting globally on an author's work versus getting into the weeds, and also the fine balance between praising your author and pushing them to keep working through. What do you think makes for good editing?

SB: I learned how to write a reader's report when interviewing for my job at Houghton Mifflin. In four paragraphs: say what the book is about, what the author's intention was, whether they achieved that intention, or how not, and then what the market is. The form is designed to take out your opinion, to meet authors on their own terms. I always think about that, in editing: What is the intention, what is the author trying to do here? And are they or are they not doing it?

In terms of my editing, that's how I think about it. Not in terms of a heavy or a light hand. But if something needs to be rewritten, or is not written well enough, I'm not going to be taking it on.

TO: And I guess you also have to consider how to approach writers when giving them feedback, too, which is part of the work of agenting. Though as you said, that will depend in part on how experienced they are or what stage they're in career-wise.

SB: A writer I am very friendly with once came to me with her work. She'd written a piece of fiction that I just thought was fine, and I told her so. But she ended up going with another agent, another woman. I asked her why.

She told me that that agent had said, "You can do this." And I thought, right, "Oh. *That's* my job."

This writer has now written a book that's wonderful, and I realize now that the other agent had seen the larger picture. She knew the writer could do it, and she knew what the writer needed to hear at that time.

And so, I know I can take on people to whom I can say, you're not there yet, but you can get there.

TO: Your mother, Nonnie Burnes, who recently died, was clearly a passionate, driven advocate, who fought for social justice in the legal field and beyond. I see a lot of commonalities between her drive and passion, and what you've done with your work. She was described in the *Boston Globe* as "a mentor to other women and to new associates" at the firm where she first worked. Did you get to witness her mentoring of others firsthand?

SB: I had a skewed vision of my mother's career there because I mostly heard about her frustrations. But young women were going to Hill &

Barlow [her firm] because of my mother. To be associated with her. She was kind of like the mama bear with the associates. It was great for the young women—she was the person people turned to for advice and counsel. Someone recently even called her "the senior partner for Good Judgment."

TO: In the beautiful words you read at your mother's memorial, you say that she didn't always understand what you were going through but also that "she got me the help I needed and, unlike her own mother, supported me as I built a life of my own on my own terms." Several of our writers discuss the boundaries between mentoring and mothering—how one role often either prevents, or prompts, the other. Does this seem relevant in any way to your situation? Did you think of your mother as a mentor?

SB: One of the things patriarchy does is frustrate women so that they start to compete with each other. I think that's also true of mothers and daughters. Attention is a scarce resource. One of the reasons why my mother became more difficult after she "retired" is that she lost this sense of her professional self. And she competed with me a little bit in a way that I think was her temperament, but it didn't feel good. This is part of why I try to build community with women rather than feel that attention and power are a scarce resource.

Honorée Jeffers and I did an event together this week. My professional colleagues called to congratulate me and say how amazing this is. And I just kept saying, "It's good for all of us that this book is working." And I said that to her, too. This book is making things possible for other people.

I think my mother did that. When my mother became a lawyer 8 percent of lawyers were women. She created a path for people.

But—and I think this has been one of the shattering things about her death—I was trying to construct my life differently from hers. I didn't want to be unhappy in my day-to-day professional life in the way she was; I didn't want to have those frustrations.

NKM: I think your mother sounds a bit like Carolyn [Heilbrun], or Carolyn sounds a bit like your mother.

SB: It's not dissimilar, actually.

NKM: Being difficult and helpful at the same time.

SB: One of the things I often puzzle over and think about are the waves of feminism and generations of feminism. There was a moment when my daughter was a teenager when I worried she was going to become a radical rightist, in rebellion against me.

My daughter is doing with me as I did with my mother, and as my mother did with her mother: we were all trying to differentiate from one another. And that creates waves. So how do we allow people to differentiate in the ways that they have to in order to become full people but also maintain enough solidarity so that we can defeat the patriarchy?

Some of that is, I think, outside mentorships. My assistant, Sophie, for example—I try to be cognizant. She's a young feminist, and I try to figure out how she can flourish so she can spread that out into the world.

TO: I love that phrase, "outside mentorship." It's a good reminder that sometimes you have to go far, away from home, from the family, to get what you need.

SB: At the end of her life, it really was the case that where my mother and I met most often and most happily was politics. We went to Iowa for a big dinner for the Democratic Party in an indoor arena. We were with Elizabeth Warren's team. It was exhilarating to be there. That was the space where we met.

Sarah Burnes is an agent at The Gernert Company, where she represents literary fiction, nonfiction, and children's and YA fiction. She is on the board of the nonprofit progressive publisher The New Press, and a cofounder of Writers and Artists Across the Country, a nonprofit that facilitates school visits for children's and YA authors. She tweets vigorously from @sarahburnes.

Works Cited

Enni, Sarah, host. "Sarah Burnes." *First Draft with Sarah Enni*, 12 Feb. 2019, firstdraftpod.com/audio-episodes/2019/2/12/sarah-burnes.

Gilligan, Carol. *In a Different Voice: Psychological Theory and Women's Development.* Harvard University Press, 2016.

Heilbrun, Carolyn G. *Writing a Woman's Life.* Norton, 2008.

Hurston, Zora Neale. *Their Eyes Were Watching God.* Perennial, 1990.

How I Came to America and Discovered Female Mentors

MIKHAL DEKEL

Feminism came late to Israel, where I was born and raised. The texts that would have instilled feminist awareness in my American colleagues and their mothers—*The Feminine Mystique* in 1963 and *Sexual Politics* in 1970—were not translated into Hebrew until the mid-2000s. Had they been translated, they would not have struck a chord with readers. The Israel of my 1970s and '80s childhood was a poor, semisocialist, two-decade-old country with no bourgeois suburbs and little mystique. In 1973, a tough, long war brought crushing devastation. Friends lost fathers. Fathers lost jobs. Demonstrations against the government, which was blamed for the war, reverberated throughout the land. To engage in politics meant to be an antiwar activist, a "Peace Now" activist. The war was a fight for the country's survival and its aftermath a fight for the country's identity. Feminist politics were not on the horizon; female mentors were nonexistent. Nor would they be on the horizon for decades.

Even at Tel Aviv University Law School, which I attended in the late eighties, nearly all of the senior professors were male, and no course in feminism or feminist legal theory was offered. Texts on feminism, gender, and sexuality began to be widely read at Israeli universities only in the early 2000s and the first feminism reader was published only in 2006 (Baum). By then, Israel had privatized its economy, acquired new wealth through its successful technology industry, and become digitally aligned with and in some cases ahead of the rest of the world. Everything seemed

91

to happen all at once—first-wave feminism condensed with second and third wave; #MeToo together with Andrea Dworkin—but I had already decamped to America.

I write all this to say that I spent the first two and a half decades of my life as an elementary, middle, high school, and university student with zero feminist awareness and without a single female mentor. One does not, of course, need feminism to have a female mentor, but the two are closely related. Women of stature were around us, including Israel's first (and only) female prime minister, but somehow we could not see them.

Mentors and role models in general figured little in the first couple of decades of my life. In the young, post-Holocaust country of Israel, the experience of wiser elders was portrayed as either gone and no longer available—"We left the past . . . behind us. We were ripped at once from our culture, which was stamped on us with thousands of years of history. We were ripped and tossed onto this dry soil, these sun-eaten fields, these naked boulders . . . and from these had to chisel our lives. The caress of a mother's hand or a father's reprimanding gaze were not available to us. . . . We were alone," a founding member of the first large kibbutz wrote—or it was portrayed as negative, oppressive, a thing to be tossed away and rebelled against (Metz 70). "We skipped school, disregarded teachers, our parents could teach us nothing," an interviewee in Yael Ne'eman's *Hayo Hayta* (She Once Was), a biography of one anonymous woman and her 1948-born, post-state generation, tells the author. In lieu of hierarchical relations with older mentors, Ne'eman's interviewees describe a world of rich and nourishing *lateral* connections between siblings, cousins, and, most significantly, friends. "We listened to each other, we read together, we taught each other, we helped each other. It was exhilarating," her interviewees say (48). I, who was born two decades after them, inhabited a much similar world.

I can't quite point to the exact moment when this world of purely lateral connections began to falter. It was in many ways an idyllic world, made of bonds that were coed and largely without hostility or schism between boys and girls. Our education system wasn't great, but it was largely egalitarian. Socialism gave a uniform shape to our lives. We ate the same meals. We lived in the same charmless apartments, in the same 1950s Soviet-style apartment buildings, with the same brown sofas and Formica-laminated kitchen tables. The fact that no one had much more than others was reassuring; it was also misleading. Inequities creeped up nonetheless: fewer women rose to top positions than men. Our canonical authors—Oz, Yehoshua, Grossman, Kenyuk, Appelfeld—were all men. Israeli culture placed young men, mostly soldiers, at the center of its cultural imagination. This, and the stated ideology of equality, made gender and other inequities on the ground invisible, and it prevented any of us from taking collective action as women.

Once we hit army years—Israel mandates two years of military service for girls and three years for boys—these inequities worsened. Our male friends entered combat units, and my female friends and I were indentured secretaries, transcribers, and social workers (today nearly all IDF positions are open to women). I was lucky to be assigned to what was called "a meaningful role" during my army service. Still, in my unit, those performing the lower ranking tasks—including kitchen and guard duty—were all women, and those to whom we reported, our commanding officers, were all men. My female army friends and I continued to have our lateral networks. Late at night in our freezing bunks, we huddled over cheap canteen snacks and bitched about our unfriendly, anxious supervisors. We saw their power over us as artificial and coercive, derived strictly from a military hierarchy we hated. If there were interesting or accomplished people among them, those qualities could find no expression within that framework, nor could they see in us anything but bodies that performed essential military tasks. But I was eighteen now, and then nineteen and twenty, and deep down inside, I began to long for more. I began to write—mostly during my guard duty shifts. Seated at the edge of the base (as we were not permitted) with my M-16 rifle resting on my knees (instead of my shoulder as required), I would scribble down language that I shared with no one. For this my beloved army buddies would not do. I wanted a more mature, less sardonic voice of authority that would help me give shape to my inner thoughts. A half-baked, intuitive feminist awareness was also emerging, but without a guide or interlocutor, I could not identify it as such.

Once, on a break during my service, I stumbled on a Hebrew translation of Simone de Beauvoir's first volume of *The Second Sex* in a used bookstore in Tel Aviv. I read it from cover to cover. Beauvoir gave words to a problem I was only beginning to sense: my second-class place as a woman. Her solution, which put the onus of changing the situation on me and me alone, appealed to me. I still, at twenty, believed unequivocally in self-reliance. I still could not imagine a female collective that worked to better my situation; and I certainly still could not imagine a powerful and empowering female mentor figure.

Four years later, after graduating from law school, I began an internship at the attorney general's office in Tel Aviv. Interns were assigned mentors in law. Mine was high strung, tough, controlling, and mediocre. Other senior attorneys—many of them smart and savvy women—veered from friendly and gossipy to indifferent, competitive, and mildly hostile. None were what I today would call a mentor. Only after I passed the bar exam, traveled to the US, traded law for literature, and entered a PhD program in comparative literature at Columbia University would I encounter, for the first time, caring, supportive, and constructive mentors.

The first was the late Eve Kosofsky Sedgwick, who codirected my doctoral dissertation in the last years of her life. To merely read Eve's writing—and I am not the first to say this—was in itself to feel mentored. Her exquisite words and sentences seeping into your fledgling ones, freeing and emboldening them. Eve is well documented as a legendary mentor. "To say her impact on me was world-changing would not be an understatement," a former student, Claudia Gonson, writes of her. In the various memorials that followed Eve's untimely death in 2009, many students lined up to demonstrate this: how a one-line critique made their book; how a recommendation letter made their career. I had not been part of the inner circle that spoke at the memorials, and though she wrote for me, Eve did not change the course of my career. Yet she changed something deeper: my capacity to be mentored.

Eve's generous mentorship expressed itself in the small, practical things. The way she said she would continue to mentor me when I transferred to Columbia after one year of doctoral studies at the CUNY Graduate Center, and kept her word. The way she schlepped from her apartment in Chelsea to the northern Columbia campus on the occasion of my orals, and climbing up the multiple flights of stairs, huffing and puffing—the elevator was broken and she was already ill and ailing—she said to me, "Don't worry; I *failed* my orals exam, and I'm just fine." And again three years later, on those same stairs, when before entering the room where my dissertation defense was to take place she said to me: "It's great. Impressive. The real deal."

What made Eve a great mentor? I think it was a combination of two qualities: the authority she exuded, the respect she elicited, her intellectual prowess, but also, her willingness to set them aside, to make room for *me*, to take a deep and serious interest in *my* interests—even when they differed from hers—to listen intently and to open herself up to my still unformed intellectual world—and to validate it. A mentor like that gives order to things.

Other female mentors followed. Geraldine Murphy, my City College of New York English Department chair, not only strongly supported my work as junior faculty and guided me through the annals of the tenure run but also, when a dean tried to fire me (and another untenured female faculty member), led an unrelenting campaign to save my job. Geraldine's was a combination of unwavering faithfulness, fearlessness, and pragmatic determination. She rallied the entire department behind her. She mobilized students. She worked every angle of every sympathetic administrator. Others were pulling strings as well, but Geraldine's role was different. It was the way she kept me informed daily, the way she patiently steered my own strategy, that made her not only a supervisor but also a *mentor*. She both exerted authority and confidence *and* remained generous throughout, helping me keep my calm and mirroring my best self back to me. Oh, and she saved my job.

The mentor who most helped me in my career, and who has stayed with me as a lifelong mentor, is neither a graduate advisor, a supervisor, nor a senior colleague from my college, but a well-known academic whose work I knew. I met her at a conference: I, an entry-level assistant professor with an article or two to my name. She walked into the venue where I presented, a small hotel room in Puebla, Mexico, where my panel had already started. I recognized her immediately, and watched her intently as she wiggled in her seat during the first incoherent, jargony presentation. I could tell she was exasperated—on her face was an expression I would come to know all too well in the coming years—and then saw her rise to leave. I shot up and began to read quickly. She sat back down. She listened intently with focus and interest I would come to know again and again in the years that followed. That split second in Puebla, Mexico, was the birth of a mentoring relationship that would change the course of my professional life.

I am now a mentor, including to occasional students in Israel. I learned to be a mentor by osmosis: to identify the student who seeks mentorship; to listen to her intently; critique constructively; compliment; to write the kind of letters that nail the grants and the jobs; to network relentlessly on behalf of mentees; to not give up on them when they give up on themselves.

In America I discovered then, both in myself and in others, the possibility of benevolent authority: hierarchical mentor–mentee relationships that gave sustenance and propelled a young person forward, psychologically *and* practically. These became, invariably, relationships between female mentors and female mentees, and they were different from anything I had previously known. They were both softer and more serious. I will not pretend they were always idyllic—no relationship is—but at their core was something entirely new to me: women in positions of power and authority who were consciously, deliberately supportive of other women. It took years for me to understand that though there are more or less generous individuals in this world, nicer and less nice, smarter and less smart, my mentors' and my own ascendance to positions of power, and our commitment to advancing others like us, are the gift of feminist politics. I had come too late to partake in the struggle of which I am now a beneficiary, but I continue the chain of mentorship.

Most of my students, including those in Israel, direct beneficiaries of feminist thought, take to mentorship naturally and without reservation. Yet in some—the poorer ones, the recent immigrants—I still see a bit of my old self, longing for something without knowing where and how to get it; reluctant to seek and receive support, especially from women. Change has not been absolute, or equal for all. Still, it has happened. In the world that both these students and I inhabit, there is now a tradition and a structure that makes mentorship relationships between women possible. There is now a sensibility that enables me to watch their proud countenances from afar, recognize their need, and be there should they need me. This makes all the difference.

Mikhal Dekel teaches English at the City College of New York (CCNY), where she directs the Rifkind Center for the Humanities and the Arts. Her latest book is *Tehran Children: A Holocaust Refugee Odyssey* (2019), published in paperback as *In the East* (2021). She has been mentoring undergraduate and graduate English and creative writing students for over two decades.

Works Cited

Baum, Dalia, et al., editors. *Lilmod Feminism: Mikra'a* (Learning Feminism: A Reader). Ha'kibutz ha'meukhad, Israeli Institute for Feminist and Gender Studies, 2006.

Beauvoir, Simone de. *Ha'min ha'sheni* (The Second Sex). Translated by Sharon Preminger. Babel, 2001. Originally published as *Le Deuxième Sexe*, Gallimard, 1949.

Dworkin, Andrea. *Mishgal* (Intercourse). Translated by Daniel Friedman. Babel, 2005. Originally published as *Intercourse*, Free Press, 1987.

Friedan, Betty. *The Feminine Mystique*. W. W. Norton, 1963.

Gonson, Claudia. "Why Eve Kosofsky Sedgwick Was My Heroine." *Advocate*, 12 Nov. 2015, advocate.com/current-issue/2015/11/12/why-eve-kosofsky-sedg-wick-was-my-heroine. Accessed 10 Dec. 2021.

Metz, D. *Ein Harod Hatzi Yovel* (Ein Harod: Semicentennial). Edited by Zrubavel Gilad and Neria Tsiling. Ha'kibbutz ha'meukhad Press, 1972.

Millet, Kate. *Sexual Politics*. Doubleday, 1970.

Ne'eman, Yael. *Hayo Hayta* (She Once Was). Ahuzat Bayit, 2011.

Rainmaker

How a Mentor Transformed My Destiny

Michelle Yasmine Valladares

I teach poetry and creative writing at the City College of New York (CCNY), as lecturer in English. For the past seven years I've also served as the director of its MFA program in creative writing. While I've worked in the arts for most of my adult life, first as a coordinator of events and later as an independent producer of three films, I never imagined that I would teach in a university. This was because no one in my family was a teacher, and it was not part of the list of possible future careers that my parents wanted me to pursue, that is, doctor/lawyer/engineer. I was born in India, raised in Kuwait, and immigrated to the US when I was thirteen. I was encouraged to excel in school for the main purpose of finding a good job that would provide benefits, like medical insurance and a pension. My parents reinvented themselves without family money or support, twice in two different countries and cultures. They both worked to pay for their children's educations, and they wanted to spare us the hardships they suffered. The path I should follow had been drilled into me at a young age. The consequences and fear of instability and insecurity hovered in our family backgrounds. My grandmother had been left a widow with six children still living at home when my grandfather died. My father, the seventh of nine, did not have the opportunity to attend college like his older siblings. Study, study, study was the mantra of my childhood.

But while there was constant pressure to succeed, the arts and sports also slipped into our lives. My mother loved classical music, and bought a piano and paid for our piano lessons and ballet classes. My father, who was a wonderful athlete, played squash, tennis, and golf. He believed that we should exercise daily so we joined a local club with a pool and access to the beach, where we would swim throughout my childhood. He was a gifted storyteller who would charm company with his adventures, like the time he sailed on a *dhow*, a traditional Arab sailing vessel, across the Arabian Gulf, or how he learned to swim in a well as a boy in India.

After I left home to attend college, I slowly began to discover what interested me, though it would take years before I was brave enough to follow my dreams to make films and then later in my life to return to graduate school to study writing. My pursuit of filmmaking, writing, and eventually teaching was entirely due to the intervention and encouragement of mentors. These included my childhood friend's mother, my second grade and high school English teachers, my thesis advisor in college, and filmmakers with whom I worked. But I want to focus on one mentor, Linsey Abrams, professor emerita and author, whom I first met in graduate school as a professor of fiction and who many years later hired me as an adjunct to teach at CCNY. My mother loves to remind me that my current success is based on three pillars: education, family, and Linsey Abrams. I agree that without the kindness and influence of a mentor like her, I would not be where I am today.

When I watch the occasional awards show on television, I'm curious about acceptance speeches and who gets thanked for an artist's success. As a culture and country, we like to think that we live in meritocracy, one in which our hard work and determination will fulfill our ambitions. I do not believe this is true. Without the intervention of a coach, guide, or mentor it is difficult, if not impossible for the average person like me to realize their dreams or maybe even to dream outside their circumstances or class. I think of the mentor as analogous to the indigenous "rainmaker," a shaman or medicine person in agricultural communities called in to intervene during a drought. The term has since been co-opted by corporate culture, but in its original meaning from shared indigenous stories, the rainmaker visits the arid lands and, through their vision, summons the rains. The mentor who selects the student or colleague identifies their potential and is able because of their own position to create or point to opportunities. They open doors that would have remained shut without their intercession. In times of drought, the rainmaker is asked to perform the ceremonies that invoke the rains. The mentor is like a rainmaker who creates circumstances and opportunities for the mentee's potential to blossom.

If you grow up between cultures as I did, or as an immigrant between languages and religions as I was, you are often confined to the parameters of those influences. My family lived in a local suburb of Kuwait in a predominantly Arab neighborhood. My mother enrolled my brother and me in the private American School of Kuwait so we could have access to a good education. I also witnessed the differences in class between my local community and the international students in the private school. It was only through intervention that I was able to move beyond the invisible boundaries of culture and class. It was due to the kindness of mentors in childhood and Linsey Abrams that I was able to imagine a life I never thought possible.

Recently I was up for a promotion, and I shared with my mother a letter of recommendation by Abrams. My mother, who is a retired college dean, immediately called to declare that it was the best letter of recommendation she'd ever read. She also said that if I were not success-ful, there was little else I could do. I did not get the promotion, but what buoys me through difficult times is the faith in my work by Abrams and colleagues like her. I met Linsey at Sarah Lawrence College where, after years of producing films, I decided to pursue an MFA in creative writing. She was the director of the fiction program, and I was accepted for poetry. I snuck up to her attic office in Slonim House one afternoon and asked her if I could take her renowned novel workshop. I had previously been rejected from graduate programs when I applied with a fiction manuscript. Though I doubted my ability to write fiction, Abrams reassured me after reading my work that I had a story to tell. The characters in her own novels possessed unique, brave voices that rallied for women's rights, defended the history of their neighborhoods, and shared their vulnerabilities. In the writing workshop, Abrams encouraged these qualities in our characters and helped us to develop their humanity. Years later I would discover that she was simultaneously and skillfully identifying and amplifying confidence in our voices as writers.

She invited me to join the staff of *Global City Review*, a journal she founded and edited. For many issues, I wrote a column on art and film. I was a woman's studies major at Bryn Mawr College, and many of the renowned feminist writers whose work I had studied were Linsey's friends and peers. Those early days of manually editing the mailing list of *Global City Review* to discover that Adrienne Rich and Grace Paley received copies of the journal were thrilling. I thrived in the MFA program under Linsey's influence as well as the opportunity to work closely with poets like Jean Valentine, Marie Howe, Joan Larkin, Vijay Seshadri, and Suzanne Gardinier. My experience in graduate school opened the door to a literary life and community. I remember those years as some of the best in my life. I found both a voice and a place in the world.

After my graduation Linsey and I lost touch. I was struggling in the bardo that is adjunct teaching while trying to complete my first book. For Buddhists the bardo is the intermediate state where one goes after death and before the next rebirth. Adjunct teaching is not a real job with adequate pay, but it is a world that many of us end up in after graduate school while hoping for full-time work. After seven years of adjunct teaching, I gave up on the idea that I would be able to find a full-time job teaching poetry in New York City. After a fifteen-year career producing independent films, I was older than most of my peers applying for the same entry-level teaching positions, and I was weary of commuting to five different colleges to make a living wage.

I called another mentor in graduate school, my advisor Susan Guma, who had helped me navigate scholarships and funding while I was there. I was hoping she could help me figure out another career. Susan took me out to lunch and said in her practical, no-nonsense way, "Of course you are having a tough time. You want to do the three hardest things in the world: write, teach writing, and live in New York City." She then wrote a list of five names on a paper napkin, handed it to me, and said, "If you don't find a job after calling all these contacts, come back and I'll give you more names." The first name on the list was Linsey Abrams.

I reconnected with Linsey, who by then had become the director of the MFA program in creative writing at CCNY. She appreciated my work in the arts, and my age was not an obstacle but an asset that she thought made me a wiser human and a better teacher. She hired me as an adjunct to teach creative writing. Unlike previous adjunct jobs, in this situation I had someone to check in with who cared how I was doing. We had a history. She observed my teaching and began to informally mentor me. I was fortunate this happened twenty years ago, before the shrinking of budgets and the cutting of full-time faculty hires in colleges. I was among two candidates hired for a full-time lecturer position to teach poetry in the MFA program. There were four hundred applicants for the jobs.

Linsey continued to mentor me by helping me edit and publish my first book of poems. We worked together and had a meaningful relationship as colleagues at CCNY for over a decade. She became more than a mentor and we developed a cherished friendship. Though I think a mentor may be a friend, not all mentor relationships turn into friendships. However, over the years we often drove home together after teaching, attended writing residencies and events, and went out to dinner with our partners. Years later, after Linsey retired from teaching, I was asked by my colleagues to direct the MFA program. I try to continue the spirit she instilled in the program, which was to honor the human story in every student and writer. On the days that we discover the enrollment has increased, or that diverse faculty hired under Abrams have strengthened the reputation of the program, or that we rank highly among other MFA programs despite little funding for marketing, I attribute these victories to the foundation created by Abrams during her tenure.

I acknowledge the difficulties of working in higher education and trying to publish. One must confront class, privilege, and connections. In both worlds, the right connection or invitation can transform a writer's career and work. Too often talent, literary success, and hard work are not enough to secure a stable job or imagine a career as a teacher and writer. There is never a day that I am not grateful to my mentor, who transformed my life, giving me the opportunity and time to develop as a writer and intellectual. Without my mentor's faith and guidance, I would not have a career in higher education.

Abrams and I continue our friendship to this day. She reminds me that the most important aspect of a writer's life is our humanity. And when I forget in the frenetic pace of working and writing in New York City, she continues to remind me where our allegiance lies. She is a lifelong activist who has been instrumental in the feminist writing community. I was inspired and influenced by her commitment to women and diversity and have made these missions my own.

Because of my positive experience of being mentored, I try to mentor my students. I see it as an essential part of my work to repay the kindness shown to me. It is not always a formal relationship. As director of a large, thriving program I meet and advise each student in the program. But I can only mentor a few and usually these relationships occur organically. Sometimes they are the students in my classes or the ones whose thesis manuscript I am asked to supervise. But more often it is the student that shows up every week in my office. They know my door is open. They know my office hours. They chat with our graduate assistant while waiting and eat the occasional cookies or sandwiches from an office party left on the table by the printer. We chat about their work, problems, and challenges.

I help find them student jobs and internships or encourage them to study with a certain faculty member. I lend them books to read. I make them hang posters up on campus for a reading. I ask for their help and in doing so they have reason to hang out long enough to ask directly for my help, about something, about anything. Mentorship is not necessarily about a job, career, or a book. It's advice from someone with experience in the world on whatever is on their mind. I have mentored students I've known as undergraduates who have become successful, each in their own way. For some it's the success of graduating with a college degree. For others it's the publication of a poem, story, or book. For others it's about creating a literary life and community.

When asked how they summon the rains, one rainmaker responds, "First I move into the community. Then I imagine that the grass grows high and the crops flourish and the clouds collect overhead. Only after this the rain arrives." We cannot predict what our mentees will accomplish, and we cannot fulfill all their wishes, but we can imagine their success before it arrives and do what we can each day to summon the rains.

I wrote this poem early in my teaching career, perhaps anticipating the role I'd one day take on as mentor.

Wishes

They gather outside
the classrooms,
smoke and talk.
Their silhouette
against the sun
as it sinks into the Hudson.
From the top of 135th Street, the light
is red. I wait and drink in the wide horizon.
Their voices reach me, excited,
insistent, young. I want to share
this sunset and their wishes to come true.
The old men sit in their chairs
on the sidewalks. The women
sit on stoops while children
run up and down the hill.
Soon the sprinklers
turn into a fountain. Soon

it is summer and school
is out. The cars on Broadway
screech, speed to make the lights.
The breeze picks up. I hear
their wishes as songs—
which rise like spring's
pollen, into the breeze,
float above the Hudson, head
for the Atlantic past tugboats, barges
seagulls, the renovated
piers, ships and New Jersey, out
to currents, eddies and swirls
of the ocean. Each wish rises as seed
or water, plants itself next door
or falls like rain.
If only they could see the power
of their wishes, that keeps the universe
connected, as their heads
reach their pillows
and new wishes rise,
the old forgotten
in the clear light of dreams.

Acknowledgment

This essay was written on lands of the Lenape, Manhattan's original inhabitants.

Michelle Yasmine Valladares (michelleyasminevalladares.com) is a South Asian American poet, educator, and an independent filmmaker. She is the owner of a badly behaved rescue dog. She teaches at the City College of New York and directs their MFA program in creative writing.

Transformative Adaptations

Tracking Fay Gale as a Teacher

ELIZABETH WOOD

The following remarks were given as a speech on December 6, 2012, at the Fay Gale Center for Research on Gender at the University of Adelaide, our alma mater. Although the occasion concluded an annual conference in the social sciences, it was a jolly family affair, for among those present were Fay's daughter and my goddaughter, Marie Gale; Fay's sister and inspiration, Edna Walker Oosting; Fay's longtime research collaborator, Joy Wundersitz; my eldest daughter, Anna Wood, and many of Fay's old friends and fellow alumni.

Fay Gale was born June 13, 1932, at Balaklava, a country town in South Australia, and died May 3, 2008, age seventy-five, at her home in Adelaide. She was a pathbreaking scholar of nontraditional Aboriginal people, and as she continued to research and publicize the living conditions of urbanized Aboriginal people, her influence went far beyond the academy. Her advocacy ranged from the rights of Aboriginal families and youth for equal justice under the law to the necessity of protecting heritage sites of Aboriginal rock art from the predations of tourism. Always, in whatever she did, Fay believed in women and our capacities.

Her career was a series of "firsts." At Adelaide University, she was the first woman PhD graduate in geography; first woman professor of geography and the very first woman professor at that university, among few women nationally; the first woman president of the Institute of Australian Geographers, the Academy of the Social Sciences in Australia, the

Association of Asian Social Science Research Councils. The list is endless. Professionally, it culminates in her appointment as vice-chancellor at the University of Western Australia and as an officer of the Order of Australia for services to the social sciences, particularly in the field of Aboriginal studies.

How fortunate I am that this teacher and mentor became my beloved friend! While writing the speech that follows, I felt I was following in her tracks, hearing her voice, its informality and warmth, on a hunt for clues to what motivated her, what made her tick. Now, a decade further on, I realize that had she lived Fay would be almost ninety, since I am now eighty-two. How ridiculous! This is a love story without end. A school-girl crush grew into love. From her, I learned what it is to be loved. Not maternally. Not sexually. Truly.

With respect for Kaurna Nation Aborigines of the Adelaide Plains and Hills

I met Fay Gale in 1954, when I was fifteen, a student at Walford, a school for girls on Unley Road in Adelaide, South Australia. I took up geography simply because I wanted to learn from her. Fay Gilding, as she was, a twenty-two-year-old newly minted BA Honors graduate in geography, was starting her first teaching job. Her approach to teaching was stunningly innovative for the mid-1950s. It took us out of the conventional class-room literally into the outside world, into a more inclusive, democratic, and transformative physical and intellectual space. She held classes out of doors whenever possible. We students circled her, cross-legged on the ground, a learning circle with no single body dominant, to listen closely and watch her draw with a stick in the dirt or mold earth with her hands to illustrate the gripping three-dimensional story she told, about how the continental shelf or a glacial landscape is shaped; how an earthquake or oceanic wave pattern is formed.

Fay was very enthusiastic about field trips. Decades before Google Maps, she took one class aloft in a single-prop airplane to survey the Murray River delta and Coorong unscrolling below. "You could see every-thing more clearly from the air," she told me, "but no one had ever done that, and the headmistress wasn't very pleased, so we didn't do it again."[1] I was in another group who took a three-day field trip to Nairne in the Adelaide Hills, with the goal of measuring and mapping an entire country town. I realized years later that Fay was adapting the then-new field of

Transformative Adaptations | 109

cultural geography to our high school education, even before she taught it as a newly appointed lecturer, in 1966, in the Geography Department of the University of Adelaide. She taught us to use generic symbols, scale models, photography, drawings; to designate, date, and tabulate every road, building, dwelling, public space; to research municipal and church records to learn the area's history; to interview residents about their work, lives, and relationships with the land and their community; to chart a locality's topography, history, and cultural identity.

Fay taught us critical observation, "one of the great tools of the geographer," that she described as an intellectual breakthrough for her in 1962, when she read a then-new textbook, *Readings in Cultural Geography* (Gale, "Textbooks"; see also Gale and Anderson). Here was a theoretical framework that made sense of what she was studying and teaching and helped explain the problems she had had in formulating her own research in the late 1950s. "For me, this body of work interrelated regional geography, based on fieldwork and observation, with both anthropology and the archival record" (234). In looking for a way forward toward alternative methods of exploring the world, and for ideas about the dynamism of cultural change, the concept of culture as a process, Fay was a trailblazer in teaching young people how to engage dynamically and creatively with the world and with our own sense of being and becoming in relation to it and to one another.[2]

Before cultural geography, there was an earlier formative experience in Fay's evolution as a transformative teacher. After I teased her once for the parsimonious postcards and scrappy shorthand memos she sent in place of meatier letters, she told me about her childhood dyslexia. Judging by her handwriting, she may also have been dysgraphic (they go hand in hand). Dyslexia is a reading disability. The child has problems decoding words, blending letters, reading fluently, reading orally, and comprehending what she has read. It is a disorder that interferes with processing language and causes difficulties with receptive and expressive language. Dyslexic people can be identified by writing that does not seem to match their level of intelligence. Dysgraphia, a writing or typing disability, is an orthographic processing deficit that can exacerbate dyslexia. Fay's problems with handwriting clearly and fluently may have been a leftover effect of early childhood problems she had with reading, possibly also with hearing, or impaired voice recognition. She always loved to be read to, more than to read her own words to others.

Tools today, such as a phonics-based reading program, memory and word games, audiobooks, and constant repetition and patience, can treat these neurolinguistic disorders. When Fay was a child, not much was known about them. They are not visible disorders. They are not written on the body in ways that another, differently abled, might "read" as disabilities. Embedded in self-identity, without the encumbrances of written words, dyslexia and dysgraphia are a secret self-knowledge that need not be expressed or communicated. Rather, they may be disguised, evaded, or denied.

Yet such invisible, interior marks of identity and difference can present alternative ways of being and knowing.[3] How did Fay cope with these disabilities? She taught herself to read, a little girl huddled beneath her father's desk while he wrote the Sunday sermon. (Jasper Gilding was a Methodist minister. Kathie Gilding, Fay's mother, worked for the church mission.) Fay's books: Arthur Mee's two-volume encyclopedia, and a world atlas. There she learned to decipher the names of things and to decode their meanings (their toponymy), and to map in her mind's eye the interrelatedness of continents and oceans, of constituent topologies. In other words, disability could act as a spur to her acquiring, in nonverbal tracking and mapping of data, the complex skills for which Fay was famed: observation, memorization, and empathy.

Theorists in cognitive psychology and critical thinking in disability studies and transformative learning suggest that an experience of a deep structural shift in our consciousness can dramatically alter our way of being in the world, of understanding ourselves and our self-locations, our relationships with other humans and with the natural world. In classroom contexts, transformative learning involves participatory discourse, a welcoming of diversity, a trusting and caring communality, development of sensitive relationships among learners, and peer collaboration, all of which Fay performed as a teacher and throughout her professional life. What if her experience of being differently abled triggered her development of an adaptive, compensatory, and holistic consciousness that transformed her own learning, field research, and scholarship? That enabled a compassionate, empathetic exchange of positionality (of self and subject, self and other) that allowed her to listen and learn—and teach us to learn—from alternative positions and in different registers of the social and material—and thereby to free herself, and subsequently us, her students, to think for ourselves by freeing us from mindless or unquestioning acceptance of conventional ideas and practices—such as she had encountered in mainstream anthropology when she was an undergraduate student?

Fay struggled throughout life with written expression. Here, I think, is another contributing component of her receptivity to the Aboriginal world in pathbreaking doctoral research that became *A Study of Assimilation: Part-Aborigines in South Australia* in 1964.[4] For I believe that Fay understood the many virtues of collaboration quite early in her professional career. In the preliminary stages of that research, she invited me to accompany her on a field trip to Nepabunna mission settlement, a parched, isolated, segregated reserve in the northern Flinders Ranges. I acted as notetaker and witness, squatting beside her in the red dust, as Fay asked questions and listened to the Indigenous women living there. A year or two later, Fay's husband Milton Gale, a Methodist minister, took on the role of notetaker, typist, editor, and more, in Fay's research and publishing. After their divorce, she invariably invited a colleague, often a graduate student at the start of her professional career, to work alongside her as collaborator, coordinator, cowriter, coeditor: a second pair of eyes and ears who took care of the words. Those she mentored, such as Jane M. Jacobs, Kay Anderson, and Joy Wundersitz, became her lifelong friends.

Fay worked by choice and inspiration in a culture that does not rely on words and require written language: one which has diverse symbolic narratives and pictorial expressions (the heritage sites of Aboriginal rock art, for example, at Kakadu, Uluru, the Flinders Ranges, Kurringai Chase, and the Pilbara) that have meaning not so much in content as in the doing, remembering, repeating, and layering over time. A culture with a different notion of time. A different concept of inside/outside. A different way of telling, learning, and teaching stories. Fay's engagement with Aboriginal culture had the most profound influence on her consciousness and creativity.

Here is a vignette of collaboration in formation, the evolving strategy of "share with us and we will share with you" that Fay discusses in "Roles Revisited" (129; see also *Woman's Role*). She first describes how she was able, on a return trip to Point Macleay in the 1950s, to talk and listen specifically to the older women on a more equal basis than before. Their main questions to her were about life on the outside, that is, outside the mission. "I remember an elderly white-haired lady at one of these camps . . . it was strong-minded women like her who first made me question. . . . As a young white woman conscious of my own secondary place in society, I asked her how and why" (129). As her own understanding grew, Fay realized that women, rarely considered in field research conducted in the past by white male anthropologists, had untold secrets and sites specific to women's experience and culture. From Aboriginal women she interviewed, Fay acquired a way of teaching and explaining (for which we Walford girls were beneficiaries) using sticks, dirt, hands, to tell stories. As Jeannie Nungarrayi Egan described for Fay her own preschool teaching of Yuendumu Aboriginal culture, "I talk to the children. Telling sand stories, talking stories, making tracks, digging sticks . . . and old people are asked to come [to her classroom] to tell the children old-time stories and about their history" (122).

Former "subjects" of Fay's research, like Jeannie Egan, would become her coproducers, for instance in the work of translating, interpreting, and planning the sessions chaired by Aboriginal women in the groundbreaking ANZAAS (Australian and New Zealand Association for the Advancement of Science) conference of 1980 (Gale, *We Are Bosses Ourselves*, "Introduction").[5] The importance of exchanging one's own positionality for another's had become apparent to Fay in 1972 as a visiting lecturer at St. Hugh's College, Oxford. She told me that her experience there of "the ivy tower's inward-looking educational claustrophobia" so distressed her that she ran off to join (and observe from within) a group of so-called "gypsy" travelers. She made it her practice thereafter to take undergraduate students outside the university in order to enhance their studies, just as she had taken Walford schoolgirls away to camp in the Adelaide Hills. As an Adelaide University lecturer, later its first female professor—all of her appointments were "firsts" for a woman—she continued the kind of hands-on teaching she developed first at Walford, taking undergraduates on camping trips to the northern Flinders Ranges, for example, "so they could learn geomorphology from a Western scientific view." She continued, "And then I would get the old Aboriginal people to come around the campfire each night and they would tell the stories of the Ranges from the Aboriginal point of view." She wanted "students to think about these alternative ways of seeing the world and how they fit together. I was trying to blow their minds a bit, and I think that's what a university should be about."[6]

If cultural geography was Fay's intellectual inspiration, and disability a triggering mechanism, Aboriginal women were her guiding and guardian lodestars. Three were indeed her sisters, Linda Vale, Gladys Mayne, and Edna Walker Oosting. Edna was age fifteen or sixteen when she became Fay's sister. Edna was an Aboriginal child of the "Stolen Generation," forcibly ripped by government decree from her mother and ancestral land in the Northern Territory and transported to a remote church-run camp in South Australia, euphemistically a mission settlement, to "rescue her from her Aboriginality" (Campbell). Fortunately for Edna, she was rescued from that camp by the Gilding family. Fay would later use her research skills to track down Edna's surviving family and reunite her to them. She and Edna were sisters in the deepest sense.

Fay found a fourth way forward, as she expanded a teaching career into academic administration, in her discovery of intersectional feminism and feminist theories about women and gender, religion, ethnicity, class, race, and power. Feminist scholars at the University of Adelaide, especially emerita professor of history Susan Magarey, helped Fay to see how feminist thinking clarifies the politics of power and gender.[7] I think Fay was already a feminist when she taught us at Walford. The way she taught our so-called scripture class made dreary old-style religious instruction vital and relevant to our personal lives and to Australia's place in the contemporary world. For example, she used controversies in the press about the unfolding Suez crisis in 1956 to present us with ways of thinking about power in terms of colonialism, empire, and comparative religion. She brought to class daily press stories covering the interventions by church and crown in the love affair of Princess Margaret and Captain Peter Townsend (a riveting, even scandalous subject for teenage girls back then) to have us discuss complicated ideas about women, marriage, divorce, the right to privacy, freedom of the press, and—yes, faced with the trembling uncertainties of young women like us—about female love and desire. She taught us to question, to be skeptical of authority and the status quo, yet to be respectful. In her subsequent career as a distinguished university chancellor, a scholar-activist, and political player in the upper reaches of academic administration, she became a voice that spoke out on behalf of all women.

When I was a teenager, curious as to why Fay was so extraordinary, she was a miracle in our lives. As I grew older, little by little she introduced me to more of her life. I visited the Gilding family's home, met her parents, her brother Wes, her sisters Gladys, Linda, and Edna. I formed and trained a choir to sing at her wedding. She asked me to be godmother to her beloved daughter, Marie, an honor I try to live up to. She lent me furniture for my first flat, and her home as a refuge years later—along with Hugo, the dog, *and* Michael, her son—while she was on sabbatical in Seattle and I was undergoing contested custody and divorce in family court. After I moved to New York, she came several times to stay with us in Manhattan and on the North Fork of Long Island.

I learned more about what made Fay different when she took me along on her travels—to the Canadian Rockies; the Flinders Ranges;

Shark Bay, Margaret River, and the dark-red jarrah forests of Western Australia—always teaching me how and what to observe in the movements of migrating ospreys, an egg-laying snapping turtle in my garden, a deceptively adorable brown bear in the wild, its mother lurking nearby. She taught me that the earth and bush, rock and cave, river and wetland pond, no less than the archive and academy, are sites of knowledge and repositories of history, learning, and myth. On my trips with her (she with camera and binoculars, me with requisite pen and notepad), I saw again and remembered how she was an expert tracker who could read the wordless notations that humans and living creatures and nature itself imprint and reprint on this earth.

I remember following behind her as she deciphered marks on the ground and trees that lined an old bush track, which she determined was made by horses pulling logs to clear a route for mustering sheep through the forest and along and across a creek that fed into the Donnelly River in southwestern Australia. We later learned that this place, the very site we chose to make camp, had been cleared a century before by the colonial poet Adam Lindsay Gordon for a sheep farm, a doomed endeavor.

Fay continued to teach me on our adventures that to isolate a narrative from its roots, as she thought many popular books of mythology do, is to destroy its soul and denude it of its meaning. Narratives belong to their own cultural and topological setting, she believed. In their telling, a narrator may, and does, assume a great deal of knowledge on the part of hearers—knowledge of how the culture works, its rules and behaviors; knowledge of what the story is all about and its place in history. Reciprocation, shared knowledge, was key to learning the Fay Gale way.

So, who was the woman I learned to know, who changed my life? Who transformed difficulty and challenge into ways of learning and forms of respect? Who taught me about her adult self; who seemed so composed, so reserved, yet was a tough determined negotiator and warrior who advised us women: "[P]ut on the asbestos suit if you don't want to feel the fire. I often put it on in my mind." Who, during the fiercest gender wars among university chancellors, carried a metaphorical see-through plastic umbrella: "Nothing can hit me then, but I see all."[8] We may smile to remember her outsized spectacles, but—with those owl's eyes, did she see *more* than we?

Fay Gale would always have been an original. Her intellect alone guaranteed that. But it was her combination of her intellect and how she played the cards that she was given that made her a transformative figure, a genius. Among the things she transformed was that fifteen-year-old Walford girl in 1954, but she transformed for so many how we learn and how we teach.

Elizabeth Wood is an Australian American music historian and conservator of a micro-habitat for wildlife on the North Fork of Long Island, where she thrives with her spouse and other varieties of birds, frogs, squirrels, turtles, and trees. Her "To Do More" list includes charcoal drawing, piano sight-reading, limerick writing, and deciding what to do with the books. The house overflows with them.

Notes

1. Fay Gale, correspondence with Elizabeth Wood, 1994.
2. Her example led me to choose an Australian topic for my doctoral research in music, for which I adapted some of her interviewing, data gathering, and archival recording techniques (Wood).
3. Guiding my thoughts is "Beyond Abnormality" by Marianne Kielian-Gilbert. See also O'Sullivan.
4. In the introduction, Gale thanks her "Aboriginal foster sisters Linda, Gladys, and Edna for their insights and inspiration" and notes how her dissertation was "an academically unacceptable topic." I was interested to see in rereading it how plain and unadorned her style of writing was. She told me decades later, "[W]riting is not all that great, and I get impatient as my thoughts just go too fast for my fingers" (Fay Gale, private correspondence with Elizabeth Wood, 6 Nov. 1989).
5. This was the first Australia-wide meeting of Aboriginal women. See also Bell and Kartinyeri in *We Are Bosses Ourselves*, and Gale, "Participation."
6. Fay Gale, correspondence with Elizabeth Wood, 1997.
7. Susan Magarey, correspondence with Elizabeth Wood, 3 May 2008.
8. Fay Gale, correspondence with Elizabeth Wood, 1994 and 1995.

Works Cited

Bell, Diane. "Consulting with Women." *We Are Bosses Ourselves: The Status and Role of Aboriginal Women Today*, edited by Fay Gale, Australian Institute of Aboriginal Studies, 1983, pp. 24–28.
Campbell, Beatrix. "Stolen Lives." *The Guardian*, 17 May 2001, theguardian.com/education/2001/may/17/tefl.beatrixcampbell. Accessed 21 Apr. 2008.

Egan, Jeannie Nungarrayi. "The Yuendumu Aboriginal Cultural Pre-school." *We Are Bosses Ourselves: The Status and Role of Aboriginal Women Today*, edited by Fay Gale, Australian Institute of Aboriginal Studies, 1983, pp. 122–23.

Gale, Fay. "The Participation of Australian Aboriginal Women in a Changing Political Environment." *Political Geography Quarterly*, vol. 9, no. 4, 1990, pp. 381–95.

———. "Roles Revisited: The Women of Southern South Australia." *Women, Rites and Sites: Aboriginal Women's Cultural Knowledge*, edited by Peggy Brock, Allen & Unwin, 1989, pp. 120–35.

———. *A Study of Assimilation: Part-Aborigines in South Australia*. Libraries Board of South Australia, 1964.

———. "Textbooks That Moved Generations." *Progress in Human Geography*, vol. 27, no. 2, 2003, pp. 233–36.

———, editor. *We Are Bosses Ourselves: The Status and Role of Aboriginal Women Today*. Australian Institute of Aboriginal Studies, 1983.

———. *Woman's Role in Aboriginal Society*. Australian Institute of Aboriginal Studies, 1970.

Gale, Fay, and Kay Anderson, editors. *Inventing Places: Studies in Cultural Geography*. Longman Cheshire, 1992.

Kartinyeri, Doreen, as told to Milton Gale. "Recording Our History." *We Are Bosses Ourselves: The Status and Role of Aboriginal Women Today*, edited by Fay Gale, Australian Institute of Aboriginal Studies, 1983, pp. 136–57.

Kielian-Gilbert, Marianne. "Beyond Abnormality: Dis/ability and Music's Metamorphic Subjectivities." *Sounding Off: Theorizing Disability in Music*, edited by Neil Lerner and Joseph Strauss, Routledge, 2006, pp. 217–34.

O'Sullivan, Edmund. *Transformative Learning: Educational Vision for the 21st Century*, U of Toronto P, 1999.

Wagner, Philip L., and Marvin W. Mikesell, editors. *Readings in Cultural Geography*, U of Chicago P, 1962.

Wood, Elizabeth. "Music Into Words." *Between Women: Biographers, Novelists, Critics, Teachers, and Artists Write about Their Work on Women*, edited by Carol Ascher, Louise DeSalvo, and Sara Ruddick, Beacon, 1984, pp. 71–84.

Further Reading

Anderson, Kay. "Gwendoline Fay Gale AO (13 June, 1932–3 May 2008)." *Geographical Research*, vol. 46, no. 4, 2008, pp. 468–70, JSTOR, doi: 10.1111/j.1745-5871.2008.00541.x.

"Fay Gale." *Wikipedia*. https://en.wikipedia.org/wiki/Fay_Gale.

"Gale, Gwendoline Fay AO (1932–2008)." *The Encyclopedia of Women and Leadership in Twentieth-Century Australia*, edited by Judith Smart and Shirlee Swain, Australian Women's Archives Project, 2014.

Dear Ant

AOIBHEANN SWEENEY

Dear Ant:

I was asked to submit an essay for an anthology a friend of mine is putting together, called *Feminists Reclaim Mentorship*. I told her you were the closest thing I had to a mentor, and naturally (because she knows your work) she was interested in hearing more about that, so I told her I'd write you, because it seemed weird not to tell you, if I was going to write about you, for the purposes of publication.

Do you think of me as a mentee? It's hardly a word, *mentee*—it's the kind of nonword I usually squint at, in a contract, to work out who is who, and sign it, thinking how strange it is that there is so much linguistic inadequacy in the law, as if language wasn't made to stand so still. Lessor, Lessee. I think of you as someone who doesn't clutter her life with inadequate words, and I doubt you think of anyone as a mentee. Though, formally speaking, there has been that sort of business between us: straightforward classroom instruction, letters of recommendation, me putting down your name on applications of all sorts. Which, by some kind of law, I suppose makes me the *mentee*?

I know I've told you I love you, countless times. I doubt this is in the definition of mentor, or mentee. Perhaps, though, I've been mistaking this ancient, nearly contractual arrangement of mentorship for love? Could be. I promise it isn't a fleshy sort of love. I don't imagine licking you or anything. But when I look at you, it's true that every part of you seems deeply admirable to me: your giant, lashy eyes, your nearly always lipsticked mouth, your changing hair, your troublesome feet, your insect legs. I love the body you have—its beauty, its fragility. Your long, bony hands, your bulky rings. Your clothes! Your capes, your black leather pants, your high heels. I'm certain I would admire them on no one else, however: they're not my kind of thing. They're simply yours.

I've certainly asked your advice, countless times—all the time, really, in my head, and a few times, on the phone. I remember asking you, when I got stuck at the end of my first book, about endings, and you left a long message on my answering machine about the problem with endings actually being a problem in the middle. You were right, of course—and I did fix it, however much fiction is ever fixed. Often, by making a writing problem into something really technical, that only another person, a really masterful person, could solve, I write my way out of it. But still, I feel I have you to thank, since you're the masterful person I have in mind.

I don't think in the end that it has been your advice that has mattered, so much as your permission. Like when I asked you if I could leave New York, and my job, and my native country, to try to write the book I'd been trying to write, for years, on the side, because I knew better than to ask you if I *should* leave my home and my job, to write a book. No one can answer that for anyone else, not even a mentor. But I remember it perfectly, standing in the warm wind of traffic on Sixth Avenue, after lunch, strangled by relief and trepidation, getting the unnecessary question out, because it felt so necessary. I was wearing a vintage dress I hoped you would like, my flip-flops facing your high heels. You said that *I might as well try*, because if I didn't, then I wouldn't have tried. I stood there with tears pouring down my face, knowing you were giving me permission, as I knew you would, and now that I had asked, I would have to write the book, all by myself.

I was stupidly honored, when you signed off on an email, a few years ago maybe, as "Ant." I assume it was you who started that. Or maybe I prompted it, cheekily pretending to be your niece, linking arms with your actual relative, and coincidently my best friend, Nell. I've always told myself that I would be your mentee with or without Nell, but really she brought us together, outside of my working for your publisher, so I suppose it's impossible to say.

Anyway, I like it that without the "u," the word Ant conjures, simultaneously, a childless older woman, and a shiny, black, cinch-waisted creature, with long, comical antennae, and industrious, but vaguely malevolent ways. I have a number of aunts, but they do not have this transformative range, perhaps because they are actual relations, or perhaps because they are not childless. My mother's sister, who is also my godmother, is very kind to me, and loves me nearly as she does her own children. I'm grateful for the contrast she provides between herself and my mother, but she doesn't have any idea how long it takes, when you are alone, to drag a crumb up a long, sandy hill and down into a teeming hole in the ground. I am certain you have experienced the heights and depths of these horrors, and when I am with you, no matter how many glasses of wine either of us has had, I always have the sense that we are crawling, companionably, free from anything *familiar*.

I'm careful, every time I write you, because I don't want to waste any bit of what you give me, or force your obligation toward anything like the aforementioned contract. So—I thought I'd write this letter, exploring the theme, just to see what you think? I'm sort of fine either way, if you're busy, or don't want to be involved, or have your name mentioned in this way, I don't need to do anything with this at all. But I'd been meaning to get in touch, so this seemed like a way to do both, albeit somewhat awkwardly, but ideally, with no harm done. To avoid confusion, you can just write me back & say nice to hear from you but no thanks on the "mentor essay" thing.

Love love love, xx yer fake niece, A.

Aoibheann Sweeney is the author of the award-winning novel *Among Other Things I've Taken Up Smoking*, which she wrote while running the Center for the Humanities at the Graduate Center, City University of New York. Though she never in fact took up smoking, she was diagnosed with cancer a few years after the book was published. She now lives in Ireland, where the health care is free, and is writing another novel, about her Irish ancestry.

Part II

Rearview Mirror

Mentoring at a Distance

Part II

Rearview Mirror

Monitoring at a distance

Ready

JOY LADIN

Fear not, I am the one who helps you . . .

—Isaiah 41:13

"7 Empowering Life Lessons from 'Buffy the Vampire Slayer'"

—www.cosmopolitan.com/entertainment/a9118169/
buffy-anniversary-empowering-heroine-moments/

Are you ready to be strong?

Are you ready to follow me beyond
the fear that warns you
to hold your tongue

when cruelty and hopelessness,
degradation and evil,
stab you through the heart?

Fear likes you this way,
self-loathing and numb,
believing you're no one

I'd ever choose,
a worm in a tunnel, dust in a gale,
a nameless pool of blood

I could never love.
I summon them all to judgment,
the fear that stalks you

to the ends of the earth,
the shame and disgrace
that nail you in your place,

everything that gets in the way
of you responding when I say
"Don't be afraid."

Don't be afraid.
I was here before fear
and I'm there beyond it,

opening fountains,
trampling kings underfoot,
calling you to me

across generations
by paths you haven't walked,
by ways you cannot imagine.

I'm the mother who really sees,
the father who understands
you, every version,

real and imagined, future and past,
cypress and desert, queer fluid light,
thresher of mountains, solitary pine.

You have nothing to fear
and nothing to prove.
Are you ready

to be strong? Time
to remake the world.

Joy Ladin's experience of being poetically mentored by the Shekhinah resulted in the completion of a book-length sequence, *Shekhinah Speaks*, published by Selva Oscura in 2022. Joy has also published nine other books of poetry, including two Lambda Literary Award finalists, *Impersonation and Transmigration* and *The Book of Anna*, reissued in a revised second edition by EOAGH in 2021; and two works of creative nonfiction, National Jewish Book Award finalist *Through the Door of Life* and Lambda Literary and Triangle Award finalist *The Soul of the Stranger: Reading God and Torah from a Transgender Perspective*, the first book-length work of Jewish trans theology.

Note

1. "Ready" comes from *Shekhinah Speaks*, a book-length effort to give voice to the Shekhinah, described in mystical Jewish tradition as the immanent, feminine aspect of God who dwells with human beings and shares our feelings and experiences. Tradition imagines the Shekhinah as a silent, passive presence, but these poems tune in to a Shekhinah who challenges, encourages, empowers, and otherwise mentors the human "you" (the pronoun represents each of us) she addresses.

Mentor Ghosts

SIRI HUSTVEDT

I am fascinated by the idea of mentorship, even though I have few of my own stories to tell as either protégé or wise counselor. The word itself, *mentor*, triggers a hunger from a time in my life that is now gone, the ache for an attachment to someone who recognized me as worthy of the life I had decided upon. Although I knew I wanted to write from a young age—thirteen—and I have read and studied and written ardently ever since, the overwhelming feeling I have to this day on the subject of mentors is that I never came home.

Home? Why *home*? I suspect that my mentor fantasy was one of longing for both recognition and repair. It taps primary desires because the two sides of the mentoring couple recapitulate the child–parent relation, but at a later stage of life and in a more conscious form. No one chooses a parent, after all. A mentor must be sought out and cajoled or seduced into playing the role. And for the one who is sought, admiration is a potent elixir. Mutuality is key in the formation of the pair, but hierarchy is also a given.

"I applaud, I mean I value, I egg you on in, your study of the American life that surrounds you," Henry James wrote to Edith Wharton, who was almost twenty years younger than he was. She loved him. He loved her. She had money. He didn't. This evened things out between her and "the master." There were some irritations between them—a low-grade rivalry—but more love than competition. No sex, but influence. Wharton grew weary of critics insisting on her likeness to James.

Sherwood Anderson wrote a letter of recommendation for the young Ernest Hemingway—I see the door open to Gertrude Stein's salon, an enchanted interior. There are paintings on the walls. I hear voices but the words are indecipherable. Alice B. Toklas is in the kitchen "with the wives." In *A Moveable Feast*, Hemingway is cruel to Stein. He punched back at his mentor, whose influence on him had been profound. She was called "The Mother of Modernism." He called his own mother, Grace Hall Hemingway, "my bitch mother" and "a dominating shrew." They say Grace Hall loved a woman. In Hemingway, love and hate, masculine and feminine, are fused together into an indistinguishable lump. He feared that lump.

In his ingratiating first letter to the great Lev Tolstoy, Ivan Bunin made a bid to be mentored, "I am one of the many who have followed your every word with great interest and respect." Bunin's groveling worked. After the two had known each other for years, Bunin wrote, "Right now I feel like crying and kissing your hand as if you were my own father!"

Samuel Beckett was a research assistant to his idol, James Joyce. "That's what it was," Beckett said about Joyce's work, "epic, heroic, what he achieved." Peggy Guggenheim noted that Beckett worked "like a slave" for Joyce. Lucia Joyce, a gifted choreographer and dancer, was infatuated with her father's handsome acolyte. Beckett took Lucia out. He appeared with her here and there, but he didn't return her feelings. He was interested in *her father*. He was humoring the *father*. This is the homosocial love story James Knowlson tells in his biography of Beckett. But Joyce accused Beckett of leading his beloved daughter on. The rift between the two men lasted for years.

Beckett had to cleanse himself of Joyce's influence. He had to become other to Joyce.

The lovely Lucia went mad. She survives among the wives and daughters in literature's kitchen.

Before I met and married him, a young writer Paul Auster met his literary hero, Samuel Beckett, in Paris. He was twenty-two years old. The painter Joan Mitchell made the introduction. Beckett was kind, interested. He looked at the young man and said, "So Mr. Auster, tell me all about yourself." "Mr. Auster" had no idea what to say.

Beckett's influence is visible in some plays Paul wrote when he was in his twenties. I read them later and told him so. After that, if it's there, the influence isn't easily seen. The complete digestion of another writer's work may mean it becomes invisible.

In 1980, when I was a twenty-five-year-old graduate student in English literature at Columbia University, I wrote a letter to Djuna Barnes. I had received her address by chance.

I was carrying Barnes's novel *Nightwood* with me on the subway. An elderly woman noticed, asked me about it, and I gushed love for the book. She said that her husband, who taught at Princeton, knew Barnes, and that if I wanted to write to my hero, she would send me the address. Two or three days later, a postcard arrived in my mailbox. *Nightwood* was still new to me. I had written a paper on it, and when I sat down at my typewriter, I wanted to convey to its author the dancing complexities I had found in her novel. My letter must have been passionate, but I was also highly conscious of the need for restraint, to keep the letter short but astute. It went through a number of revisions until I felt it was just right, and I sent it off.

Two years later, after I had moved to Brooklyn, a letter typed on what I guessed was an old Underwood arrived in the mail: It said, "Dear Miss Hustvedt, Your letter has given me great difficulty." Another line followed with the signature, "Djuna Barnes." How I managed to lose that letter I cannot say. What was wrong with me? Why don't I recall the second line? I know I didn't take her response as an insult either. I read it as a tribute to me, the youthful letter writer who had disturbed the peace of the old recluse at 22 Patchen Place. She died a month later at the age of ninety. I remember reading the obituary in the *New York Times*.

I didn't expect the famously isolated, crotchety Djuna Barnes to mentor me. I was surprised that she wrote back. And yet, I am glad she received the letter and glad it gave her difficulty. Djuna Barnes is my phantom mentor.

The vagaries of my desire for someone to recognize me as worthy of the life I had chosen are painful on hindsight. What was the life I had chosen? I could have attended a writing program, given myself up to the instruction of older poets and novelists, but I didn't. I went to graduate school for a PhD. I wanted to study, to read hard and think well. I also wanted to pay the bills in that place known as the future.

"I'm not sure you want to become a professor," my father said to me after I had been in graduate school for years. He was a professor. Did he mean he thought I wasn't cut out for it? Did he think I should write and not eat? Did he feel bad about his own career? Did he think I would be unhappy? I couldn't form the words to ask any of these questions.

After he had read my dissertation, my father said, "It doesn't read like a dissertation." That was it. Nothing more. I should have spoken up then, asked him to explain, but I didn't.

On hindsight, my memories on the subject of mentors have acquired a bitterness, which I didn't feel when I was young and eager and floundered toward likely candidates who regularly resisted or slapped away my overtures.

Several times I approached the attractive young professor and Joyce scholar my first year of college. She had a head of dark curls. I did not interest her the way the young men in class interested her. She chose one of them. Young professor L. didn't last long at St. Olaf College in Northfield, Minnesota. It was a Lutheran place with Lutheran mores, which didn't mean Eros wasn't rushing madly around the classrooms. It meant you couldn't let on that you were running after him, especially if you were a teacher and a woman.

I remember another college professor from whom I hoped to get some direction. He was a large, sweaty man with thick-rimmed glasses. I sat in his office as he excoriated a paper I had written on Theodore Dreiser's *Sister Carrie*. His teeth on edge, he spat venom in my direction and never took his eyes off my breasts. Why so hostile? What I wrote about that second-rate writer has long vanished. The paper may well have been bad. What I remember is that I couldn't understand why the professor was so angry at me. The breast business should have been a clue, but I just felt stunned and puzzled.

And then there was the professor I visited during my first year at Columbia. I had a letter of introduction from one of his colleagues at another university. Although cold, curt, and stiff, Professor S. agreed to look at my work. When I returned for his comments, he led me, page by scrawled-over page, through an evisceration of the prose, the argument, and the sorry mind that had produced such drivel. I said nothing, although I no doubt thanked him before I left.

Again: his inexplicable rage. I think he smelled my ambition.

Even at the time, I knew the paper wasn't as bad as all that. With a few revisions that had nothing to do with Professor S.'s campaign of carnage, I delivered it in a seminar on nineteenth-century literature and philosophy. The prominent curmudgeon, Professor M., in charge of the lit-phi seminar thought the paper excellent. And yet, during office hours, M. was stiff, reluctant to talk, forbidding. I did not dare ask him to be my dissertation advisor, although he was the expert in my field. He ended up as head of my defense committee, however, and lauded my thesis in front of his five male colleagues. "There are sentences here I wish I had written myself."

I remember his sentence. Once uttered, some sentences stay for a lifetime. In an essay I called such phrases "brain tattoos."

A brain tattoo: "What are you doing in graduate school? You look like Grace Kelly." I did not look anything like Grace Kelly, but the comment ended all hope of my working with Professor H., who had spoken it, one of a handful of women in the English Department and a feminist. I was and am a feminist. It was in her class that I gave the Djuna Barnes paper, and it was after I had given the paper, and we left the room together, that she spoke the words I remember. She seemed to think *Nightwood* was incomprehensible, so it might not have worked out between us anyway. Many years later, I came to know that she had been mistreated and was unhappy in the department. The sentence may have carried other meanings I was in no position to read.

In my twenty-seven years of school, there was a single teacher who responded to my bid for instruction, help, dialogue, mutuality. I was a junior in college. The subject was Russian intellectual history. The professor's classes had a reputation for being difficult. The rumors had spread that he was hard to please, graded low, bristled at platitudes and lazy answers, all of which attracted me. He taught with a stringent vigor I found electrifying, and for two years I felt the soaring pleasure of being recognized by him as a student of unusual gifts. He pushed me to read closely and to argue carefully. Under his guidance, I wrote on the nihilist strains in Tolstoy's work. That was when I ran across the adoring apostle Bunin for the first time. I felt my intellectual powers bloom.

We met for coffee. We talked about ideas, literature, life. Our relations were warm, respectful, and correct. We became friends. He read the essays I wrote when I applied to graduate school. I loved him for encouraging my ambition, for taking me in, for praising my writing, but I never told him to his face. I never said, "Right now I feel like crying and kissing your hand as if you were my own father."

The ghosts of the familial haunt these ties between student and teacher. As a young woman, I longed for approval and affection from paternal quarters, from those who had authority. I now think it is a good thing that my yearning went mostly unanswered.

This memory from 2017: I am standing on a balcony looking out over Lake Como talking to a German colleague, a professor of American literature. We are at a conference where we are both giving papers on narrative medicine. It turns out he is a friend of Professor M. at Columbia, the one who admired the reviled paper and later my dissertation. My colleague says, "I saw him last week. He is so proud of you." I feel a thrill of happiness, followed by irritation. Why didn't he let me know he had followed my work? It would have meant something to me if I had known. Then I am further annoyed. Why should I care? I am sixty years old with the feelings of a child.

Professor M. died last year. I intended to go to the memorial. I had it written on my calendar. I forgot. The better word for what happened, I suspect, is repressed.

"I applaud, I mean I value, I egg you on . . ." This came as a fulfillment for Wharton because she had sent her work to the master, but the story to which he was referring in the letter he came across himself, and he wrote his admiration spontaneously.

Fathers and mothers, but also fathers that are more like mothers, and mothers that are more like fathers, at least if one takes the point of view of literary canons and our ideas about mothers and fathers and feminine and masculine. Henry James swam in what we have come to think of as the feminine, and Stein in what we imagine is the masculine. It is supposed to be the boys and men who duke it out in an Oedipal battle for literary or scholarly or scientific prominence. I have seen iterations of all these—the slugging and the pissing. The girls and women stand outside the ring or stay in the kitchen. But really the feminine and the masculine are all mixed up. It is impure, a mélange, a mess. Aren't we all lumps of the two?

No wonder people long for living as a person truly in-between. We called it androgyny back in the day, but I didn't look or dress the part; it was/is psychic: the mutations of gender are all over my work from the beginning. One of my early poems published in the *Paris Review* in 1983 is titled "Hermaphroditic Parallels."

An oddity of my personal story is that from a distance I was assigned a mentor who is not, was not, and has never been my mentor: my husband. I am the humble student in this fantasy that pops up regularly in articles, reviews, papers, other kinds of traveling literary news, and interviews.

More brain tattoos:

The most painful: "I think your husband wrote it." I was on tour in Germany for my first novel, *The Blindfold*, in 1993. The journalist was insistent, and I could feel his rage. He said my husband ran "a literary factory" in Brooklyn. At the time I thought he meant it. Now, I am convinced it was a ruse to hurt me. He thought the book was very good.

"Your first two novels are just like your husband's," a journalist in Holland said to me in 2004. "Please explain to me why you think so?" I asked him. The man reddened. "I was just trying to be provocative."

"Everyone knows you learned psychoanalysis from Paul Auster," a friendly woman confidently stated in an interview.

Words from a journalist in Chile in 2017: "Your knowledge of neuroscience comes from your husband? Mr. Auster reads neuroscience, doesn't he?" Mr. Auster has never read a neuroscience paper in his life.

I attend a lecture by my husband. The academic who introduces him tells the audience that Paul Auster is an expert on the work of the French psychoanalyst Jacques Lacan. Afterward, I explain to the man that Paul read one essay by Lacan in 1966. I read Lacan carefully. Some of his work informed my dissertation. The man was annoyed. I was supposed to remain silent.

A breathless Auster fan approached me at a party in Copenhagen. He wanted to talk to me about my husband's knowledge of the Russian theorist M. M. Bakhtin. "But," I say, "Paul never read Bakhtin. I read him. Paul borrowed the story from me." (In his introduction to *The Dialogic Imagination*, Michael Holquist explains that during the siege of Leningrad, Bakhtin used his manuscript on the German Bildungsroman as cigarette paper. In the screenplay for the film *Smoke*, into which Paul inserted the tale, he made the story memorable, a brain tattoo: "He smoked his book.") "I love Bakhtin," I said to the man, in hope of further conversation. But the man did not love that I loved Bakhtin. His face fell. He looked stricken and ran away.

I have hundreds of not-my-mentor-become-my-mentor stories. It can't be *you*. It couldn't have come from *you*. It must be the hero-mentor-man. It is comic, and it is tragic. To grant authority to the wife undermines the husband's authority, even if the actual living breathing husband does not feel that way at all and says so in print. In *A Life in Words*, a book-long conversation with I. B. Siegumfeldt, "Siri is the intellectual in the family, not me, and everything I know about Lacan and Bakhtin, for example, I know from her." They project onto the hero. If I, woman-writer-wife, am given authority, he, and by the magic of identification, they, are emasculated and shamed by the "dominating shrew."

We all have our phantoms.

Epic. Heroic. That's what it is. It's love. It's hate. It's a mix.

I have taught only rarely, so my opportunities to mentor have been few. I am lucky to live from my work. I am fond of the young residents I teach every month in a seminar on narrative psychiatry in a hospital in New York City. No doubt, the doctors in my class have physician mentors. It happens that young writers and scholars approach me for a favor. I read. I write blurbs and endorsements. Sometimes I detect the light of admiration in their eyes. In my case, anyway, such admiration is an elixir that must be drunk slowly, carefully, and rarely.

I remember the pleasure of that brief time when I was mentored. I also remember the sting of rejection and the paternal ghost who haunted my mentor fantasy and those who foisted their own angry-man husband-as-mentor fantasies onto me. I will stick with the phantom I never knew and from whom I received only two lines. She is a mentor of the purely literary kind, the kind that never leaves the pages of a book or a letter.

Siri Hustvedt left the Midwestern boons for New York City in 1978 seeking adventure and a degree in English literature to secure a way to make a living while she wrote the books she then only imagined writing, but in fact came to write over the decades since—a book of poems, seven novels, four collections of essays, and two works of nonfiction (some of which have been anointed with minor and major prizes). The PhD led to no job but came in handy later, when, due to several turns in the road of life, she developed a passion for the science of the so-called "mind," which turned out to mean delving into the body and its various organs, and she found herself writing and lecturing on the mysteries of neuroscience, neurology, psychiatry, and their necessary companion, philosophy—as it is always better to be Dr. Somebody at a conference even if your degree is in English literature, especially if you're a woman. In 2010, she did land an actual appointment at Weill Cornell Medical College where she teaches a seminar to psychiatric residents. She is still alive and has popped out another book of essays, *Mothers, Fathers, and Others*—available now at your local bookstore.

Writing Letters to Ghosts

On Meena Alexander's Posthumous Mentorship

ASHNA ALI

During most of my graduate career, the late celebrated poet and scholar Meena Alexander was the only South Asian professor teaching literature at the Graduate Center, City University of New York, where I earned my PhD. Meena was born into a Syrian Christian family in Allahabad, and lived and worked in Allahabad, Kerala, and Khartoum as a child. She studied in England, taught in India and France, then settled in New York where she lived and taught until her death in November of 2018. These biographical details are important because Meena was not "just Indian" in the way that I am not "just Bangladeshi." My parents had their first child, my brother, in New York, a place that they had never expected to see when they were newly married in Dhaka. Life soon took them to Italy. Invested in the American Dream and concerned about the familial fragmentation that might result from having two children of different citizenships, they chose to orchestrate an American birth for me. I was born in New Jersey, raised in Italy, and have spent the last seventeen years in New York City studying, teaching, and building a life as a writer, researcher, and educator.

Like Meena, I have always carried the feeling that I am fated to belong nowhere. Both of our origin stories produced lifelong concerns with migration and the question of home. Our work overlaps in its consideration of whether and when it's possible to find oneself in language, and the stakes of allowing the heart to plant its flag anywhere on a globe fraught with ever-hardening borders and definitions. Meena often referred to herself as having an "illiterate hear," because she, like me, could not read or write her mother tongue, Malayalam, despite being a fluent speaker and having dedicated her life to literature in other languages. I have the same relationship with Bengali. I speak with polish, but struggle to so much as write my name to match the skill of the average six-year-old. Like me, Meena was interested in the relationships between the nation, language, the body, and memory. Like me, Meena turned to language and poetry to make sense of what she called "impossible lives," or lives rarely represented in most available narratives. We were fundamentally similar in that we felt marooned in a world that we had the privilege to see more of than many but could never experience a true settling. In short, I felt like I had been waiting for Meena my entire life.

I could not wait to meet her and approached her with trepidation when I did. I expected someone apparently tough, worldly, the kind of woman who sees straight through your soul upon meeting. I was immediately taken aback not only by her appearance, but her speech patterns. Meena referred to herself as speaking in a tongue both broken and forked, and clearly chose to allow for these violences to live on her American tongue in an act of decolonization, a form of truth. What does this sound like? Meena explained herself with a light wave of the hands that punctuated her clauses as she spoke. She raised her eyebrows as if sharing an inside joke, though she was often describing experiences she herself deemed "impossible." Her speech tumbled out of her mouth in a breathy, mellifluous pitch that sounds the way floral and vanilla notes smell. It held South Asian and Commonwealth rhythms and notes, picked up various Francophone habits, and rolled its r's in patterns that matched no language I could identify, and that were not always consistent. I was stunned and frustrated by both its beauty and its improbability. I suspected that it was some kind of guise. I could not digest an affect so ornate and delicate. It grated against a need to protect myself and others like me from the exoticization, and against my own internalized misogyny—an issue I didn't learn to address until far later. I had imagined that her approach to the world, her appearance, and her language would be hard, sharp, formidable in part for being a little fearsome. To put it another way: I thought she would be more like I wanted to be, or the way many described me as being already. I didn't know then that said hardness was more an indication of being afraid than being fearsome.

I know now that Meena was unafraid as a personality default; living as an exaggerated version of the irreconcilable parts of her life was both a choice and something she could not help. To me, she seemed exposed. She wore kurtis and long shawls that reminded me of my aunts in Bangladesh—aunts whom I love but with whom I cannot be honest, whose judgment I fear, whose very presence turns me into an excruciatingly polite, formal, and reserved animal who is better if rarely seen, and certainly not heard. Meena did not expect such behaviors of me, but I couldn't help performing them. Her dense, fluctuating accent, not too unlike mine before I beat the lilt and song out of it to sound like an American, stuck a finger deep in a wound I was not ready to acknowledge.

I still tell the story of how in my first year of college, I stood in front of a bathroom mirror in my New York University dorm on Washington Square Park, toes digging into the linoleum, practicing a standardized American accent in imitation of the actor Tia Mowry. I cried my way through it, frustrated by months of trying to make new friends and thinking I did, only to find that they had drawn me close so that they could display me like an exotic bird, ultimately less interesting to them than how interesting it *made* them to have brought me along. I stopped wearing my many kurtis and my Bangladeshi jewelry. I learned to look neutral when Americans made references to television shows, commercials, music, or common high school experiences that I could not relate to. I avoided talking about my childhood in too much detail. I took an enormous eraser to my biography, found a way to stick out less. Soon, it took many months before people asked where I was from, often assuming that I was born and raised in New York. I was passing.

Today, I am ashamed of these erasures. The kurtis and jewelry are back, as are linguistic turns I would not have allowed even two years ago. Meena did not pass and would not have tried to. I was dumbstruck as she casually called me *beta*, a Hindi word also used in Bengali meaning "son," and a term of endearment for a younger male person. This was a common slip for her—everyone was *beta* rather than *beti* regardless of their gender—but in the first instance, Meena hit a nerve. I remember feeling a shock of recognition that registered at the time as alarm. My level of education, assertiveness, and agency outside of my father's desires makes me a fairly anomalous character in the greater context of my family. In so many ways, I was raised as a boy in a girl's body, with many but not all of the double standards imposed on desi girl children.

When I finished high school, I was not only allowed but was expected to leave home and live in a different country. I was provided with the kind of financial support and encouragement to pursue higher education that few women in my family ever received. For a long while, I did what I wanted and seemed to get away with it by failing to ask for permission and lying by omission. My ability to live this way felt so distinctly male that I experienced frequent gender dysphoria that extends beyond my social roles and to my face and body. I was resisting full acknowledgment of my queer identity when I met Meena. Today, I identify as agender and use they/them pronouns, and spent years teaching teens about the many ways that gender can manifest in global contexts—but none of this was on the horizon at the time.

Meena's use of *beta* broke an invisible professional barrier. It occurred to me very briefly that she might have mistaken me for a boy, a possibility I feared and hoped for at the same time. More importantly, she was signaling insidership; she knew I knew the word and that it intended warmth, familiarity, and closeness that we were yet to build, and that she was generous enough to offer despite not knowing me. In my experience, this is not a common response. Until I met South Asian academics who worked on the region and explicitly tied their work to their biography, other South Asians did not acknowledge our racial similarity. In job interviews, classrooms, or at parties, we spoke to each other cordially, in sharply guarded, dominant American accents, and never referred to our shared race. It's likely that we all have the passing thought: "Indian? Pakistani? Gujarati. No, Punjabi. No, Bengali. Hindu? Muslim? Christian? First generation?" We never ask. For three years, I taught at a New York City public high school where the second most spoken language after English is Bengali. My Bangladeshi students watched me closely but only acknowledged the similarity with embarrassment, staring at their feet, when their mothers came to parent-teacher conferences relieved not to have to rely on their child as a translator. Otherwise, we held our shared origins between us in an emotionally dense silence, as if we shared an unspoken pact never to speak of it lest the consequences be too intense to bear.

Mentorship between students and professors of color have a complicated double bind to navigate. The terms and structures of traditional mentorship in academia have been shaped by white masculinity. The standards for professional speech, clothing, and behavior are white and Euro-American. If we fail to perform proximity with these ideals, we risk not being taken seriously as thinkers and writers, offering others yet another opportunity to show us that we do not belong while we ingratiate ourselves and work twice as hard for the same kind of acknowledgment and attention that our white peers receive. Meena writes about her own experience of a department chair questioning her about whether she publishes in the area in which she was hired, British Romanticism, which of course, she did. White superiors do not believe we are capable of doing the intellectual work of the Western tradition, but we receive pressure and sometimes censure when we attempt to work outside of it. Meena was ultimately denied professional advancement from the institution she described, in part for publishing not only on British Romanticism, but poetry, and addressing the problem of apartheid.

In my own department, I showed up hoping to write about South Asian literature in English. I was anxious to separate myself from experiences of alienation and racism and become closer with my own history. Instead, I was pushed for years to become a scholar of the Italian Renaissance because of how marketable I would be—how rare of an exotic bird—as a South Asian Italianist. When I gave it a go, every native Italian in my classes looked at me with suspicion. One went as far as to reiterate at every turn how American I was for bringing up issues of gender and the question of sensual experience in Medieval and Renaissance philosophy. I eventually reached a compromise with my department: I wrote a dissertation comparing the work of contemporary migrant women writers of color writing in English and Italian. This is the part of the story that we hear the most; it is news to no one that the academy is in dire need of decolonization. However, there is little discourse about how the social codes of professionalism affect relationships between mentors and mentees of color, or among peers. So often, we reproduce the same behaviors expected of us elsewhere despite having a chance to be seen with greater complexity, or to acknowledge one another's struggles. The result seems to be that we exacerbate the conditions of our own alienation for fear of being unable to advance if we make too much trouble, or if we become too visible *as* scholars of color.[1]

I find a useful example of this complication in some of the problematic valences of Mindy Kaling's show *The Mindy Project*, in which Mindy Kaling plays a self-involved and immature South Asian OB-GYN obsessed with rom-coms and dating. The show received criticism for the whiteness of the protagonist's friends and love interests, while also receiving praise because Kaling claims to operate with the confidence of a mediocre white man. (She has since produced multiple television shows that center South

Asian female experience, though they come under similar criticisms.) Over time, the show made some superficial gestures toward addressing Kaling's race, but stopped short of exploring the subject. Kaling was the first South Asian American actor to star in her own show but not allow her racial identity to get in the way of doing what all of her white peers do. The idea is that we shouldn't *have* to make our work *about* our race in order to be successful, which, to be fair, is a legitimate argument. In retrospect, I realize that I am Mindy's character on that show in my encounter with Meena.

And I grew closer to her over nine years while maintaining a studied distance. Throughout, she checked in on me, asked about my work, and offered unflagging support for a student group I ran that curated lectures on postcolonial studies. I felt her love and I loved her in the way I might one of my warmer aunts; *I don't have to understand or agree with you to love you.* This too, I felt silently, and communicated by implication. Meena, always one to blow my assumptions open, simply brought it up point blank at the end of a lecture when I thanked her for coming despite her busy schedule: "Of course, we're family, *na*?" Just like that. I had lived so long without a sense of family that the casual toss of this offer almost broke my heart.

My response to her was not shared by the other desi students who started to pour into the English program in the last year of my time there. Watching their arrival and their relationships with each other and with Meena stung me. They all knew each other, and seemingly every other South Asian academic in America through a variety of familial and professional connections. This new crop of students shared a language and an attitude—they felt comfortable and entitled to their place, their work, and their communities. One of them said to me, "Oh, I know that she drives you crazy but Meena's like all of my aunts and my mom, so it's totally normal for me." Did all of these students really know and love so many other elders who were *like* Meena? Had I missed out on far more than I even knew how to imagine? I stood alone with Meena in an elevator a year after this influx, and she asked me, not making eye contact, "Have you met all of these new Indian girls in the English program? They are all excited to meet you." I murmured in the affirmative, and she responded in a half question, half statement, "They're so sure of themselves, *na*?" I still wonder if she felt the same twinge of jealousy that I did when I looked at them, or whether she was simply sharing that she knew our time to feel that way had long passed.

While Meena and I maintained our odd faraway closeness, my other mentors were men; European men whose investment in the system and the kinds of self-sacrifice it required aligned with mine. American men who admired my specificity and rigor. I was routinely described as a "tough cookie." One advisor made frequent comparisons between me and Olivia Pope from *Scandal*, which both thrilled and frightened me. These were men I chose because they admired my ability to keep my feelings stitched as far inside me as possible so that I could be seen as smart, conscientious, responsible, and dependable, even when showing at the seams. They created opportunities for me because I spoke to them in their language. They did not ask who I was or what I wanted. A massive pane of identitarian plexiglass sat between us that we could see through but could be assured we would never breach. As I moved further and further into my research on migration and its poetics, I felt wounded by their sanitized approach. I felt that I was begging them to hear me, and while they nodded and praised, what I needed was altogether different.

Eventually, the distance I maintained from my mentors began to backfire. There were no open channels through which I could communicate how personal the work was becoming, and how painful. Writing my dissertation stripped away every layer of the self-protective armor that allowed me to perform my robotic professionalism. I had no ability to ask for the kind of mentorship I needed more than I needed revisions or line edits. *I needed someone to tell me how to survive coming into the pain of my own story.*

By the time Meena noticed that I was writing at the Graduate Center every day and looking increasingly haunted, she was experiencing her own haunting. Her chemotherapy treatments forced her to cut her hair to look much like my own, a close pixie cut ill-suited to her romantic, willowy femininity but elegant, nonetheless. She had lost a lot of weight. Regardless, she came in to work, she taught, and seemed to be doing readings all over the city during which she made good-natured jokes about her condition. She made time for me. As she did with everyone, she asked me to join her for tea. When I mentioned to her that my work had been delayed by a divorce, that I was working several jobs, and living alone for the first time, she did not, like my other mentors, tell me this would give me more time and space to focus my attention on the work. She did not suggest, as one mentor did, that I channel my anger into my writing. She told me instead, "You have to be very, very gentle now. Ask yourself seriously what's at stake for you in this work, because you are working very close to the bone, *na*?" *Close to the bone*. A matter of marrow and connective tissue of risk, a set of questions that draw blood. She knew exactly what I was doing, having read none of it.

Meena saw through my elaborate charade and emaciated selfhood from the moment she met me. She knew where the pain was far better than I did. I realize now that the reason I could not bear Meena's supposed performance of selfhood is that it came from too similar a clot of traumas and existential wounds. Her speech patterns and clothing operated as a kind of transparent veil, a way of hiding that doubled as the scream of an honest self into space. She describes it in visceral terms in her memoir: "Sometimes I think of the English language as a pale skin that has covered up my flesh, the broken parts of my world. In order to free my face, in order to appear, I have to use my teeth and nails, I have to tear that fine skin, to speak out my discrepant otherness" (73). She let her otherness sing in a closely calibrated construction of identity that served as both expression and protection. She knew I was using my work to pull at a face scrubbed of all identity and let the tumult of the histories beneath see the light of day. She knew well my abject fear of feeling too much and feeling *like* too much, and the freedom that comes from letting it happen, allowing poetry to hold you while it does.

By the time I finished my dissertation, I found my kurtis, started wearing my old earrings, using plural pronouns, and otherwise came out in a variety of ways to myself and to the world. Ironically, this all took place while I lived as a true hermit, glued to my computer and stepping out only for a little air and food. I saw Meena in the hallways sometimes or would catch her in the elevator. I heard snatches of rumors about her health and promised myself to go see her. I got busy. I got sciatica. I opened my first chapter with an excerpt from one of her poems. I waited too long.

I never had a chance to tell her how she contributed to my slow and necessary emergence from a state of constant self-negation. I never had a chance to show her my poetry. Her family requested that after a memorial reading the Graduate Center community held in her honor, her students and mentees be allowed to ransack the books in her office before everything left behind was donated to the library. To my surprise, I was among the students chosen to do so. I inherited several of her books after her death. Their pages are covered in her annotations and marginalia, Post-its, scribbles. They are books on the history and philosophy of South Asia, on South Asian feminism, and of course, books of her own poetry. I have not stopped reading and rereading them, coming to a series of epiphanies I had hoped to come to in graduate school and am only coming to in the process of immersing myself in Meena's understanding of the networks of pain, joy, and ambiguity that make up our "impossible lives."

What mentoring I could not accept from her in life, she has managed to find a way to imbue me with in death. I meet with her almost weekly now, arguing with her at length in death as I had briefly in life about diaspora, poetics, Teresa Hak Kyung Cha, Shailja Patel, Joy Harjo, A. K. Ramanujan, Arun Kolatkar, about America. I think of her when my American accent breaks and my forked and broken tongue lives out in the open. She lives in so many of my poems, and I know she would have pushed, berated, and encouraged me if she could read them. Recently, I have begun to write to her as her work explains me to myself, sharing something of the bone, blood, and sinew of this moment. I run my hands over her marginalia, ask her what she thinks. I write to her.

Ashna Ali is a queer, agender, and disabled diasporic Bangladeshi writer, poet, and scholar raised in Italy and based in Brooklyn. They hold a PhD in comparative literature from the Graduate Center, City University of New York, and have taught at several colleges around New York City. They are the author of the chapbook *The Relativity of Living Well* (2022), and their poetry and scholarship appear in several academic and poetry publications. They live in Kensington with their sphynx familiar, Kubo Avatar.

Note

1. The scholar who has done the most radical and fruitful work on the subject is Sara Ahmed, whose work has fomented extraordinary relationships around the truths she exposes.

Work Cited

Alexander, Meena. *Fault Lines*. Feminist Press, 1993.

Part III

The Traffic in Mentors

Horizontal Scripts

Widening the Way

An Interview with Dána-Ain Davis

NANCY K. MILLER

Dána-Ain Davis and I are colleagues at the City University of New York (CUNY) Graduate Center, but this interview was conducted on Zoom since our building was still closed as of June 11, 2021. We met at the Graduate Center in 2017 when Dána became the director of the interdisciplinary Women's Studies PhD certificate program in which we both teach. She also directs the newly created MA in Women's and Gender Studies, as well as the Center for the Study of Women in Society. If that sounds like a lot, it is, but Dána makes the task appear effortless. In one of our drop-by chats between women's studies meetings, I invited her to contribute to the mentorship book that Tahneer and I had just begun coediting. Dána did not hesitate to tell me how much she disliked the word *mentor*, but nevertheless generously accepted to be interviewed for the anthology.

It was clear to me that what I'd observed of Dána's charismatic presence at the Graduate Center meant that she had the very qualities that made for an outstanding academic mentor in its most familiar incarnation. So her resistance to the term puzzled me. Was it the term or the practice? As the interview unfolded, I came to realize that what Dána preferred to the discourse of the classical model was language that turned resolutely away from all forms of hierarchy and individual pairings. Her language moved instead toward metaphors of accompaniment and the less predictable but more rewarding outcomes of encounter and collaboration, acts

147

of building community, that had in fact characterized her entire career. In other words, she had already lived a reinvented vision of a mentorship in need of renewal.

As it turned out, the student assigned to me for research assistance this year, Sharifa Hampton, happened to be a student in Dána's spring semester seminar, and a fan of mentorship herself, so we invited her to sit in on the interview. (Sharifa has also contributed to the volume.)

Nancy K. Miller (NKM): Our colleague Leith Mullings, a distinguished anthropologist at the Graduate Center, and cofounder of the Association of Black Anthropologists, died in 2020. In "A Remembrance," the piece you coauthored with Alaka Wali (the curator of North American anthropology at the Field Museum in Chicago) and published in *Transforming Anthropology*, you describe Leith as a "friend, mentor and truly a sister." You also explain that she mentored not just you, but many other students in the late 1990s. I know you have mixed feelings about the word *mentor*. How do you remember her style of mentorship?

Dána-Ain Davis (DD): Leith Mullings was my thesis advisor. In the formal or classical sense of how we might understand a mentor, Leith was that. But her style of mentoring was more like opening paths.

When I think of a mentor, I think of someone who guides you on a walk, on a path. Leith just paved a way and let you walk on it yourself. An example of her style would be a casual exchange. She might say, "I'm on the board of the journal *Souls*," which came out of Columbia, with Manning Marable, her husband [a leading scholar of Black history and race relations]. "We're looking for people to be on the editorial board. Whom could you recommend?" And when you gave her a list of names, she might ask, "Oh, do you think *you* would be interested?" Like that. She'd say, "Oh, it's not a lot of work," and when you would get on, there *would* be a lot of work. Then, if you're me (and I had just gotten out of grad school), you would find yourself on the board with Angela Davis and Robin Kelley and all of these amazing people. She would never give a directive, but then you'd find yourself as an editor of a special issue on, say, Black gender and sexuality. And you'd wonder, how did that happen?

It was about an opening of a way. Whether you decided to go down that path or not was up to you.

NKM: You talk a lot in your writing about paths—walking, opening doors—and you say in the acknowledgments to *Reproductive Injustice*, "My tendency is to walk closely with the people I have met." The word *close* comes up again when you describe partnering with people on various projects. Is the question of proximity key to what you've spoken to me about in the past—your resistance to the discourse of traditional mentorship?

DD: I resist the hierarchization and power dynamic embedded not just in my discipline but in disciplines generally. I believe in walking with people, walking alongside them, not leading. For me it's about being in dialogue, conversation, but not necessarily leading. And it's not because I'm afraid of power. It's because I think it's important to widen roads.

NKM: I love those metaphors—walking with, not ahead of others. I can't help wondering, though, at this point in your career, being a senior faculty member here and at Queens College, director of the Women's Studies certificate program, the MA in women and gender studies, and the director of the Center for the Study for Women in Society, how you avoid the dynamic of the classical mentoring situation. Other people are likely to put you there, whether you want to be in it or not.

DD: When I think about how I work with students in the MA program, for example, I widen the way. I write grants and because I know people in the philanthropic world, I get money and try to use that money to facilitate students' access into projects that interest them.

NKM: That's great, especially here at the Graduate Center where money and resources to support student research are scarce. Let me shift directions now and ask you to talk about how you got here. Early in an interview in July 2020 with the Women's Power Toolkit Podcasts, you were asked what drew you to teaching as a profession. Your answer took me by surprise. You said that you had started out in television! How did you move from television into academia?

DD: I'm an accidental academic. This was not the trajectory I was on.

As an undergraduate, I majored in film, but I didn't end up going into it. I was pregnant when I was in college, and my first job with a one-year-old was working at the old *Village Voice*. Then I went from the *Voice* to the YWCA in New York, where I embarked on a bit of a fundraising career, then left and went to work at WNYC-TV. Then I went to work at *Essence* magazine, and finally decided to get a degree in public health.

NKM: Okay, oops, that's a leap!

DD: Leap, yes. Let me explain. When I was working at *Essence*, I had to prepare presentations for potential advertisers showing the market share of Black women's utilization of cigarettes. I just couldn't do that, so I quit and took a job instead at the Village Nursing Home, which had one of the first HIV/AIDS day treatment programs in the country.[1] At the same time I was so deeply offended that the magazine had wanted to perpetuate the ill health of Black women that I applied to get a degree in public health.

I studied public health at Hunter College where I met Rosalind Petchesky and Beth Richie, and I took a class with Ida Susser at the Graduate Center. While I was getting my MPH, I started working for the Reproductive Rights Education Project [at Hunter College]. Beth Richie, who was at the Graduate Center at the time, said I should get a degree in sociology, but Ida said no, get a degree in anthropology instead. I didn't know what either discipline was because I had a degree in film.

NKM: Are we in the '90s now?

DD: Yes, the '90s. I came to the Grad Center to meet with the executive officer of sociology, but he wasn't in his office. So I went to meet with Jane Schneider who was the executive officer of anthropology. She encouraged me to apply, which I did. I was accepted, but as a full-time student you weren't supposed to work, and I had a thirteen-year-old. Although I also received a fellowship, I still didn't think I could afford to go. Then, out of the blue, I was hired as a research assistant for a National Cancer Institute–funded study on breast cancer, a consulting job. This meant I could go to school and create my own hours. I worked there for three years and that's how I ended up in grad school.

NKM: So, you're there and you take courses, and meet Leith Mullings?

DD: Yes, I met Leith. At the time she was working on the Harlem Birthright Project, which I liked.

The people in the department were all committed to social justice. I learned how one could be a "pracademic" through practice and activism from them. I'm not an organizer but I am an activist, and I learned especially from Leith Mullings, who was an amazing organizer and really committed to Black liberation, that those two things could operate simultaneously. This made sense for the kind of life I think is important, and somewhere in all of that were also links to my own family history that combined work and community.

Other people have jobs and do community work, so why should academics be different? It made sense, and I've never had to shift out of my commitment for justice because I was an academic.

NKM: In writing about Leith you defined yourself as a Black feminist scholar and elsewhere you described yourself as a feminist activist ethnographer. I'm wondering where the feminist part emerged for you.

DD: When I was admitted to the anthropology program, I had a selection of texts on my bookshelf that are probably not purchased by the average person doing HIV/AIDS work. I had books by Trinh Minh-ha, *Native, Woman, Other*. Because I wrote poetry and came of age in the 1970s, I was also reading poets Audre Lorde and June Jordan. My feminist sensibility emerged out of my engagement with those writers. Wherever Nikki Giovanni was, I was there. If Ntozake Shange was walking down the street and I could follow her, I would follow her. I went to see *For Colored Girls* seven times. And the funny thing is, I have since been honored to support her daughter, Savannah.

My connection to feminist work has been long and deep. But for me, it isn't just about feminism, or a Black feminism that's opposed. It's about a vision toward.

I identify as a feminist activist. I do ethnography. I am Black. I pretend to know something about theory although my theoretical genealogy doesn't go back very far. I cannot sit up here and talk to you about Aristotle. But I can have a longer conversation about Gauguin and his grandmother Flora Tristan, who wrote *Promenades dans Londres*, which came out in 1844. That was four years before Engels wrote *The Condition of the Working Class in England*, and Tristan was doing the exact same thing.

NKM: Gauguin's grandmother. I had no idea.

DD: Yes, I can talk about her for a long time.

NKM: That would make a great title for a book, "Gauguin's Grandmother." But let me see if I can tie a few threads together. In the preface to *Reproductive Injustice*, you tell the story, you mentioned it earlier in this interview, about being pregnant at twenty-two.

DD: I was.

NKM: You write that after giving a lecture about the book in Illinois, a young Black woman came to talk to you about her experience with pregnancy, which reminded you of your own experience, which led you to include it in the book. How do you see the connections between feminism, pregnancy, and what you call reproductive injustice?

DD: Part of what makes me a Black feminist is the fact not only that I am Black but that I am focused on Black people, and I am particularly interested in Black women because I still believe what the Combahee River Collective said, paraphrasing, that if we meet the needs of Black women, everybody else's needs will be met.

In my encounter with this young woman, Ashley, I was reminded of what it had felt like to be that girl, that young person in college. It was as though I had really put the experience out of my mind: how the doctor made me feel, how I was made to feel by others. It wasn't the first time I had been made to feel that way because I was also pregnant when I was in high school. I got pregnant the year after *Roe v. Wade* was decided, and I knew how fortunate I was to be able to get an abortion. And shortly after *Roe v. Wade* and watching the public's desire to dismantle it, I became active in reproductive rights. I was the copresident of NARAL NY in my late twenties, going to marches and signing petitions. I've always been interested in how Black women live policy.

NKM: Living policy. That's a great expression and describes a lot of your work.

DD: Back when I was working at Bronx AID Services, we were addressing the needs of women on Rikers Island, some of whom were pregnant. In fact, while I was getting my master's in public health I toyed with the idea of training to become a midwife. My grandmother had wanted to be a nurse midwife, but she was a domestic instead. And at some point, I had wanted to be a midwife.

I wanted to assist women who were HIV positive in their pregnancies at a time when, if a person gave birth at a hospital and tested for HIV, the hospital had to inform their partners. I was working against that policy with a bunch of people. But when I checked out midwifery schools, most of them were in Connecticut and were very Christian. I wasn't up for Bible verses, so I didn't go to midwifery school. I did other things instead, creating what I thought was a comprehensive approach to how I would meet the health needs of Black women. In some ways I was already training to be a doula.

But then there I was, years later, writing this most recent book. I went to a conference and heard Chanel Porchia-Albert, the founder of Ancient Song Doula. I was close to the end of data collection for the book and I thought, "Well I'm not busy in August. Let's go get trained!" Being a doula met both my need to be in community with people and to fulfill this other dream. I love being a doula. I have two clients a year, and I'm about to get a new one now. I helped support three families through childbirth during COVID, two in person, one virtually.

NKM: In one of the interviews, you speak about "a politics of radical empathy." How do you see this connecting with feminism and community?

DD: I first used that phrase in relation to Manning Marable around the time of his death, but I have mixed feelings about empathy now. We start out from a position of care and once we arrive at a place of empathy are we trying to make a change or are we just sitting in the feeling? What do we do with the feeling?

I guess I would hope that if as an empathic person you were to imagine yourself in someone else's position you might be more likely to do something, to widen the road, to open a door.

NKM: It sounds to me that you belong to many worlds. You talk so often about walking and being close by, do you feel that you're in something or that you're in several things?

DD: That's such a great question. Did you see *The Pieces I Am*, the documentary about Toni Morrison?

In it, Morrison is asked why she does so many things. And she answers, "I'm only doing one thing." That's how I feel. I'm doing a lot of things and it may look as if I'm in many worlds, but I'm really only doing one thing, and I'm only in one world. The world I'm in is the one moving toward justice, moving toward possibility. While it may seem that I walk a lot of paths, most of the days I feel I'm walking only one.

NKM: I can't help wanting to ask whether mentorship—whether you like that particular word or not—isn't inevitably part of that world. In terms of mentorship and the politics of race, Roxane Gay, for example, in *Bad Feminist*, talks about being committed to taking on the role, to "showing young black students there are teachers who look like them" (7). But this also means that faculty of color can feel disproportionately burdened. Does this problem seem relevant to the mentorship roles that you've taken on?

DD: Yes and no. I can only talk about this as a Black woman. To be a Black woman in this place where I live, where we are all living, is to bear a burden, and it's a burden of responsibility. But it's also an opportunity to bear witness to potentiality and to the future.

I think of a mentor as an uneven positionality, an unequally positioned relationship where the wise person guides you. Generally speaking, I like to enter into things, into engagements, even in my classroom setting, saying I don't know everything, because I don't know everything!

I'm not embarrassed to say that because I don't need to know everything, my brain is full of other things. I have a granddaughter, and sometimes I'd rather be thinking about her than, say, Marx.

My thought about mentoring is that it is hierarchical, and I want people to be engaged with me so I can engage with them, and we're doing something collaboratively. Does this mean that I don't at times assert the power and/or the privilege? It doesn't mean that. It means that when somebody reaches out for something I try to operate as if we are walking together, not as if I'm leading. That's all.

NKM: That sounds like a gorgeous dance.

DD: I get asked to do things all the time, and I'm on all kinds of people's committees. Sometimes I think it's funny that people call me when it's not in fact my area of expertise. But here's the bottom line: I was raised to be generous, and generosity is important to me. I hope that somewhere I'm remembered as a person who was generous and gave of her time. I have nothing else. I'm not leaving anybody money, there's not going to be a building in my name. All I have is time.

I was a Black woman in a PhD program and my cohort had more people of color than there ever had been before. We got each other through in an environment that wasn't hostile, but it was complicated, and it was hard. I can't imagine not spending time with people to help them through. It doesn't actually sit with me. Now, does that mean I say yes every single time? No.

But there are so few Black full professors in anthropology, there are maybe sixty of us in the country. So when I'm asked to write a tenure file for a professor, am I going to say no?

The politics of race is such that there aren't enough people, there aren't enough Black women to spread the work around. So we all do what Christen Smith, who started the Cite Black Women movement, calls "invisible labor." But the thing is, it's not so invisible because the people we work with see us. People in the academy like Christen Smith, who teaches at UT Austin, Ruthie Gilmore or Amber Musser here at the Graduate Center, we all see each other. The work is invisible to the white world. It's invisible to the academy. But we see each other.

Dána-Ain Davis is professor of urban studies at Queens College and on the faculty of the PhD programs in anthropology and critical psychology at the Graduate Center, where she serves as the director of the Center for the Study of Women and Society. Her most recent book, *Reproductive Injustice: Racism, Pregnancy, and Premature Birth* (2019), received the Eileen Basker Memorial Prize from the Society for Medical Anthropology. Davis is also a doula who supports birthing people and their families/partners, and in 2018 was appointed to New York governor Andrew Cuomo's Maternal Mortality Taskforce.

Note

1. The Village Nursing Home, which operated an adult daycare program for people with HIV/AIDS, later became known as the Village Centers for Care.

Work Cited

Gay, Roxane. *Bad Feminist: Essays*. Harper Collins, 2014.

Navigating Distance and Self-Doubt through Multiple Mentors

ANGELA FRANCIS

After successfully defending my dissertation, I reached out to several professors to thank them for their years of guidance and support. I addressed each as "Professor" as I always had, but two replied that it was time to use their first names instead. I was so shaken by the idea that I couldn't wrap my brain around a response. Looking back over my emails, I realize now I never made one.

Instead, I disappeared for three months.

At the time, I couldn't have said why I was thrown for such a loop. Now I know it was a matter of distance. More specifically, it was the shock of realizing there could be and perhaps should be less of it. If that seems to suggest that I wouldn't have welcomed such a shift, let me be clear: that's not the case at all. Instead, I recognized this as a moment when people I viewed as exemplars—as living examples of the sort of person I wanted one day to become—had indicated it would be more appropriate for me to think of them as mentors and friends. I wasn't ready, not because I didn't want to make this transition but because I didn't think I was worthy of it.

I didn't truly open myself up to being mentored until more recently. Of course I had benefited from people's help before then, but they were always in my mind advisors or informal coaches. I couldn't see them as mentors even when they were willing to be exactly that. If you're going to be mentored by someone, you have to be able to admire them while also looking at them and seeing your own potential. You can't elevate them on a pedestal that's so high you have no hope of ever reaching it yourself. This is easier to manage when you aren't consumed by self-doubt. It's likely also easier when you have examples of people "like you" in the spaces you want to eventually inhabit.

In the time since my disappearing act, I've made progress when it comes to my self-doubt. Through that progress, I've come to understand why it was so difficult for me to accept the close, more equal relationship involved in mentorship: low self-esteem. Equally as important, I've also learned what form mentorship needs to take for me as I fumble my way forward. I do best when I am mentored by a handful of individuals with whom I share one or two important aspects of my identity but with whom I can only partially identify. This creates the right degree of distance for me through the expectation of a greater difference between who they are and who I will hopefully become. It makes obvious the key differences in how we experience the world so that I don't feel encouraged to follow in their footsteps rather than forging my own path.

Through this, I can also avoid the kind of idolization Mindy Kaling jokingly describes in her second book, *Why Not Me?* There, she portrays meeting her mentor in part by telling the reader: "You know when you meet someone so smart and cool that all their tastes and opinions seem like the correct ones? And you instantly think: those are my opinions now too!" (87). For me, such idolization paradoxically imposes too much distance and not enough—too much because it stands in the way of genuine relationship, and not enough because it might lead me to lose sight of my own goals, blinded by the brilliance of my mentor. I'd say this is what my mentorship story is really about: navigating self-doubt and gaining effective mentorship when you're the only neurotic unicorn in the room. Identifying with your mentors (ideally plural!) but only so much.

I enrolled in graduate school with the dream of becoming a college professor and the deeply held belief that women like me didn't succeed at goals like mine. This wasn't purely due to demographic concerns although I am visually identified as a "double minority"; while anti–affirmative action narratives primed me to wonder if I hadn't actually earned my space in any room I was in, I had also been taught to prove I deserved my seat once I was in it. Instead, my certainty that I was unworthy can be traced to a failed attempt at gaining mentorship as an undergraduate student.

I had worked with a scholar who was known for guiding students through the graduate school application process and, when I decided to apply to graduate schools, went to them to ask for their guidance about both graduate school and the professorial career path. I was hoping, I realize in hindsight, for mentorship. Instead, I was informed that, while the scholar was usually happy to work with students, it wouldn't have benefited anyone for them to try to help someone they already knew would fail. I left the scholar's office quietly crushed. Ultimately, I walked away from that meeting and into graduate school having learned the wrong lesson: that girls like me didn't, and shouldn't, get to places like that.

I am older and wiser now with the benefit of a successfully obtained PhD behind me, so I can view this moment differently. Yet I know that without the support of two other professors, that scholar's statement could have discouraged me from applying to graduate school. One of these professors was my formal honors advisor who spent a great deal of time engaging my academic pursuits, not as something she needed to evaluate but as something she was interested in discussing. The other professor gave me a copy of the recommendation letter he wrote for my graduate school applications and told me to read it, perhaps because of some sixth sense. I remain endlessly grateful to them both, and I keep in mind both the potential of a single sentence to tear someone down and the amount of hard work necessary to build them back up.

I also recognize that some readers might believe I simply needed to have more "grit" in that moment. However, it takes a lot of grit for those of us who occupy multiple minority subject positions to attempt to occupy spaces where we are infrequently represented, and even the roughest sandpaper gets worn smooth eventually. I am not suggesting that the scholar's statement was evidence of deep-seated racism; I assume that they genuinely doubted my ability to meet graduate school's demands. But I am suggesting that there are more constructive ways to communicate those doubts. More than fifteen years later, having watched the effects of similar moments on other minority women, these statements frequently seem more like weapons designed to reinforce self-doubt until we believe what a brilliant young woman later told me in the aftermath of her own unpleasant meeting—roughly, "Girls like me don't make it to places like this"—and close the doors in our own faces.

Having engaged mentors helped to convince me otherwise, and perhaps that's why I'm so bothered by the stance that people should take mentoring where they can get it even if those "mentors" do not want to help them. It's commonly suggested, particularly to people who can't build close mentoring relationships, to watch people in positions you want to attain and glean knowledge that way. Even Kaling's mentor gives her readers this advice, telling us to "take your mentoring where you can find it, even if it is not being offered to you. . . . If you have the opportunity to observe someone at work, you are getting mentoring out of them even if they are unaware or resistant" (89). Yet even beyond the importance of acknowledging the emotional toll of needing to rely on sneaking lessons from people who do not want to teach them to you, we risk understating the difference between this sort of observational learning and what mentorship is, in my mind at least, supposed to be.

Put bluntly: learning by observing someone is very different from being mentored because mentorship necessarily includes a relationship and the decision to relate must be mutual. The only aspects of mentorship accessible through such observation (the answers to the question: What did she do?) have been the least useful aspects of mentorship in my life. For example, my most recent mentor provides me with guidance regarding how to design effective teams and how to navigate people's changing expectations and reactions to me as a relatively young racial minority taking on positions of increasing responsibility. His focus hasn't been on the specific choices he's made but instead on the principles and lessons that undergirded his decisions. If he hadn't agreed to mentor me—if I were instead simply regarding him despite his resistance—the lack of relationship would leave me guessing at his reasoning, and I wouldn't be able to reflect on how his choices might play out differently in my own life. Calling observations "mentorship" obscures these very real differences between the two and, if someone has never actually been mentored, can create a false understanding of just what that relationship can be.

In fact, my experience of mentorship has been more akin to friendship than anything else. And while I have had mentors who have simultaneously held other positions in my life—supervisors who have been mentors, for instance—my relationships with them are warmer due to their viewing me as a mentee. In each case, there's been mutual fondness in a relationship that is increasingly reciprocal; each mentor seeks to learn from me at the same time that I learn from them. Admittedly, this often begins with my helping them with technology (I am a somewhat stereotypical elder millennial), but ultimately I find they call on me for more specialized knowledge. Indeed, one of my mentors will sometimes joke that he is getting to tap into other mentors' expertise when he speaks with me. While I may have learned not to idolize my mentors, this remains its own special type of validation.

It also highlights another benefit about having multiple mentors: it requires you to be deliberate about what role each mentor will fulfill as you work toward your goals at the same time that it also widens the field of people you can ask for mentorship. None of my mentors have the career that I've begun to see for myself, but each has knowledge that will help me be more effective on my path. One mentor works in a completely different field, but that doesn't affect her ability to provide insight about enjoying a rich career and social life while also navigating a chronic illness. My mentors who are tenured faculty or college administrators without research agendas can each help me as I learn to balance the demands of administration and a research agenda. None are my particular combination of Black, Hispanic, biracial, and female (most of my mentors have instead been white women or Black men), but I am able to learn about how each of them approached navigating nondiverse spaces and consider how to adapt their experiences into lessons I can use.

As I begin to enter those spaces, it has become increasingly important for me to find people who had some insight into navigating them. After all, microaggressions don't suddenly disappear because you're promoted, and sexism doesn't vanish from your work life just because you earned tenure, but the ways that these affect you might be different as you gain more institutional power. My mentors' openness about the situations they have faced—and their insights when I come to them wondering about something I've experienced—have been invaluable, especially during moments of transition in my career. For example, one of my closest mentors has helped me prepare for a leadership position by balancing her guidance about skills like systems thinking with her insights about the more human costs and considerations that arise when you move up in the organizational chart, particularly as a woman. There's a trust and an openness to her invitation for me to learn from her experience, and as I continue to chart my own path, I am increasingly grateful for the combination of her lessons on skills, considerations, and strategies for how to navigate spaces as someone who is not necessarily always expected to take up that room.

I've also been grateful for the times that my mentors have helped bring me into those very places. This same mentor periodically pulls me forward into roles that would be unavailable to me without her intervention. In this way, she's modeled what it's like to put Toni Morrison's advice into practice: to remember that in the workplace, we should attain power and then use it to empower someone else. Through this, she's modeled the type of person I hope to be, and I've been surprised at some of the positions I've found myself in as a result.

Earlier this year, I learned that someone viewed me as her mentor. I was flattered but surprised. Beyond feeling like I'm not too terribly far along on my own journey, I've always been open about the large roles that chance and good fortune have played in my career trajectory. While I'm hopeful enough to believe that luck is more likely to favor the prepared, my life seems to be less deliberately directed than that of some of my peers. If you were to try to chart my path thus far, you would be left with less of a map than a puzzle that creates an unexpected picture only in hindsight.

If I hadn't learned from being mentored by multiple brilliant people, I would probably feel deeply unworthy of the title. But looking at the people who serve that role for me, I've come to realize that some of them also didn't know where they were going until they got there. Some of them arrived, looked around, and marched right off for what they hoped would be a better-suited position. All of them made missteps and mistakes, all of them have flaws, and I am still flattered to have each of them in my life as a mentor and a friend. Equally important, I've realized that if each of them independently decided I was worth the time involved in their mentorship and valued my expertise enough to ask for my assistance at times, then I guess I can be a mentor for someone else.

Now I mostly wonder about my mentee's view of mentorship. How does she relate to me as her mentor? Does mentorship for her involve the sort of idolization that Kaling describes in her book? The sort of pedestal placement that prevented the relationships I would have liked to have with potential mentors in the past? I hope not. Instead, I hope that she has added me to a slate of people that she knows would be glad to help her if we can. And because being her mentor does not suddenly make me infallible, I hope she isn't any more likely to take my word as gospel than she would be if I were simply her friend.

With one major exception: if she needs someone to tell her that "girls like her" can excel in "places like this," I hope she takes me at my word.

Angela Francis has benefited from the seemingly endless patience of her mentors while settling into her role as the assistant dean of general education and first year experience at the City University of New York (CUNY) School of Professional Studies. Previously, she spent more than ten years pestering her academic mentors while earning her PhD in English from the CUNY Graduate Center. When she isn't busy making these kind souls question how someone in her thirties could maintain the curiosity of a five-year-old, she enjoys drawing, playing party games, and serving as a most dutiful cat food can opener.

Work Cited

Kaling, Mindy. *Why Not Me?* Three Rivers Press, 2016.

All the Angry Young Women

Elizabeth Alsop

In my early twenties, I worked for an editor at *Vogue*. He wrote a regular food column for the magazine and preferred to do his writing from home, rather than the Condé Nast headquarters. When I arrived at his apartment in the mornings, it was not unusual to find him sitting at his desk in a white terry-cloth robe, or sometimes still sleeping, in the Murphy bed at the back of the loft, just off the kitchen where I made his coffee.

I was grateful to have gotten the job as his assistant—incredulous, in fact. I had no culinary training or expertise, and none of the usual connections. The interview had consisted of two long conversations at the editor's kitchen table, where he asked about my favorite restaurants and the correct preparation of crème anglaise, and tested my knowledge of the romance languages listed on my resume. It all seemed impossibly eccentric, glamorous in all the ways I had imagined New York would be, and that my gig in textbook publishing most definitely was not.

My peers, likewise, thought the job was a coup. "You've begun well," a friend's boyfriend told me, approvingly. Privately, I agreed. On the one hand, I understood I had won this position—from among hundreds of applicants—because I shared certain characteristics in common with the editor's previous assistants: I was young, female, white, well educated, and attractive. But I didn't allow my consciousness of these facts to interfere with an emergent sense of entitlement, the belief that I was deserving of these rewards, and that, so long as I continued to abide by meritocracy's rules, future successes would follow.

That belief sustained me through the following two years I spent as his assistant. During that time, I tested recipes, sourced ingredients, and fact-checked stories; I also collected the editor's dry cleaning, bought him scotch, and reordered his favorite cigars and Turnbull & Asser shirts. There were regular occurrences that might have caused me to question the job, if not quit. When I traveled with him on assignment to Italy, he booked us a single hotel room; he remarked often on my looks, my clothes, my "time of the month"; he berated me but also paraded me, a tall twenty-four-year-old, at restaurant openings and appointments with his realtor. All the while, his wife lived and worked on the West Coast.

At the time, none of this seemed to rise to the level of a problem, the kind of egregious offense that I understood as "harassment," and that I thought, frankly, only happened to others. I could handle this. Indeed, I took perverse pride in our relationship. If anyone asked—and they did, since it was the early 2000s, an era in which magazine publishing still retained some vestige of glamor and *The Devil Wears Prada* was considered an aspirational tale as much as a cautionary one—I presented myself as a Girl Friday: spunky, resourceful, impervious to machismo or casual misogyny. He could only make inappropriate comments about my appearance, after all, because we understood each other so well. I was in on the joke!

I felt sure I was the real beneficiary in this arrangement. I had learned so much, about food and food history, about cooking, about the world of professional restaurants and professional writing. And there was, he assured me, a *really good* job in my future. Was it really worth protesting just because he had, say, grabbed another editor's ass at the company Christmas party? Wasn't the point of feminism to allow me to *choose* to disregard this kind of bad behavior for the sake of my own professional advancement? Couldn't I *decide* to be empowered enough to overlook it?

When the time came, I found my own job, a decent one, but he never made the calls or wrote the emails of introduction he said he would. I explained away his inaction as carelessness, and continued to treat him as a positive force in my life. I invited him to my wedding; I called him for advice. And when I eventually wrote about the job, I called the piece "The Apprentice" (no relation to the show), and presented our relationship in a wry, affectionate light—a two-year lark, *Talk of the Town*-style. At one moment, it looked like the *New Yorker* might publish my essay, but then they passed, and it ended up at a small journal. Shortly after, I learned it had been chosen for inclusion in the annual anthology of *Best Food Writing*. The catch was that the volume's editor needed my editor's permission. She didn't say as much, but it was clear she was scared enough of my former boss, who wielded power in New York's insular food world, to want his blessing.

Without thinking, I sent him a copy of the journal, with a lighthearted note tucked inside—it probably said something like, "I hope you enjoy this portrait of our time together!" I never heard from him directly, but I did hear from the volume's editor. Apparently, my old boss had called her to accuse me of fabricating the story, and lying outright. A former lawyer, he might have threatened litigation. In any event, he forbid her—I think he used that word—from publishing my piece. She was sorry, but it was never a great fit anyway, and she hoped I would find another home for it. That was that.

He and I never spoke again. I wrote him once, asking to talk. Instead, I got an email from his wife so mean it took me weeks to read the message all the way through. In the decade since, I've considered contacting him a few times—when I had a baby, when I published a book—but then I remember. Not only is he dead to me, in the tradition of my Italian ancestors, to whom I had never felt as spiritually proximate as in these moments. It was a mistake to think we had been close in the first place.

He never cared, not really. This person I thought was my mentor wasn't. All the time I thought he was looking out for my career, he was looking out for his own.

❧

The particulars of my experience aren't unimportant, but they're also not definitive. Ultimately, what is most significant about this episode isn't how singular it was, but how generic. What I experienced at the time as a unique betrayal I now recognize as a banal one: a grievance so familiar, it's a cliché.

I thought about the banality of bad mentors when watching Kitty Green's recent film, *The Assistant*, an account of a Harvey Weinstein–like predator from the point of view of his lowliest female hire. Although the protagonist's boss exists at one criminal extreme, and mine, within a more permissible range of male misbehavior, the story's outline is much the same. Like the film's heroine—like any number of young women—I worked for low pay and little respect, in too-close proximity to a powerful man, who exploited my time and talents, manipulated my feelings, and appreciated my ambitions only insofar as they could advance his own.

In other words, we were both part of the Female Assistant Industrial Complex—a structure that depends on the exploitation of mostly young women's labor, and their willingness to tithe endlessly in the hopes of future reward.

But it also depends, crucially, on a distorted idea of mentorship, in which abusive treatment masquerades as care. Tough love, exacting treatment, punishing standards—all are presented as tactics to ensure the mentee excels sufficiently to earn the payoff continually promised and deferred.

What Green's film made me realize, in other words, is how often, and for how long, we've let patriarchy co-opt mentorship for its own purposes. And the innumerable ways in which young women, in particular, have been gaslit into embracing as natural and necessary conditions that will never allow them to prosper.

Near the end of *The Assistant*, the unnamed heroine receives a series of emails from her demanding boss, in quick succession: the first two chastise and threaten, but the final one flatters ("you're good, you're very good"), by way of explanation. "I'm tough on you because I'm gonna make you great," he writes. *That* is the love language of the false mentor.

Of course, that's not to say dues-paying can't vault people into desired careers, or the upper strata of their industries. But it is to say that those very strata—the hierarchies they constitute—are gendered, as are the tactics used to sustain them. The most dangerous of these tactics might be this myth of the mentor as *maker*, as someone with the power to make or, treacherously, unmake the mentee. It is the fear of undoing, after all, that keeps so many of us loyal to bad mentors, even when we have all the evidence we need of their antagonism or neglect.

I wish I could say I learned all this quickly. I didn't. It took years of graduate training and professional experience for me to realize how regularly institutional structures—which is to say, ideological ones—warp what should be supportive relationships. I have had generous mentors, but also those who were jealous, ineffectual, or absent.

What took me so long? In a recent interview, about the slow crescendo of the #MeToo movement in France, actress Adèle Haenel notes, for her own part, "[I]t took me a long time to make the personal journey to look at myself as a victim" (Peltier). That wasn't my journey, precisely, but I knew what Haenel meant—raised in an era of postfeminist assurances, it took me too long to see myself as anything other than empowered, to recognize the structures aligned against women's success.

Mentorship for me, now, is expansive and diffuse; it is not bound up in auratic individuals or professional mandates. I don't have a mentor, but I do have *mentors*. This decentralized model, discovered in my middle years, feels infinitely more sustainable than any of the overburdened alliances to which I previously entrusted my well-being. Whatever I did or did not learn from the editor has since been eclipsed, I realize, by the guidance I've received from another, more unexpected source: a network of women who at various points *also* worked as this editor's assistant—a group with whom I am still friends, and whose counsel I seek out and trust.

If I had it to do over again, then, what I would write about that early experience would look less like a loving tribute than like a text characterized by dispassion, in its presentation of facts, but also by deep anger. Anger at my own powerlessness, to be sure, and my failure to confront it. But mostly, anger on behalf of all the young women, at all the false mentors, at the ones we thought we had, but who were never really there.

Elizabeth Alsop is a writer, professor, and recovering foodie. She lives with her husband and daughter in Brooklyn.

Works Cited

Green, Kitty, director. *The Assistant*. Bleeker Street, 2019.

Peltier, Ellen. "Adèle Haenel: 'France Missed the Boat on #MeToo.'" *New York Times*, 24 Feb. 2020, nytimes.com/2020/02/24/movies/adele-haenel-france-metoo.html. Accessed 10 Dec. 2021.

Mentoring and #MeToo

LEIGH GILMORE

Harvey Weinstein, former Hollywood producer and convicted rapist, is the poster boy of bad mentoring. For decades he sexually abused women who sought work from or were employed by him. When they resisted, he escalated his attacks, threatened to ruin their careers, silenced them with nondisclosure agreements, and retaliated through concerted smear campaigns (Kantor and Twohey).[1] Widely known as a bully, Weinstein yelled at everyone, but he only sexually assaulted women (Farrow).[2] Men were not only spared sexual abuse, but they were also allowed to shrug off the open secret of Weinstein's predations and continue to benefit from his considerable influence and resources.[3] At his trial in New York, Weinstein's defense team tried to obscure the fact that Weinstein targeted women who worked for him, or hoped to, and assert, instead, that his contact with them represented consensual sex between adults, as if his abuse did not take place in a professional relationship. In their testimony, several women used the word "mentoring" to describe the actions through which Weinstein groomed them, including meetings to discuss their careers, auditions, and networking opportunities.[4] The Weinstein case reveals that *for him* sexual abuse was indistinguishable from mentoring. Certainly, Weinstein emblematizes the outsize role gatekeepers play in women's careers, but his exploitation of this position highlights the asymmetries of power, influence, and status built into mentoring relationships generally.

#MeToo opened a new perspective on mentoring that goes beyond a single Hollywood producer to reveal the connective tissue that links abusers and the systems that protect them. Historically, mentorship is gendered and hierarchical and because of this linkage, women are at heightened risk of having their careers derailed or ended before they begin. The Weinstein case demonstrates that men associate their control of women's access to work with their sexual entitlement to them. Certainly some men use their mentoring role to replicate the asymmetry of power they enjoy elsewhere, and through it, extend their claim to women's bodies, emotional labor, and silence, as well as their own impunity to censure.[5] These links were the foundation of the unanimous 1986 US Supreme Court ruling in *Meritor Savings Bank v. Vinson* that defined sexual harassment as the creation of a hostile work environment and a violation of federal civil rights law. The case concerned Mechelle Vinson, who was hired as a bank teller when she was nineteen years old by Sidney Taylor, a married father of seven and church deacon who had been hired at the bank ten years prior as a janitor and worked his way up to bank manager and assistant vice president. Shortly after Vinson began work at Meritor, Taylor took her out to dinner, which, as Vinson described it, concluded with this demand: "'I want to go to bed with you.' I said, 'I don't want to go to bed with you.' . . . And he says, 'Just like I hired you, I'll fire you, just like I made you, I'll break you, and if you don't do what I say then I'll have you killed.' . . . And that's how it started" (Battiata). Vinson endured three years of forced sex. When she took sick leave and refused to return, she was fired. Taylor cultivated a mentoring relationship with Vinson. After he hired her, he guided her through teller training and encouraged her to share professional and personal concerns freely. Grooming, under the guise of mentoring, enabled Taylor to gain leverage over Vinson and learn about her vulnerabilities, the better to coerce her into sex and silence.

Although it may seem unfair to lump together male sexual entitlement with mentoring, consider that the #MeToo movement's outcry against workplace sexual harassment prompted some men to renounce mentoring women altogether. The *refusal to mentor* women is neither new nor unique to the activism grouped under the sign of #MeToo. It has until recently been the norm. During the 2016 presidential campaign, an interview with Mike Pence surfaced in which he referred to his practice of not dining alone with a woman who is not his wife. Pence's stance exemplifies the refusal to acknowledge women in their professional roles and to place them, instead, in quasi-personal relations of sexual or filial attachment (LeFevre). Only two years into the #MeToo movement, 60 percent of male managers said they were "uncomfortable participating in a common work activity with a woman, such as mentoring" ("Working Relationships in the #MeToo Era"). To be clear, this is in response to the exposure of widespread sexual harassment and a new demand for accountability. Many companies have reviewed mentoring guidelines to address the "silent workplace scourge" of sexual harassment in all its myriad and insidious forms (LeFevre). Yet according to a host of professional journal articles on mentoring in the #MeToo era, most workplace cultures are long overdue in providing guidelines and protocols to address sexual harassment.

Much media coverage of #MeToo has focused primarily on famous men despite the existence of sexual harassment across class, race, and workplace. Nonetheless, high-profile stories can offer a window on sexual violence in specific work cultures. Consider how the exposure of Matt Lauer and Charlie Rose at NBC revealed cultures of enablement built around protecting powerful men, silencing the women they abused, and norming abuse as a feature of the work culture (Folkenflik and Dwyer). Ronan Farrow began reporting on Weinstein while employed at NBC, which sought to squelch the story. After years of denial, Mario Batali admitted to a pattern of groping women and retaliating against those who complained, saying, "[M]uch of the behavior described does, in fact, match up with ways I have acted" (Chapman and Pisani). His participation in sexual harassment traces a path through the sexual abuses endemic to restaurant culture (Hakim and Moskin). Similarly, Louis C.K. spent years denying allegations that he sexually harassed women comedians who sought his mentorship, claiming instead, as several male comedians did in his defense, that comedy was a man's world (Kilmartin). When he admitted to the accusations five women made, a spate of articles exposed the working conditions for women in comedy. Bill O'Reilly and Roger Ailes's use of nondisclosure agreements and settlements to silence women they sexually harassed exposed the culture of abuse at Fox News. Class action suits at the Ford factory in Detroit, the walkout at Google to protest the company's handling of sexual harassment, and the strike led by McDonald's workers lack a celebrity abuser, but they reveal the same pattern that all the examples represent: cultures that tolerate sexual harassment and abuse by powerful men send a signal that such behavior will not carry consequences.[6]

In *Tainted Witness*, I describe how judgment sticks to women, tainting them with bias as they bring forward accounts of injury and seek justice. In networks designed to protect male privilege and power, women's testimony is vulnerable to doubt due to disparities in credibility. These disparities represent epistemic violence (Dotson), or the harm inflicted on knowers by hearers who fail to recognize their legitimacy. In the case of women's testimony, epistemic violence names a structural bias built into law and borrowed as a standard in cultural discussions; namely, that the benefit of the doubt is offered as easily to the accused as it is withdrawn from the accuser. In extrajudicial settings where organizations have an obligation to ensure workplaces free of sexual violence, the accused is not only offered the presumption of innocence but can rely on a presumption of doubt to be directed at accusers. This transfer of credibility from women to men is so routine that any alteration in it strikes the empowered as evidence of unfairness. Because culture is saturated in default narratives of women's unreliability, abusers are readily excused, sexual harassment is the norm, and survivors who speak out are marginalized, fired, blacklisted, and otherwise erased. Mentoring does not exist outside these conditions. It is embedded within them and can incubate sexism, racism, homophobia, and misogyny in a relationship charged with defining who can and cannot succeed.

In this context, the refusal to mentor represents a desire to protect the freedom to abuse. In my first job as an assistant professor in the late 1980s, I raised the question of faculty (in this case, men) sleeping with students (in this case, women) as there seemed to be a general institutional narrative about its frequency, and students were routinely describing to me classroom experiences that sounded like grooming, including boasting about sleeping with students. When I brought this up in a department meeting, a tenured male professor said that one of the best parts of his job was the prospect of meeting a "lovely" student in class and having sex with her. He saw sexual access to women students as a job perk. He was not embarrassed by the topic; he publicly declared his embrace of it. I will point out the obvious: this particular professor was in a position to mentor students and junior faculty members, including me.

In June 2018, a study entitled *Sexual Harassment of Women: Climate, Culture, and Consequences in Academic Sciences, Engineering, and Medicine* documented how unexceptional sexual and gender harassment is in science, engineering, and medicine. The study found that more than 50 percent of women faculty and staff and 20 to 50 percent of women students experience sexual harassment in STEM fields, with women of color and nonbinary, queer, and trans people experiencing more sexual harassment than their white cisgender peers. In addition to analyzing the conditions that allow harassment to go unchecked, the study provides a range of "power-diffusion" (National Academies 135) transformations in the structure of mentoring, including replacing the single-supervisor model with community-based advising. Sexual harassment within mentoring within academia is tied, too, to the exploitation of graduate student labor, in particular, through an assertion by those in power to define the relationship and the leeway granted to supervisors, heads of labs, department chairs, and others with the ability to retaliate. Taken together, the range of cases enables us to reframe #MeToo beyond its force as a collection of stories about sexual abuse by particular men, and to situate critiques of it in the context of abuses of power.

The scope of sexual harassment documented in STEM fields is similarly pervasive throughout academia. In her recent study that draws on her experience at Goldsmiths University of London, Sara Ahmed describes a process seemingly designed to drain those seeking to report sexual harassment of energy, time, and resources without offering any remedy as recompense. Ahmed ultimately resigned in protest over the university's failure to address complaints. In this context, it is jarring to read Amia Srinivasan's hypothesis that the "real" harm in sexual relationships between faculty and students is the misdirection of the erotic quality of pedagogy from teaching to harassment. Survivors have few tools at their disposal to respond to harassment in higher education. Yet Srinivasan asserts that "rather than look to the law, professors might look to themselves." She recommends soul searching and conversation as if those are preferable to the admittedly limited policies feminists have worked decades to put in place that enable students, faculty, and staff to appeal to federal civil rights law (Title IX in the US context) to report sexual harassment, assault, and rape.[7] In Ahmed's terms, refusing to hear what women, and survivors of all genders, have been loudly saying about sexual harassment in higher education and, instead, calling for a new round of talk demonstrates that sexual predators will continue to exploit the good faith of those willing to educate them on the true joys of teaching, as if they did not have their own views, as my colleague did, of what those are.

Debates about whether it's reasonable to connect sexual harassment and rape, as some have accused #MeToo proponents of doing, or whether insights about the prevalence and harm of sexual abuse will threaten due process for specific men, are invested in preventing an alternative perspective on sexual abuse from emerging: one centered in the perspective of how survivors experience sexual violence as an enactment of asymmetries of power. In other words, if we train our attention primarily on threats to the accused, we will fail to recognize how #MeToo represents women's (and nonbinary, trans, and male survivors') assertion that sexual exploitation within hierarchical relationships is not "bad sex"; it's unethical, harmful, and wrong behavior enabled by systemic bias. The confusion of sexual harassment, assault, and even rape with "bad sex" would mean that replacing sexual abuse with "good sex" is the solution. It is not. The issue, instead, is that the freedom to abuse ought to be removed by policy and accountability from those with power, and this includes power over students, advisees, junior faculty members, trainees, researchers, and other mentees.

In addition to contributing to the long overdue rethinking of the mentoring relationship and the concerted effort to mitigate how degrading, stressful, and career-destroying it is for many women, I want to build on the recommendations of the 2018 study discussed earlier and recognize an alternative form of support arising through the direct effort to confront abusers and bring their decades-long and institutionally protected harm to an end. Namely, the MeToo organization founded by Tarana Burke that laid the foundation for the viral tweet in October 2017 and opened a new chapter of feminist advocacy and activism. In 2006, Tarana Burke founded a nonprofit organization support girls and women of color who were victims of sexual violence. At the core of her program was identification of advocates with victims and empathy as a basis of healing represented by the words *me too*. This coinage and versions of it have long circulated between survivors and advocates as a token of shared experience to break down the isolation of trauma and restore belonging. Burke's condensation of an intersectional feminist stance on empathy into a compact, shareable phrase found a global audience. Comprised of millions of survivors, #MeToo disrupted the routine mechanisms of shaming and precipitated a shift from the coerced, passive, and morally injurious position of watching victims be discredited without being unable to prevent or stop it to an invocation via survivor advocacy to witness and act.

Data from Twitter shows that more than half of all people who disclosed an experience of sexual violence did so in response to seeing others in their social network disclose. Further analysis shows "that the more disclosures an individual potentially saw prior to disclosing, the more likely they were to share details with their disclosure" (Gallagher et al.). Witnessing the voluntary formation of a virtual community of survivors was critical to the spread of the hashtag. Through MeToo, millions of survivors showed up for each other and what began to take shape in response were communities of collective witness, formed in solidarity to speak out against abuse. Understood as "repeated resistance" (Jackson et al.), the circulation of the hashtag enabled the formation of a counterpublic that would soon appear in the voluntary, embodied assembly represented by silence breakers in multiple locations of protest.

In February 2018, Judge Rosemarie Aquilina invited victim impact statements during the sentencing phase of Michigan State and USA Gymnastics team physician Larry Nassar's trial. Delivered after the verdict and before sentencing, such statements inform the court's view of what a victim's suffering is worth. In cases of sexual violence, they provide an opportunity to counter the law's notorious bias in favor of men not just on trial for but convicted of sexual assault and rape. Rachael Denhollander, the first of Nassar's victims to go public and the last of the 156 to offer victim impact statements, asked, "How much is a little girl worth?" Questions of women's worth confront cultural norms upholding male primacy in adjudicating sexual abuse cases; but also, as #MeToo resistance has demonstrated, the answer to "how much are women worth?" lies at the heart of exploitation in work cultures broadly.

In her landmark study *Trauma and Recovery*, Judith Herman argued that the degree to which trauma is taken seriously by a culture depends on the perceived value of those who suffer. The persistent refusal to believe survivors of sexual abuse, address the causes of sexual violence, and provide trauma-sensitive and adequate care for healing was directly tied to the low status of women, children, and men who were victimized. In this context, it is interesting that Simone Biles and the more than 150 women who testified against Larry Nassar formed a supportive collective, mentoring each other in effect, to rise together and emulate what their value looked like to each other and in court. The statements by each woman as she came forward cited the courage gained from the others. Similarly, in their effort to get women to go on the record and to break the Weinstein story, *New York Times* reporters Jodi Kantor and Megan Twohey noted the same aggregation of women moving from isolation and silence to a justice-seeking collective witness. Annabella Sciorra, whose testimony in the Weinstein case carried the charge of sexual predatory conduct and a potential life sentence, came forward "with the strength of the eighty plus victims of Harvey Weinstein in my heart" (Quealy). The formation of a collective witness represents a horizontal form of mentoring, one that emerges from shared experience and that overcomes epistemic and material violence through the identification and empathy Tarana Burke crystallized as "me too."

The slow emergence from pain and silencing speaks to the texture of witnessing as unstuck, unstrangled voices take shape together in a recognizably new formation. Removed from contexts in which they were doubted and discredited—by family members, complicit administrators, coaches, and those who protect institutions and enable abuse to continue— the witnesses reknit together. These are examples of survivors exposing abuses cloaked by the camouflage of mentoring. In contrast and as an antidote, survivors became visible to each other as a support and a new form of advising emerged. The insights and experience of survivors that Tarana Burke places at the center of the #MeToo movement point a way to restructuring mentoring.

Leigh Gilmore is an American literary scholar, feminist theorist, and expert on the literature and theory of life writing. She is the author of *Tainted Witness: Why We Doubt What Women Say about Their Lives*, *The Limits of Autobiography: Trauma and Testimony*, and other books, as well as a new book, *The #MeToo Effect: What Happens When We Believe Women*. Her writing also appears in *Cognoscenti*, *The Conversation*, and *Public Books*.

Notes

1. Annabella Sciorra, Jessica Mann, and Miriam Haley testified to the pattern of Weinstein's abuse and to acts of sexual assault including rape at his New York trial. Jodi Kantor and Megan Twohey document Weinstein's use of NDAs, as well as the offer by self-described feminist lawyer Lisa Bloom to use her knowledge of survivors' vulnerabilities to help smear Weinstein's accusers.

2. Ronan Farrow documents the pattern of Weinstein's sexual predation. Typically, Weinstein books a professional meeting with an actress through the agency that represents her. Because he travels frequently, the meeting is often scheduled in the public area of a local hotel. When the actress arrives, she learns the meeting has been moved to Weinstein's hotel room. When she arrives there, Weinstein is often in a bathrobe, insists on a massage and/or a shower, removes his clothes, and, as the actress tries to escape, he gropes her. If he can bar her escape, he sexually assaults her. This is the pattern testified to by silence breakers Ashley Judd, Rose McGowan, Rosanna Arquette, Gwyneth Paltrow, and many more.

3. See Valiente and Williams on Matt Damon and Sharf on Quentin Tarantino, for example, on their complicity.

4. Dawn Dunning, for example, described Weinstein as a "mentor." After a few business meetings to discuss her career, which established their relationship as professional rather than dating, Weinstein lured her to a hotel room under the pretext of a business meeting and sexually assaulted her; see Ransom.

5. Roman Polanski was awarded the French film industry's best director award in 2020. Polanski is a convicted child rapist. He drugged and raped a thirteen-year-old girl and, in 1978, pled guilty to this charge. He fled the US before sentencing and remains not only a fugitive but an active filmmaker.

6. For an account of the Detroit case, see Chira and Einhorn. For an account of the Google walkout, see Wakabayashi et al. For an account of the strike at McDonald's, see Haddon.

7. In a response to Srinivasan on Twitter, Amulya Mandava argued that academia is a workplace like any other. She observed that suggesting professors ought to look to themselves to solve their sexual harassment problem obscures how unexceptional such behavior is across workplaces and how inadequate a response it is to ask abusers to monitor themselves rather than focus on developing a clear and transparent process for reporting: "Would you ask Hollywood to look to itself? . . . We are people in a workplace that like any other is full of predators (your prof who groped you may not just be an innocent fool with good intentions overwhelmed by erotic energy, but an actual predator reveling in the pleasure of transgression, of leveraging power)."

Works Cited

Ahmed, Sara. *Complaint!* Duke UP, 2021.

@amulyamandava. "Would You Ask Hollywood to Look to Itself?" *Twitter*, 5 Sep. 2021, twitter.com/amulyamandava/status/1434556745347747843.

Battiata, Mary. "Mechelle Vinson's Long Road to Court." *Washington Post*, 12 Aug. 1986, washingtonpost.com/archive/lifestyle/1986/08/12/mechelle-vinsons-long-road-to-court/b5fa7c5b-c0cf-412b-b40f-a3811e042884/?utm_term=.9d392d3c59ea. Accessed 10 Dec. 2021.

Burke, Tarana. *Unbound: My Story of Liberation and the Birth of the Me Too Movement*. Macmillan, 2021.

Chapman, Michelle, and Joseph Pisani. "Mario Batali Takes Leave from Businesses, 'The Chew' after Misconduct Allegations." *NBC Boston*, 11 Dec. 2017, nbcboston.com/news/national-international/mario-batali-taking-leave-restaurant-the-chew/1923885/. Accessed 10 Dec. 2021.

Chira, Susan, and Catrin Einhorn. "How Tough Is It to Change a Culture of Harassment? Ask Women at Ford." *New York Times*, 19 Dec. 2017, nytimes.com/

interactive/2017/12/19/us/ford-chicago-sexual-harassment.html. Accessed 10 Dec. 2021.

Dotson, Kristie. "Tracking Epistemic Violence, Tracking Practices of Silencing." *Hypatia*, vol. 26, no. 2, 2011, pp. 236–57.

Farrow, Ronan. *Catch and Kill: Lies, Spies, and a Conspiracy to Protect Predators.* Little, Brown, 2019.

Folkenflik, David, and Colin Dwyer. "Matt Lauer Accused of Rape in New Book; Former NBC Star Denies 'False Stories.'" *NPR*, 9 Oct. 2019, npr. org/2019/10/09/768527936/matt-lauer-accused-of-rape-in-new-book-former-nbc-star-denies-false-stories. Accessed 10 Dec. 2021.

Gallagher, R. J., E. Stowell, A. G. Parker, and B. F. Welles. "Reclaiming Stigmatized Narratives: The Networked Disclosure Landscape of #MeToo." *Proceedings of the 22nd ACM Conference on Computer Supported Cooperative Work and Social Computing* (CSCW19), Article 96, 2019, ACM Digital Library, doi: doi.org/10.1145/3359198.

Gilmore, Leigh. *Tainted Witness: Why We Doubt What Women Say about Their Lives.* Columbia UP, 2017.

Haddon, Heather. "McDonald's Workers Strike to Protest Pay and Harassment Complaints." *Wall Street Journal*, 23 May 2019, wsj.com/articles/mcdonalds-workers-strike-to-protest-pay-and-harassment-complaints-11558627417. Accessed 10 Dec. 2021.

Hakim, Danny, and Julia Moskin. "State Investigates Sexual Harassment at the Spotted Pig." *New York Times*, 20 Aug. 2018, nytimes.com/2018/08/20/dining/mario-batali-spotted-pig.html. Accessed 10 Dec. 2021.

Herman, Judith. *Trauma and Recovery: The Aftermath of Violence—From Domestic Abuse to Political Terror.* Basic Books, 1992.

Jackson, Sarah J., Moya Bailey, and Brooke Foucault Welles. *#Hashtag Activism: Networks of Race and Gender Justice.* MIT P, 2020.

Kantor, Jody, and Megan Twohey. *She Said: Breaking the Sexual Harassment Story That Helped Ignite a Movement.* Penguin, 2019.

Kilmartin, Laurie. "Being a Female Comic in Louis C.K's World." *New York Times*, 10 Nov. 2017, nytimes.com/2017/11/10/opinion/sunday/louis-ck-harassment. html. Accessed 10 Dec. 2021.

LeFevre, William. "Mentoring in the Age of #MeToo." *US Official News*, 18 Oct. 2019.

National Academies of Sciences, Engineering, and Medicine. *Sexual Harassment of Women: Climate, Culture, and Consequences in Academic Sciences, Engineering, and Medicine.* National Academies Press, 2018.

Quealy, James. "Handcuffed and Humbled, Harvey Weinstein Could Spend the Rest of His Life in Prison after Rape Conviction." *Los Angeles Times*, 25 Feb. 2020, https://www.latimes.com/california/story/2020-02-25/handcuffed-and-humbled-harvey-weinstein-is-convicted-of-rape. Accessed 1 July 2022.

Ransom, Jan. "These Are the 6 Women Who Are Testifying against Harvey Weinstein." *New York Times*, 26 Jan. 2020, nytimes.com/2020/01/26/nyregion/
harvey-weinstein-trial-accusers-testimony.html. Accessed 10 Dec. 2021.

Sharf, Zack. "Tarantino: I Wish I Told Harvey Weinstein 'You Can't Do This, You're
Gonna F*ck Up Everything.'" *IndieWire*, 1 July 2021, indiewire.com/2021/07/
quentin-tarantino-harvey-weinstein-spoke-up-1234648215/. Accessed 10 Dec.
2021.

Srinivasan, Amia. "What's Wrong with Sex between Professors and Students? It's Not
What You Think." *New York Times*, 3 Sept. 2021, nytimes.com/2021/09/03/
opinion/metoo-teachers-students-consent.html. Accessed 10 Dec. 2021.

Valiente, Alexa, and Angela Williams. "Matt Damon Opens Up about Harvey
Weinstein, Sexual Harassment and Confidentiality Agreements." *ABC News*,
14 Dec. 2017, abcnews.go.com/Entertainment/matt-damon-opens-harvey-
weinstein-sexual-harassment-confidentiality/story?id=51792548. Accessed
10 Dec. 2021.

Wakabayashi, Daisuke, Erin Griffith, Amie Tsang, and Kate Conger. "Google
Walkout: Employees Stage Protest over Handling of Sexual Harassment."
New York Times, 1 Nov. 2018, nytimes.com/2018/11/01/technology/google-
walkout-sexual-harassment.html. Accessed 10 Dec. 2021.

"Working Relationships in the #MeToo Era." *Lean In*, leanin.org/sexual-harassment-
backlash-survey-results. Accessed 10 Dec. 2021.

The Mentor as Mirror

Melissa Coss Aquino

If I had to give only one quotation to a student, or a mentor advising students, it would be this one: "do not be misled by details / simply because you live them."

It is a line from an Audre Lorde poem that has been with me for more than thirty years. I have written it in countless journals and taught it in spaces as varied as ESL classes, teen poetry workshops, and college-level creative writing classes. It also served as bedrock for my dissertation on exclusion and belonging in American autobiography. I would offer it with the advice that seeing and being seen is the single most powerful element of transforming lives, your own, and those of others.

If we begin in the middle, as any good story should, we begin with me now: tenured associate professor of English at Bronx Community College. It is a campus that holds the many parts of our current academic and socioeconomic challenges as a country in close proximity. It is also three blocks from where I grew up, and across the street from my first public library. An unusual event in the life of an academic is to both stay so close to home and travel so very far to get there. During any given semester I have two or three students, sometimes more, navigating housing crises like evictions, temporary shelters, and domestic violence displacement. We have a very large and heavily utilized campus food bank. These are not the majority of my students, but they are a significant number every semester. Their economic struggles are also not the most interesting or relevant things about them. That so many of them reach out about missing a deadline or class, write brilliant papers, and support each other in the classroom as they navigate these struggles always astonishes me. They are, despite the wildly unfair and complex circumstances of their lives, the classic college students striving toward a goal beyond their current condition, but only if you know how to look beyond "the details."

Their "details" often exist on the extreme end of a spectrum of material, social, and psychological challenges to be expected on a campus situated in one of the top three poorest congressional districts in the country. A district that often beats places in Mississippi or Alabama or West Virginia for the poorest, as if that is a contest anyone wants to win. I admire my students, not for any inherent nobility, but for believing in a system that has failed them so often.

If what I do is called mentoring, it is really a mirroring, in that I see their light and power beyond the details they may be living and exhibiting, in ways I work to mirror back to them. Their willingness to receive what I offer mirrors that light back to me. We enter a mutual act of witnessing, exchanging something of value, precious even, and worth sharing. While the fairy-tale mirror on the wall seeks beauty in "the fairest of them all," the mentoring mirror seeks core truth and potential even before it is visible, or perhaps still packed inside a tiny seed. I did not invent this idea. I was mentored.

Bronx Community College is the only college in New York State—and one of the only campuses in the US—designated as a National Historic Landmark because of its collection of architecturally valued buildings. It was formerly owned by New York University, complete with rooms that once served as dorms for the elite but now serve as classrooms for the mostly working class and poor. Size and space are most definitely an issue, despite its thirty-four buildings across forty-five acres. The campus is also about a ten-minute subway ride from Yankee Stadium, and a twenty-five-minute ride from Midtown Manhattan. The proximity of this inequality in New York City, in stark geographic terms, is a useful visual. Mentoring requires knowing your students, but also knowing both the world they are navigating through and the one to which they hope to be guided. That my students traverse, often inadvertently, the architectural relics of wealth and power that are more highly valued than they are, and are also the source of their struggles, as they attempt to become "educated" is not ironic; it is cruel and unjust. However, it is also reality. Mentoring, especially as a feminist practice, requires always grounding goals and dreams in the reality that is clearly built to keep us from them. The systems matter; otherwise, all failures feel personal when they are not. That I grew up a few blocks from our campus also matters, but that I was mentored matters more. I was taught to see the as yet unseen, a cornerstone of mentoring, by being seen, not as I was in that moment but as it was possible for me to be.

I was twenty years old, freshly returned from a study abroad to Brazil that had been financed by summer jobs temping on Wall Street, working at Lord & Taylor, and financial aid. The trip served as an incredible experience of intellectual growth, but it ended in violence and an attempted sexual assault. I returned to my home campus in New York City, after nine months of a planned twelve, feeling like I had failed (despite sixteen credits, fluency in Portuguese, and no missed semesters). I was, at the time, being misled by the details I was living, still unable to see the bigger picture already taking shape. I submerged myself once again in the troubles of my family, who were now only a subway ride away in the Bronx. I was deeply distracted and unsure if I would even make it through the semester, having arrived only one day before it was set to begin. I qualified for emergency housing as my mother and aunt in the Bronx were in the process of losing their housing due to drug dependency issues, and my grandmother, who had raised me and always provided stability, was making her plans to return to Puerto Rico, overwhelmed and unable to take on any more of the challenges.

These were my "details" when I encountered my soon-to-be mentor, Suzanne Oboler, a Peruvian woman with Jewish American heritage, and a feminist who had also studied in Brazil. She was teaching a class across the hall from the class on the French Revolution I was sitting in. Her course was on the origins and conflicts around the use and application of the terms Hispanic and Latinos. Everything from the sound of her voice, complete with a soft Spanish accent that reminded me of my grandmother, to the content of her lecture, made me think I was absolutely in the wrong class. I went across the hall and asked if I could, since it was only day one, transfer into her class. I was wearing a Zorro-like black hat, and she said, "How could I say no to a girl in such a cool black hat?" Weeks later, when she confronted me about a missed paper, I cried and gave her all my "details," and she was not misled. She looked at me and said, "That sounds very difficult, but you will have to decide if you are in college or not, because they are not here, and you are." It was a moment of illumination and being seen I have never forgotten but only found words for through the spiritual practices that led me to the concept of Darshan.

In Hindu spiritual traditions Darshan has many complex layers of meaning, but primarily it is the act/experience of feeling seen by a Holy Being. Though it may seem a stretch, it has meaning worth considering deeply in the context of mentoring in academic environments.

On the website Ananda.org the first line of the definition of Darshan offered is: "The blessing which flows from the mere sight of a saint." In the context of mentoring in Western Eurocentric higher education models in the masculine tradition, it would take on the meaning of being given importance by being valued or singled out (blessed) by elite institutions ("holy beings"), and being allowed to lay eyes on the vaunted men of power and prestige, albeit via teaching assistants and large lecture halls. Of course, this is not the intended meaning, but the shape/structure of the guru–devotee relationship is both much older than the teacher–student, mentor–mentee model of Western education, and undoubtedly a source of inspiration for its shape and form. Although most would not go as far as proclaiming a mentor a saint, many behave as if they were and are distraught to discover the contours of their flawed humanity. The stories of failed or dramatically disrupted mentor–mentee breakups are too numerous to track, but many have been very public, and always there is a shock as if a mere human should have been somehow above human failures like ego and abuse of power. The important part of this for me is that I was seen by a feminist first, and as such she made light of what we both knew were part of the rules for women, physical appearance. She illuminated our shared context as women, not herself in any holy light, and as such made me visible to myself, which is the deeper layer of meaning in Darshan.

Ananda.org continues: "Darshan is derived from the Sanskrit word *darsana* meaning 'sight,' 'vision,' or 'appearance.' In the Hindu tradition, darshan refers to the beholding of a holy person, sacred object, natural phenomenon, or deity especially in imaged form. Darshan implies a mutual interaction between the viewer and the perceived object or being. Although it requires nothing more than the performance of seeing, darshan is considered a powerful form of worship and process of spiritual fulfillment." The single most important idea to be taken from Darshan in the spiritual context to mentoring in the educational context is that "Darshan implies a mutual interaction between the viewer and the perceived object or being." This is not the traditional hierarchical model of mentoring, which is a singular transference of value given to the invisible (powerless) by the visible (powerful). I don't, by any means, want to imply traditional gender norms with these uses of the masculine and feminist traditions. Darshan in mentoring can have a multidimensional presence across gender and sexual identities. My first fiction writing mentor in college was Jaime Manrique, who identifies as a gay man, and who offered a similar experience of Darshan when he said to me, "It is clear you are a writer, but you will have to figure out how to give yourself a decent life first." I was nineteen, coming to class straight from nightclubs, and confused by the seriousness with which he delivered this pronouncement. He was seeing me, telling me exactly what he saw, and allowing me to see myself. This is the Darshan of mentoring.

Both of these experiences were more than thirty years ago, and they marked the start of the longest and deepest mentoring experiences of my life. I have regular contact with Dr. Suzanne Oboler and periodically reach out to Jaime Manrique, most recently with the wonderful news that my novel will soon be published, and that it took a while because I did, in fact, focus on giving myself a good life first. These experiences deeply shaped my ability and willingness to be mentored (seen, revealed, and illumined by challenges to what I thought I saw / was living). I had deep work mentors as well from my first job out of college in Carol Joyner, an African American woman who organized and founded youth development programs and pioneered a groundbreaking childcare fund within the labor movement. I was only twenty-two years old when she hired me. She made it clear that she saw me as a leader and thrust me into roles that required me to rise to that image, and to her example. My last supervisor before I left for academia, Maureen O'Brien, saw me as the writer, teacher, academic I longed to be, though my career had led me in another direction. She insisted on making me see it in my own reflection and future plans. This experience of feeling/being mentored (seen and received for what value I had and offered, not by what value I gained by being seen or associated with them) also impacted what I came to understand about my role mentoring my students.

Mentoring is not about me being of value to my students for who I am or who I know, although I work hard to help them with letters, jobs, and even housing in a few cases. The act of mentoring inspired by my experiences, and deepened by my encounter with spiritual practices and Darshan as a concept, is about me seeing in my students what perhaps they don't yet see and mirroring that back passionately with greater faith and belief than they can currently muster for themselves. This is not one-sided. I am changed by every student I mentor, and more so each time their gifts go on to be revealed to them. This gives me the energy to do it for the next one. Seeing and being seen illuminates the spaces where the seeing is taking place. The space of mentoring is charged and vibrant with the exchange of energy, and it reinvigorates the classroom, and the act of teaching, by extension.

In a community college it is also a process of illuminating dark and shadowy corners of self-doubt, as there is no badge of prestige with which to walk through the front door just for having been accepted. Many students in this setting did not get into their first choice, went away and did not do well, and came home to regroup in community college or are returning as adults after having made a myriad of life choices they often deem as not enough. I have had countless students tell me that no one had ever told them they were good writers or deeply intelligent, and many don't believe me when I say it. I have only my own memories of not quite "believing it" about myself for some time, despite what my mentors would tell me, to guide me forward in insisting that they see what I see, if only to give me the benefit of the doubt.

Most of my work mentoring students has been in the context of being the faculty advisor for the literary journal at Bronx Community College. I have now known several former students for at least ten years and keep in contact with others through all the various modern means of social media. I am holding a ten-year reunion of students who have worked on or been published in the journal to celebrate the milestone of the tenth volume. Many whom I am in contact with are currently high school English teachers, published writers, in or have completed MFA programs, and one I just heard from is starting law school in the fall. None of this is my doing. This is who they always were. My only job was to insist on not being "misled by details" they were living when they were at BCC and asking them to share in my seeing of the details that were in fact the reality of who they are. It could easily be argued that I carry the poem "For Each of You" as its own source of mentoring. I have a long list of literary mother/mentors I have left for another essay, and Lorde is unequivocally one of them. Lorde opens her poem by advising, "Be who you are and will be." She does not stop at the idea of being who you already are but joins it with a future self already present, yet still becoming. This is the spirit that infuses the mentoring mirror I hold up each day.

Melissa Coss Aquino, PhD, is a daughter of Puerto Rico via the Bronx; an associate professor of English at Bronx Community College, City University of New York; and a novelist. *Carmen and Grace* is forthcoming in 2023 from Harper Collins / William Morrow. For more, see www.melissacossaquino.com.

Works Cited

Lorde, Audre. "For Each of You." *Chosen Poems Old and New*. Norton, 1982.
The Yogic Encyclopedia. "What Is Darshan?" *Ananda*, ananda.org/yogapedia/darshan. Accessed 4 Oct. 2021.

Among Friends

SARAH CHIHAYA

I've never quite understood the idea of the mentor, but I've almost always understood the role of the friend. Mentors, if we follow the origin of the term in the *Odyssey*, are guides who are older and wiser than us; they are charged with our care, either by their own will or another's. Yet "older" and "wiser" are not categories of person I've typically felt comfortable around, and I've often been embarrassed by or suspicious of care offered by those more powerful than myself (I'm not proud of these facts). As a child, I was afraid of adults, and even older children; teachers, babysitters, and most of my relatives frightened me, and I rarely spoke in front of them. I discovered somewhere around sixth grade, however, that there was no greater pleasure than to talk with the other weird girls in my class who found me interesting, or at least bore my long flights of fancy patiently. Ever since, I've continued to have a troubled relationship to conventional "mentorship"; as a younger woman, my career-minded parents encouraged me to ingratiate myself to professors or employers, but I was uniformly terrible at it, ending up dry-mouthed and mortifyingly dull in office hours or at networking coffee dates, smiling my toothiest, most gormless smile. Female friendship, though, has remained a social mode in which I engage with merciful ease, and from which I draw comfort and confidence.

And it is friendship more than anything else that has seen me through nearly a decade and a half of professional life in the university, as both a student and as a teacher. I have at times also been lucky enough to find support and guidance from far more advanced colleagues, who

191

192 | Sarah Chihaya

have been invaluable to my progress as a scholar and as a woman in the academy. Yet overwhelmingly, working in a new field—twenty-first-century literature—in an uncertain, new moment in the life of the American university, I have found my closest and most trusted mentors to be the friends of my own generation, who've moved alongside me on equal footing through the years of graduate school and beyond, with whom I have shared all manner of personal and professional disappointment, insecurity, and hard-won triumph.

✿

We entered the academy as it was about to fall apart. Not that it had been particularly stable to begin with, but in the brief and wobbly history of American public education, it was mere moments before the big crash. I started graduate school at the University of California in the autumn of 2007, the year before the financial crisis and the attendant fee hikes, hiring freezes, and labor struggles that continue to proliferate in our universities today. The other program that accepted me, at a private university, had nonchalantly brushed off questions about job placement during the prospective student weekend, noting that their stellar record should make all of us feel assured of academic employment after five years of well-funded graduate study. Berkeley made no such promises and also offered relatively little financial support during the seven years of ridiculously named "normative time" they predicted it would take to finish the PhD in comparative literature. There was something about this arrogantly brusque honesty that I respected, even if it made me queasy about the receding prospect of life after grad school. As a questing twenty-three-year-old from an unimaginative Rust Belt suburb, I was romanced easily by the Berkeley mythos of truth telling and collectivity, or perhaps by the smell of night-blooming jasmine as I walked slowly up to the department cocktail party at a professor's beautiful Craftsman bungalow in the hills. I decided to ignore the future and move to California, lacking in funding and confidence but overfull of nervous excitement.

It turned out I had chosen exactly the right field for my own intellectual uncertainty. Comparatists are always on the outside. We are dedicated drifters who move between languages, disciplines, and points in history, constellating ideas and lighting up connections. Some might challenge me on this assertion for good reason, but I have personally—irritatingly, no doubt—always believed that we are astrologers, not surveyors. This naïve belief is no invention of my own; I absorbed some version of it from one of the discipline's sacred texts, Erich Auerbach's *Mimesis*, written when the theorist was in exile from his native Germany, teaching in Istanbul during the thirties and forties. The creation myth goes that Auerbach fled the Nazis without any of his books and wrote his long meditation on the traditions of representation in European literature from memory. Elements of this myth have been disproven, but it was powerful nonetheless to the intellectually unrooted graduate student that I was, longing to be part of this mystifying vocation and wanting to believe that my accruing credit card debt would someday have some esoteric literary payoff. This was also part of the early romance of graduate school to me, as was my own feeling of particular misfitness even within this hermetic order of misfits. I had only haphazardly found my way to the field of comparative literature and had never taken a class in literary theory; I didn't, and perhaps still don't, really know what theory is. It seemed very clear to me from the start that I was there on forbearance. My offer of admission came with fewer semesters of funding than that of my cohort, and, perhaps in keeping with the implied commodification of our relative intellectual value, I felt certain that I had fewer good reasons to have chosen graduate study. Nobody in my family, myself included, understood what graduate school was, and yet I'd ended up there, among geniuses fluent in two or three languages more than me, or fresh-faced prodigies who arrived with master's degrees in hand, not yet old enough to rent a car. Everyone else was brilliant; everyone else was terrifying; everyone else seemed to interest our professors more than I did.

I felt out of place, but out of place was a feeling with which I became increasingly comfortable and, later, even confident. At Berkeley, I discovered myself to be at home with fellow misfits among misfits, friends who were also often uncomfortable, and who also grated, sometimes gleefully and sometimes despairingly, against the nonrules of our uncertain discipline, or the unspoken rules of academic propriety. With only one or two exceptions, these friends who felt closest to me in heart and mind were women. As seminar students, we talked about how difficult it was to make oneself heard in a classroom full of theory bros, so seemingly assured and voluble about the importance of their thoughts. As teachers, we lamented the tendency of our undergraduate students to describe male professors as serious or brilliant, and female professors as sweet or, its assertive inverse, bitchy.

These are, of course, very obvious observations on the nature of being women in an institution built by and for men. This is a story all too familiar to anyone who does not fit the precise specifications of the original mold of the white, straight, male scholar. Yet it has become increasingly clear to me that, like any other generation, the women I grew close to in that time have been particularly marked and drawn together by the historical circumstances of our upbringing in the academy. Our professional educations were shaped by political and often personal misfortune as the 2008 financial crisis and its lingering aftershocks rippled destructively through the interrelated economies of academia. Of course, this affected workers and students of all genders and ages. As graduate student workers, we talked to classrooms full of confused and upset undergraduates about the importance of civil disobedience and peaceful protest, despite coming exams and threatened GPAs; we held classes outside or at coffee shops to respect the picket line; we fought in meetings and around kitchen tables about what we could or could not do.

But there were also specific, seemingly gendered experiences that my female friends, especially women of color, and I encountered with greater and greater frequency in those years. More and more of our students came to office hours to tearfully disclose how they would have to take a semester or year off from school to work full-time to pay for their rapidly rising university fees; or to express their frustration at alarmed parents, like my own, who urged them away from literature into "practical" majors that they hated; or simply to tell us that they felt crippled by financial, familial, and social anxieties—a marked intensification of the usual personal confessions that rarely came to bear upon our male colleagues and friends, or, we gathered, upon our tenured faculty. This was meaningful affective labor that, of course, we could not and would never refuse; all the same, it was labor that our male colleagues, especially the straight ones, often did not even know we shouldered. The more our students needed us, the more we needed each other—for long hours spent reading and writing together, or longer ones spent drinking, talking, laughing, crying.

As my friends and I approached the dark and still-darkening academic job market, it became clearer and clearer that in some ways, we might be our own most trusted advisors in this most recent iteration of the American university. While our tenured professors, years or decades away from their own experiences of the market, had the best of intentions and strove to teach us everything they could about the obscure and ever-shifting rules of the profession, they evinced a certain confidence in the prospect of a life in the university that fewer and fewer of us could imagine. We felt no such confidence, and even those of us who had started graduate school with the optimistic reassurance of employment, in the pre-2008 era that seemed suddenly so far away, could not remember what it was ever like to feel it. The acute instability of academia in the moment of our emergence into it, mixed with the insecurity of being a woman in the university at *any* moment, resulted in a particular alchemy of companionship that I have found essential and life-sustaining over the last several years. I imagine that a similar sense of highly specific solidarity must have circulated among the waves of female scholars who came before us, separated inexorably by gender, race, or generation from their might-have-been mentors further up in the academic hierarchy. There is a certain unique recognition of experience that I've found in the community of female writers who have come up in this particular moment, ranging from my dissertation advisor (herself fresh out of graduate school in 2008, and only two years older than me), to my three coauthors in our collectively written book, *The Ferrante Letters*, to advanced graduate students and postdocs navigating the job market in recent years.

These relationships, more than any others, have shaped my understanding of what it means to be a young(ish) woman of color participating in, and at times implicated by, the unpredictable and often unjust structures of academic life. Rather than learning from the transmission of experience that often emerges from a generational gap in mentor–mentee relationships, the deep knowledge that circulates among my group of close friends and collaborators, some of whom remain in the academy and some who do not, is embodied knowledge that we have gathered and shared, often through failure, mishap, and dumb luck or circumstance. We learn as much, or sometimes far more, from the frustrating fits and starts of our own careers and those of our friends, than from the shining successes of the established scholars we admire or strive to emulate; we learn these lessons from sharing with each other honestly, from real vulnerability, and from the generosity of mutual care.

৬

I recognize that it's rich for me to make these observations about professional disappointment and heartbreak. I miraculously lucked out on the job market and so cannot ever truly understand the agonizing years of fruitless applications, exploitative adjunct positions, or impossible personal choices forced by the profession. I was not so lucky when it came to tenure, and, after a long stretch of relative stability in my academic job, I now find myself facing a version of the challenge many of my friends faced earlier: what to do after leaving academia. In this moment of uncertainty, I feel more grateful than ever for the relationships that sustained me in graduate school and after. My experience as a junior faculty member at an unreasonably wealthy university, and my increasing understanding of my small and temporary role there, was shaped almost completely by these intimate relationships that efface the boundary between the personal and the professional, among the friends I traveled with through the last several years. Though they are marked most clearly by emotional closeness and vulnerability, these relationships demand a sense of unsentimental perspective and communal awareness that is particularly necessary—a moral imperative, even—to anyone in a position of relative safety in the profession. Those who stay in the academy must remain open and uncynically empathetic to the experiences of their peers inside and outside the cloistered walls of the university. When I was a tenure-track faculty member, I had to remind myself daily that I was not special by nature, despite what the institution might have encouraged me to believe, nor were my struggles with mental health or work-related anxiety unique. Some of this understanding came from survivor's guilt; I was ashamed by the fact that nothing at all differentiated me from the friends who ended up leaving the university after years of unfair and untenable struggle on the market; those who left were just as fit, or sometimes far more so, than I was for the tenure line that I temporarily occupied. Some of it was the pressure I felt, whether real or imagined, to succeed in the profession not only for myself but specifically for the friends who supported and believed in me with unstinting generosity, even in the face of their own difficulties. Some of it, too, was simply the painfully quotidian understanding that I shared with the lucky few who also spent the last several years as junior faculty at various institutions, that we were all eminently and instantly replaceable in today's university economy, in which brilliance and creativity are buyer's markets more than ever before.

And so it is, as I approach the end of this particular path, that I find myself again wondering if I have any kind of future in academia. Yet this time, stripped of the naïve romantic hopes I took away from that long-ago first visit to Berkeley, I approach the uncertain years to come with something far better and more sustaining: the guidance and kindness of my peers, the women who have grown up with me in the last strange and bewildering decade; my mentors, my friends.

Sarah Chihaya is the author of *Bibliophobia* and one of four coauthors of *The Ferrante Letters: An Experiment in Collective Criticism.*

A Chorus, Not a Monologue

Melissa Duclos

Jamie once told me that dating me made him feel like a grown-up.

When he and I met in 2004 I was twenty-five years old and had just moved to New York. I'd spent the previous three years since I'd graduated college waiting tables, tending bar, working briefly at a bookstore, and teaching English in Shanghai. Though I'd attended an Ivy League university and had studied creative writing with some wonderful professors—many of whom I maintain connections with today, more than twenty years later—the one piece of career advice I heard in college came from a counselor who told me the only job I could get was teaching English at a private high school. She gave me the name of a recruitment agency and sent me on my way. I wanted to be a writer, though, not a teacher. None of my teachers told me how to make a career out of writing, maybe because I didn't ask them, or maybe because they didn't know. They were all writers who'd made careers out of teaching.

I reasoned that to be a writer I didn't need a specific career path or a mentor. I just needed time to write. So while my friends became consultants or headed to law school, I got a job at an Italian restaurant and started writing a novel. When I moved to New York three years later, I had a terrible manuscript and a copy of *The Insider's Guide to Getting an Agent*. I took one part-time job after another; I was a literacy coach for an education nonprofit, an after-school homework club instructor, a private English and SAT prep tutor. I started mailing off query letters for my terrible novel and began writing a second, based on my experiences living and teaching in Shanghai.

Jamie offered me career support before we'd even met. After he suggested in the same online chat that we meet for coffee and that I submit my book to his agent, I began buzzing around my apartment with nervous energy. Looking back, I'm not sure which offer excited me more.

When we started dating, Jamie was twenty-eight and the only other aspiring novelist I knew. From the very beginning most of our chemistry was based on our conversations about writing, the first I'd had since leaving school. We met for happy hours at the bar around the corner from his house and talked about our books. We developed characters while we were out for dinner, scrawling notes in tiny moleskins about the people around us.

We commiserated over rejections and celebrated every small success. He gave me advice on submitting to agents (including his) and edited my grad school applications. After I was accepted into an MFA program, we moved into a one-and-a-half-bedroom railroad apartment in Brooklyn, a ten-minute walk from the train that would take me uptown every day.

⁂

Grad school should've been a place for me to find a new mentor. Not that Jamie had stopped filling the role. We set up our two writing spaces in our Brooklyn apartment—mine a compact desk with drawers and cubbies beside our bed, his a smooth five-foot table in a small adjoining office—and continued to support each other's writing, emotionally, practically, and financially. We made a joint decision about my student loans; he introduced me to his accountant and gave me advice about what to write off on my taxes.

Still, in my MFA program I met other writers—teachers and classmates—whose career experiences and insights could've been useful to me. I could've found a new mentor there, but I didn't. The missed opportunities were partly my fault. I hate asking questions because I hate admitting what I don't know. During the one-on-one conferences I had with professors after each workshop critique, I would listen to whatever they said about my pages and then leave their offices as quickly as possible. In many of those meetings, I rarely spoke at all.

There were other factors that made it difficult for me to find a mentor in grad school, starting with the program's aggressively masculine vibe. I don't know what the actual percentages were, but in my memory my workshops were almost always filled with men talking loudly. I lost track of the number of stories I read about hapless men getting laid by flatly drawn female characters whose breasts were always somehow heaving. I do remember exactly how many graphic, gratuitous rape scenes I was asked to read and comment on as a student—three—and exactly the number of times the professor addressed the problematic nature of this work—zero.

After I sat through a workshop in which a classmate's feedback consisted of an admission that he wanted to be in bed with my characters and a thinly veiled joke about masturbating on my work, I began scurrying out of offices more and more quickly. Why would I have asked the professor who presided silently over that critique for career advice?

Instead of seeking new mentors in school, I went home to Jamie; he'd finished four novels by then and had found his second agent. He had answers to the questions I had, or at least a willingness to share his own experiences. He commented on my writing without degrading me or the work. Most important, I trusted him enough to admit to him what I didn't know. I trusted what he would teach me. After I finished my MFA coursework, Jamie and I got married and moved from New York to Portland, Oregon, a city we'd never visited and where we knew almost no one. We hoped it would be a more affordable place for two writers to live.

*

Fast forward five years. By the fall of 2014, Jamie and I had been together a decade, and he'd lost his career lead on me. We both had MFAs now and neither one of us had an agent. We both had stacks of rejections. We both worked from home, our matching tabletop desks on opposite ends of the loft in our apartment. He still had only one job as a freelancer and I still had several, working as a freelance editor for multiple clients and as an online adjunct writing instructor at two different schools. Beyond the number of clients and variety of work, our careers mirrored each other, just as our desks did. We had two children, ages four and two, and we divided up our parenting responsibilities to give each other time to write.

While Jamie remained focused on writing and submitting novels for publication, I began thinking more broadly about what I could do to develop my writing career. I started publishing book reviews and author interviews, and took a class on how to pitch short nonfiction that led to a few publications. More and more, I found myself with questions about my career that I didn't think Jamie could answer. I needed a new mentor. The problem was where to find one.

In 2015, I attempted to find career support for myself by launching a mentoring program for writers called the Clovers Project. My clovers had three leaves, not four, and the tagline of the project was "Good support is better than good luck." Over the course of two six-month "seasons," the Clovers Project matched ninety-nine writers into groups of three, each comprised of a college student interested in pursuing writing as a career, an emerging writer, and an established writer. Participants were given discussion prompts for each month of their season on topics focused around career development: pitching, publishing, finding an agent, earning a living.

Meanwhile Jamie also sought new connections with other writers. While I was recruiting for the Clovers, he joined a weekly critique group where he met the woman he would eventually have an affair with.

Running the Clovers for two years taught me a lot, though not about how to develop my writing career. First, I learned that it's (unsurprisingly) more difficult to find mentors than people who want to be mentored. I'd hoped my decision to match writers in groups of three instead of two would mitigate this. The common understanding that younger professionals need mentoring while older people have expertise to bestow doesn't fit with how writing careers actually develop. A writer can have decades of experience and still need career guidance. Our paths aren't straight lines; they are spirals. I opted for three-person groups to create a more fluid dynamic, encouraging the idea that everyone has questions *and* answers.

Still, I had far more applicants who were either students or working writers who identified themselves as emerging, both groups looking for monthly conversations with someone more experienced. I had so many more emerging than established writers that I didn't feel right putting myself in a Clover when there were other writers I couldn't match. The first year I ran a mentoring program, I didn't get a mentor.

In the second year of the Clovers, I joined a group, but I still didn't get a mentor out of the deal. That year, I again had far more emerging than established applicants. I began to notice other patterns too. Women, who accounted for 91 percent of all my applicants, tended not to describe themselves as "established" in their careers, no matter how long they'd been writing or what they'd accomplished. This was true of myself, too. As I recruited other writers—including Jamie—to help fill my Clovers, I realized I had just as much experience as many of the people I was asking to be mentors, and so I took the role of established writer in a group.

I wish I could tell you what I got out of that season of the Clovers. I talked with my group every month during the spring of 2016, but I have no recollection of any of our conversations. The mentoring season launched one month before I learned of Jamie's affair. Instead of conversations about pitching and publishing, I remember the things he told me in our therapist's office and on the weekly dates we went on throughout our separation. I remember the panic attacks I started having before every meeting and the way the details of his affair came out slowly over the course of weeks. I remember my fear of what I didn't know, of what Jamie would teach me next.

In one of those conversations in therapy, Jamie told me he no longer wanted the "role" of husband. I still don't know what he meant by that, but I wonder now about how his concept of the husband role relates to other roles he played in our relationship. By 2016, some of those roles had shifted. Did he miss being my mentor, or had he resented it all along? When he'd told me all those years ago that I'd made him feel like a grown-up, I heard gratitude in his voice, but maybe I was wrong.

❧

After the Clovers ended and Jamie moved out, I stopped looking for a mentor. Maybe because I finally found something better. Over the summer of 2016, I was living alone (with my kids half the time) for the first time in twelve years. I didn't know what to do with myself, but I knew I needed support. I invited all the women I knew in Portland to come to my house every Monday night for drinks and snacks and the occasional burnt offering in my backyard fire pit.

I don't know what to call what I was asking for, though I know it wasn't mentoring. It was a chorus of us all howling at the moon together. It was reassurance that my community was strong. Each week, women came—not always the same women and not always many, but every week more than one. The most frequent attendees were other writers. When we weren't talking about what a jerk my ex-husband was, we talked about our work.

When I first started this essay about the mentoring I've sought and received over the past fifteen years, I didn't expect to write about the women who held me up while my life fell down around me. But as I have written in circles around this question of mentoring—what I hoped for and needed, what I failed to find in the places I'd been taught to look—I've had trouble differentiating between personal and professional support. Because success as a writer requires both.

Perhaps it took my divorce from my mentor to realize I could get better support from a community of women than I ever would from an individual man. In March of 2019, three years after Jamie started sleeping with a woman in his writing group, I started a writing group of my own. The line from those weekly summer gatherings of friends, many of whom were writers, to the monthly writing group I host now is another spiral.

We call it the Coven. I've tried and failed to remember how or when we first came up with the idea. I searched my email archive and found nothing, the lack of a paper trail suggesting Coven was planned in person, likely over whiskey. Of the few close friends I know who were involved in its conception, I don't know who came up with the name. But what else would we call a group of women we hoped to convene on a regular basis for the purpose of supporting the performance of magic with sentences?

We didn't want a workshop. We were all clear on that. No deadlines or obligations. No penalties for missing a month. We wanted to come as we were, to a space full of other women juggling all the same demands— jobs and partners and kids and parents and overflowing septic systems. At Coven we ask questions: about our works in progress and which residencies to apply for or agents to query. About how to make time for writing, and sometimes whether to. And we celebrate: book deals and award nominations, or the completion of one wonderful paragraph. At Coven I heard my first ISBN number read aloud in a sexy voice. I still have the recording. The conversations among the group aren't so different in their content than the ones I used to have with Jamie, but they are richer in their texture, a chorus instead of a monologue.

Jamie and I are amicable coparents now. We talk on a regular basis, but never about our writing. I can track our parallel career paths through our public milestones: his debut novel came out in 2016, mine in 2019. I got a full-time job at a nonprofit working in communications, a huge shift after more than a decade of freelancing. He grew his editing work, registering as an LLC and hiring an employee. But I don't know anything about his process or his goals, his private triumphs or defeats. He doesn't know anything about mine.

Sometimes I miss being in a romantic partnership based on a shared love of writing. I miss the way we talked about characters in our novels over dinner, as though reporting to each other what old friends were up to. I miss not having to differentiate in my own mind whether I need personal or professional support because I was getting it all from the same person anyway. Surrounding this grief at what I've lost, though, is gratitude. I'm grateful that divorcing my mentor led me to make space for a Coven. All those years I longed for an individual mentor to guide my career, what I really needed was a community to support my growth.

Melissa Duclos is a cofounder of Amplify Writers, an organization that seeks to support the career development of writers with lived experiences, identities, and backgrounds that are underrepresented in publishing. Her debut novel *Besotted* was released in 2019 and her essays have appeared in the *Washington Post*, *Salon*, and the *Offing*, among other venues. She and her partner live in Portland, Oregon, amid the happy chaos of four kids in a newly blended family.

The Group (Text), or the Small Stuff

Sarah Blackwood

Would you put a bra on your friend's corpse in preparation for her burial? This is the morbid question asked at the end of Mary McCarthy's bestselling 1963 novel, *The Group*, which tracks eight Vassar graduates as they live out their tumultuous young white womanhood in the 1930s. Kay Strong—whose wedding opens the novel—has died, either falling or jumping to her death, and the remaining members of the titular collective have gathered to sort through all the gruesome, social details of her funeral. "It seemed against nature, somehow, to bury someone in a brassiere . . . and yet, as Ross pointed out, the Fortuny gown was clinging" (462).

The question of the burial bra belongs in the category of questions that shouldn't be questions at all. Couldn't we universally stipulate that of all the times a woman might wish to be free of socialized constraint, death is the ultimate? What would a bra provide in this scenario? To Kay, who is dead, probably nothing. Certainly not comfort. And yet, despite such certainty, the question the Group finds themselves considering does not, in fact, have an obvious answer. This is because the question of the bra is not just about Kay. For once, the "everyday support" that bra manufacturers are always promising consumers seems to finally really be on offer. This is a form of support that is also a form of protection: protecting Kay, and all of her friends, not only from the thoughts of others about women's bodies but also from their own.

The Group's final chapter is a crescendo of detail at the end of a novel comprised almost entirely of the small stuff. McCarthy herself described it as "a crazy quilt of *clichés*, platitudes, and *idées reçues*" (Gelderman 253). How and when to lay out the "funeral meats," what hymns to sing, what flowers to have, "sherry or Madeira, biscuits or sandwiches" (McCarthy 462). The strange group consciousness that narrates the novel remarks, of the Group's absorption in these minutiae, "You found that you got so obsessed with these petty details. They were supposed to distract you from your grief."

And so goes womanhood. The image of the bra, lingered over, comes to seem like metonymy for the Group itself. Feminine, supportive, and protective in the everyday, while at the same time symptomatic of some larger social problem, symbolic of the world's capacity for hating, berating, and surveilling women.

It reminds me, today, of nothing so much as group texting.

&

Don't worry, I am not going to write about the details of what happens in my group texts. I'm no Norine Schmittlapp. But given the objective to write about mentorship and feminism, I found myself contemplating their existence and centrality. While I have been lucky to have had many intellectual and professional mentors, and while I have tried to mentor my undergraduate students in similar ways, if I'm being totally honest, the most robust forms of mentorship in my own life are the horizontal ones that take shape through my phone's messaging app.

My group texts, in fact, do a surprising amount of the traditional work of professional mentorship. They are places where, together, we navigate how-tos (how to write a grant, when and how to advocate for a raise), cultivate insider knowledge, and share successes and failures. The group text is the most reliable professional pressure valve I know of: a space in which to express the rage about my workplace that too often courses through me. My group texts help me metabolize a world in which the question "Should we put a bra on her corpse?" remains only just a slightly amped-up version of the impossibility many women face in the workplace, the crescendos of daily details that often threaten to topple us.

In 2001, Nancy K. Miller published an essay considering *The Group*'s groundbreaking fictional representations of women's contraceptive and sexual lives. In it, she suggests that it is "instructive to revisit McCarthy's project through the prism of seventies feminism and nineties postfeminism" to explore the continued relevance of a "paradox in the privacy dramas that attend, even structure women's lives." Describing this paradox, Miller elaborates: "[W]omen's privacy often needs to be both protected and exposed. . . . It is, perhaps, the founding dilemma of privacy in women's lives that women sometimes need to have the details of their intimacy revealed to protect themselves against a much wider injustice: the ignorance and vulnerability produced by silence" (186). These themes—private/public, protection/exposure, intimacy/vulnerability—have long animated white women's domestic fiction in the US, both before and after *The Group*. Recently, as critic and writer Lydia Kiesling has pointed out, we've seen a boom in novels that tie these same domestic themes to plot and character arcs and settings that explore women's positions within a workplace. These dovetailing genres highlight how much gendered professional life continues—bizarrely—to rest on the precariously balanced fulcrum that Miller describes as a "privacy drama."

Yet the element of paradox present now in the privacy dramas of lean-in feminism of the 2010s and early 2020s is not exactly the tension between secrecy and exposure. Rather, the paradox lives inside these dramas' totally disordered sense of scale, in large part stimulated by the encroachment of work and professional attainment into every element of public and private life. Kept nearly equally private, in networks of professional women mentoring one another, are details that range from sexual abuse, harassment, and discrimination to irritation at men who refuse to figure out how to electronically sign a work-related PDF. I'd argue that the result of this disorder is less a feeling of vulnerability than it is a feeling of futility: these are realities that can come to feel simultaneously too big and too small to do anything about. A novel like *The Group* held out the promise that exposure of intimate gendered details, up and down the various scales, might have salutary political effects. This promise was explored by many midcentury feminist thinkers and writers, like Muriel Rukeyser in 1968 ("What would happen if one woman told the truth about her life? / The world would split open" [462]) and Audre Lorde, whose 1977 speech "The Transformation of Silence into Language and Action" described the power she found in putting into language the intimate details about her life as a Black lesbian: "The transformation of silence into language and action is an act of self-revelation, and that always seems fraught with danger" (42).

Yet the world does not seem to have split open, despite plenty of truth told both publicly and privately. The aftereffects of #MeToo have brought this home, as mass public revelations of intimate details related to sexual harassment and abuse have ultimately had limited (though importantly not nonexistent) societal impact. In a review of a group of books on #MeToo, consent, and sexual violence, critic Parul Sehgal identifies a "wariness of narrative" as the key shared element of some of the most searching recent feminist thinking on the topics. In an interview with Sarah Jaffe, organizer and abolitionist Mariame Kaba notes that revelatory personal narrative is unlikely to build the capacity needed to change social and political structures, arguing that such narratives too easily cultivate an atmosphere of what she terms "compulsory confession" that has nothing to do, really, with justice or repair.

Writer Emily Gould captures the texture of this narrative wariness in a 2020 essay partially about what she has found to be the deflated promise of first-person writing by women: "I no longer think there's value in the mere fact of getting people to pay attention to what I have to say. . . . I still do this kind of writing, I am doing it now, but I no longer hope for any outcome other than my own relief. This is because I have lost faith in the idea that there might be anything an individual can say or write that will change the minds of people who, consciously or subconsciously, believe that women matter less than men."

꙳

Strangely, I think that it is within this context of wariness that both *The Group* and *my* groups have the most to say about what feminists might want to preserve from the long, vexed histories of both mentorship and the privacy dramas that structure so much twentieth- and twenty-first-century femme written expression. Both the novel, *The Group*, and the contemporary social phenomenon, the group text, spin intimate webs of stories as a way to build networks of support and protection, all woven out of the small stuff. This is a human response to injustice, and insofar as these stories and networks repair and build up individual people they are to be treasured as the good work of a life. This form of horizontal, web-building mentorship is, importantly, not transactional and not linear. It may only provide individual relief—the feeling of being seen, heard, and understood on a human scale, rather than a public or political scale. And in "only" (ha!) providing that, this form of mentorship reveals the lie of traditional mentorship's emphasis on ambition and success.

If traditional mentorship has tended to value a kind of backroom clubbiness, the extended group conversations that comprise the type of mentorship happening in a group text take on an interestingly para-private/

para-public quality. The group text is sometimes a rehearsal and sometimes the main act itself. Sometimes it's shared recipes and cute snapshots and sometimes it's professional advice. Such a mentoring platform is not an unmitigated good. Coteries can be exclusionary and wagon-circling, and while my group texts are populated not only by white women, I'd be remiss if I didn't acknowledge that when white women do group up, we are viciously good at claiming gendered victimhood while simultaneously wielding immense cultural power.

Sometimes I wonder how and why talk about work—and here I include creative and intellectual work, too, not just the stultifying stuff—takes up so much space inside some of my most intimate give-and-take relationships. But other times I consider how this kind of talk restores work to the realm of the ordinary, one of the things I do in my life but not the only, or even remotely the most important, thing that I do. If traditional mentorship sets work and professional/intellectual development and achievement on a pedestal, informal, horizontal, texty feminist mentorship returns work to its rightful place.

Maybe I reveal a bit too much about myself in dwelling on how remarkable I find the question about the bra. It's simultaneously so morbid, so abject, and also, well, *ordinary*—a question that only the cluckiest hens might cluck over. But, for me, the question crystallizes so much about the privacy dramas of twentieth- and twenty-first-century womanly life that have continued to shape those lives. It's an impossible question to answer, because the framework within which it is asked is an impossible place to live. The question about the bra, in the end, is a trick question. There is no right answer, there's only the talk about it. And the talk doesn't necessarily *do* anything; it alone moves the social needle no further, makes no transactions, follows no law of progress. But it does draw us together—for good, for bad, and also for, simply, a way to pass the time—on a human scale.

In the end, the Group decides to dress Kay in a bra for her burial. But the job of actually putting the bra on the corpse falls to Ross, the longtime servant of downwardly mobile Polly Andrews's Aunt Julia. Kay's corpse goes into the ground, nipples sheathed. The casket remains closed at the funeral. The amount of talk I could produce about these details seems, sometimes, inexhaustible. ;)

Sarah Blackwood is associate professor of English at Pace University. She is the author of *The Portrait's Subject: Inventing Inner Life in the Nineteenth-Century United States* (2019), a number of scholarly essays on nineteenth-century visual culture and representations of selfhood, and the introductions to Penguin Classics editions of Edith Wharton's *The Age of Innocence* and *The Custom of the Country*. Her cultural criticism has appeared in the *New Yorker*, the *New York Review of Books*, and the *New Republic*.

Works Cited

Gelderman, Carol. *Mary McCarthy: A Life*. St. Martin's Press, 1988.

Gould, Emily. "Replaying My Shame." *New York Magazine*, 26 Feb. 2020, www.thecut.com/2020/02/emily-gould-gawker-shame.html. Accessed 10 Dec. 2021.

Jaffe, Sarah. "From 'Me Too' to 'All of Us': Organizing to End Sexual Violence without Prisons." *In These Times*, 17 Oct. 2017, inthesetimes.com/article/incarceration-sexual-assualt-me-too-rape-culture-organizing-resistance. Accessed 10 Dec. 2021.

Kiesling, Lydia. "The Office Politics of Workplace Fiction by Women." *New Yorker*, 27 July 2016, newyorker.com/books/page-turner/the-office-politics-of-workplace-fiction-by-women. Accessed 10. Dec. 2021.

Lorde, Audre. "The Transformation of Silence into Language and Action." *Sister/Outsider: Essays and Speeches*, Crossing Press, 2013, pp. 40–44.

McCarthy, Mary. *The Group*. Harcourt, 1963.

Miller, Nancy K. "Women's Secrets and the Novel: Remembering Mary McCarthy's *The Group*." *Social Research*, vol. 68, no. 1, Spring 2001, pp. 173–99, JSTOR doi: www.jstor.org/stable/40971444.

Rukeyser, Muriel. "Käthe Kollwitz." *The Collected Poems of Muriel Rukeyser*, edited by Janet E. Kaufman, Anne F. Herzog, and Jan Heller Levi, U of Pittsburgh P, 2006, p. 462.

Sehgal, Parul. "Yes, No, Maybe So. A Generation of Thinkers Grapples with Notions of Consent." *New York Times*, 21 June 2021, nytimes.com/2021/06/21/books/literature-about-consent.html. Accessed 10 Dec. 2021.

On Leaning Out

LAURA LIMONIC

In 2013, I was a graduate student and a mother to two young children. I never slept, my children never slept, my dissertation was an unfinished shell of a project, and I was on the academic job market. I was drowning. In desperation, I picked up a copy of Sheryl Sandberg's book *Lean In: Women, Work, and the Will to Lead*. As I read, I felt that Sandberg was speaking directly to me. She "gets me," I remember thinking. Rather than see the differences between us (namely her corporate, very well-paid job), I concentrated on the traits we shared—age, religion, and most importantly motherhood. The fact that we were both Democrats and that we both breastfed our babies sealed the deal. In Sandberg, I had found my feminist guru.

As I dove into the book, I came to believe that my inability to find balance in my home life and success in motherhood and academic pursuits was entirely of my own making. I was an inadequate mother and academic because I was not leaning in enough. I did not advocate for myself. My success as a scholar, a mother, and a wife depended on me taking charge, on following Sandberg's advice to "sit at the table." But merely participating and demanding equality, she cautioned, was not enough. Equality at home must be pushed for in tandem with leaning in at the workplace—which for me at the time was graduate school. Moreover, I needed to find an advocate and a mentor following Sandberg's proclamation that "mentorship and sponsorship are crucial for career progression" (40).

I was eager to initiate my lean-in plan. I began at home, where I tried to equally share childcare and household responsibilities with my husband. I demanded equality—a fifty/fifty split, a breakdown-of-the-hours kind of division. If I was taking my kids to preschool two days a week, he needed to take them the other two days. Never mind that the preschool was in the same building where I was a graduate student, and I just followed them on the next subway train, often meeting up with them as we passed through the subway turnstile. I was adamant that my husband share in all aspects of parenting, and commuting on the New York City subway with a toddler in a stroller during rush hour was something we both needed to suffer through.

I translated Sandberg's message into a mantra that I repeated to myself on a daily basis—"lean in, take a seat at the table, be ambitious." To succeed I needed to exert my will and power, regardless of the consequences this might have on our family's time. I leaned in, I leaned in so far my husband and I almost toppled over one another. My husband had a demanding job and also taught in the evenings. He did not have flexibility over his schedule. But I did. So it made sense that, at that time in our lives, I take responsibility for more childcare—even if that meant slowing down my dissertation for a bit, attending fewer conferences, or even delaying my job market applications. But it felt as if every minute I was not using toward scholarly work was time I was shaving off my future as an academic, as a professional woman. Equality, however, is not the same thing as equity. Our division of labor problems went much deeper than commuting on the C train with a child in tow, arranging babysitters, or getting dinner on the table.

❧

I came of age in the 1980s—a time when, as my iron-on mall T-shirt slogan said, "Anything boys can do, girls can do better." I was primed to have an accomplished career, be a nurturing, hands-on mother, and have deep friendships and a fulfilling marriage. So, when I reached a point in my life where I had a career of sorts and children and a marriage yet felt that I was floundering, my inclination was to blame myself. Postindustrial capitalism values paid over unpaid labor, and women unproportionally bear the brunt of the housework and caregiving performed in the after-paid-work hours of the "second shift." A myriad of factors such as inadequate social policies; inflexible work schedules; increasing costs of housing, healthcare, and education; and a gendered labor market all work to create imbalances in the household division of labor (Hochschild and

Machung 7–10). I certainly demand equity in our family life, but I was not able to see that my imagined failure at traversing the motherhood/career dichotomy was the result of historical and social factors and not a lack of personal will on my part.

After asking my husband, as Sandberg counseled, to "sit at the table—the kitchen table" (71), with mixed results, I turned my focus to my graduate studies. According to Sandberg's theory (or my reading of her theory), the reasons my dissertation was not finished, my articles not published, and my grants not funded were not because I, as a mother to two young children, had too much on my plate. I was not achieving my academic goals because I lacked confidence and self-advocacy, because I was, essentially, sitting on the sidelines. I needed a seat at the academic table, and I needed a mentor to invite me there.

In chapter 5 of *Lean In*, "Are You My Mentor?," Sandberg discusses the importance of mentorship in advancing women's careers. We (women) should not just expect that a mentor will fall into our laps and we will succeed. In fact, it is just the opposite, advises Sandberg: "Excel and you will get a mentor" (42). But of course, I was not excelling—I was lagging behind, and I feared I would never shine enough to find a true mentor. As this was graduate school I had advisors, people who were supposed to steer me in the right direction, professionalize me into the academy. My dissertation advisor was always willing to read my work, offer thoughts on new theoretical paradigms, suggest fresh perspectives on methodology. But I rarely had any work to show her. I was embarrassed when my deadlines were not met because I had been up for ten days with a flu-ridden toddler. Or when my drafts were full of typos because my brain could not process information from lack of sleep. I was ashamed that I fuddled my way through oral qualifying exams because I was more worried about making it to daycare pickup in time than I was about Marx's theory of alienation.

I was emotional, I was tired, I was underperforming. I wanted a mentor who could tell me how to be a mother, a wife, and a scholar—and in that order. But my advisor (rightly) did not see her role as one of all-encompassing life coach / mentor. She signed on to help me learn to be a scholar, not to manage the ins and outs of balancing motherhood with a successful career in academia. Rather than pin hopes on that elusive female graduate advisor who could be a therapist / career guide / copy editor and surrogate mother all at once, I reached out to friends (and a licensed therapist). I took up running and joined a running group comprised of mothers with young children. Two days a week I made my way to the local park to meet up with other mothers and run. I liken my running group to a very loose contemporary version of a '70s feminist group, minus the vulva self-examinations.

None of us in the running group had enough access to quality childcare, preschools were expensive, our partners worked long hours and sacrificed family time for work time. We were disappointed, sad, and really angry—at our partners for not stepping up and at ourselves for not leaning in. Those of us that worked full time scrambled to find coverage on the myriad of days off, half days, and vacation days—a school schedule that assumes one parent, grandparent, or paid childcare provider is always available. We were tired, cranky, underperforming, and overzealous. We read too many blogs and were enraptured by the mommy wars over gender colors that took over the local parent Yahoo group in 2006 and were still making headlines seven years later. We ran, and we talked—about kids, breastfeeding, menopause, ADHD diagnoses, and ailing parents. Until this point I had, for the most part, blamed myself for what I saw as an underperformance in all areas of my life. Of course, as a sociologist, I rationally knew that the patriarchal capitalist social structure exerted a force that I, as an individual, could not lean into. But somehow, I still felt that it was my fault. It was not until I found myself with a group of women experiencing similar difficulties that I understood that my "underperformance" was a product of a social organization that does not value unpaid labor such as childbearing and rearing, demands too much from the overextended labor market, and provides little in the way of social support for families.

I wanted my husband to be home more, to take care of the kids more. I wanted my adjunct salary to pay enough to cover the cost of childcare so I could actually write a dissertation. I wanted to live in a city where housing was both affordable and afforded more than a closet-sized bedroom for two kids to share. We all did. But I had none of these things. Yet it was precisely these factors that were preventing me from achieving a precariously balanced life of motherhood and academia. It was not, as Sandberg admonished, a result of not "leaning in."

In fact, the lean in adage is the root of the problem—by placing the responsibility on the individual, Sandberg's advice and teachings fail to take into account the structural problems (in this case in the United States) that work to keep mothers at the sidelines. Yet her book has proved so successful because if we see the problems as individual ones then we, ourselves, have the power to fix them. Structural and societal problems seem out of our hands, but individual approaches to improving our lives and careers—by seeking mentorship, self-advocacy, and equality in the household—seem much more achievable. Even if it is just a tale we tell ourselves.

I finally found my way to a mutual mentorship that is built into many of my friendships. Mentors are often perceived as older, experienced advisors who can lead the way for the younger generation. The group of women in the running club guided me in immeasurable ways. Some were a few years older, others more than a decade younger. We mentored each other. I came to see our experiences as ones that widen the definition of mentoring—where we are at once both mentors and mentees. I did not need these women to have years of experience navigating the workforce and the New York City public school system; I just needed them to have a bit more experience than I did. At the same time there was a reciprocity to our relationships that was immediate—we gave and took freely. Some of the advice we shared was trite, such as tips on what to pack for lunch or nonperishable snacks. Some was lifesaving, like pushing for mammograms even if our lives seemed too busy to schedule them. We shared information like how to get off a preschool waitlist, what the most affordable summer camps were, what kind of life insurance made the most financial sense. This information sharing was certainly worthy, a type of social capital that is instrumental in helping women navigate motherhood and careers. Yet it was the sense of social solidarity and shared experiences that allowed me to stop blaming myself for the impossibility of achieving incredibly lofty goals and allowed me to work within the limitations of the current social system.

In the years that followed, I somehow managed to cobble together a dissertation, get two grants funded, and eventually land a tenure-track job. The women in my running group were able to support me as a mother, filling the void I no longer needed my advisor to fulfill—giving my advisor the space to do her job and serve as my academic mentor. The process was not smooth. I struggled with producing decent chapter drafts, and one was so awful that my advisor's comments included a terse "try again." My dissertation defense was rushed and unceremonious, and the first day of my new tenure-track job coincided with my son's first day of kindergarten. But I no longer felt that I was a poor excuse for an academic or a terrible mother. I simply told my advisor that I was doing the best I could under the circumstances. And I let my husband take my son to kindergarten. Sometimes the best way to lean in is to lean out.

Laura Limonic is a sociologist, professor, mother, and runner. She balances these roles by reading and then rejecting self-help books. She is currently channeling her feminist rage through a research project examining the effects of the COVID-19 pandemic on mothers and motherhood. For more, see www.lauralimonic.com.

Works Cited

Hochschild, Arlie Russell, and Anne Machung. *The Second Shift: Working Parents and the Revolution at Home.* Viking, 2012.

Sandberg, Sheryl. *Lean In: Women, Work, and the Will to Lead.* Alfred A. Knopf, 2013.

A Special Place in Hell

Women Helping Women and the Professionalization of Female Mentorship

Angela Veronica Wong

I would love for us to be a symbol of redemption and forgiveness.

—Katy Perry to Taylor Swift

In 2019, Taylor Swift and Katy Perry patched up their five-year feud, one that spawned numerous headlines and warring stan tweets, and placed the fickle nature of female friendships in the spotlight (Mizoguchi and Todisco). The Swift–Perry schism was magnified by Swift's magpie-like collecting of mostly white, pretty, famous female friends.[1]

Swift's ever-changing group of celebrity friends popped up on each other's social media feeds like whack-a-mole. Voyeurs, we played a game of peek-a-boo into their lives. There was Swift and her #squad in a staged Instagram photo on the beach. There they were, at an awards show, on a runway, in the real world with sunglasses on and never looking directly at the camera. And there they were in the "Bad Blood" music video, a song we all know is about Perry. This was commodity feminism at its most appealing, when it creates a fantasy world where embracing gendered expectations equates to fighting oppression.

White girls and white girl friendships. White girl sisterhood. That's what was celebrated, destroyed, and rebuilt in all the movies my adoles-

219

cent self grew up loving and seeing as feminist girlpower: *Buffy, Charmed, Sex and the City, Friends, Bring It On,* the underrated but vicious Rose McGowan–led *Jawbreaker,* the similarly underrated Christina Applegate, Cameron Diaz, and Selma Blair rom-com vehicle *The Sweetest Thing.* Sometimes, there would be a token friend-of-color: *The Craft, Clueless.* The late '90s and early 2000s, after all, were the pinnacle of *white* girlhood in our national imaginary—the years of *My So-Called Life* and Courtney Love, of *Seventeen* magazine and Delia*s clothing catalog. The era of *Girl, Interrupted* and *Reviving Ophelia.* Even today, I can clearly recall *Reviving Ophelia*'s cover, this book I devoured looking for pieces of myself in it. I can picture the young white girl with blue-gray eyes cast downward, with wisps of blond hair against a purple-black book cover background, with her face underneath the all-caps subtitle: SAVING THE SELVES OF ADOLESCENT GIRLS.

Like Swift and Perry's friendship was rumored to, these white-girl movie friendships often curdled when boys, who usually didn't deserve either girl, were at stake. Even my beloved sardonic soulmate Daria faced a storyline where she and her outcast BFF artist Jane Lane briefly fell out over a boy. Like Swift and Perry, these white girls would make up, and in the case of *Mean Girls,* provide a smart lesson in pop feminism: don't tear each other down, girls, because the world will do that for you. *Heathers* came to a similar, darker conclusion.

Movie and television portrayals of young women replicate socially ingrained sexism. The gendered concept of frenemies views women as untrustworthy and somewhat unstable. I need not state that women's friendships are not inherently toxic, and yet, the narrative persists. It makes for better TV. These relationships suggest that women's friendships always hold the kernel of competition that might, under the right pressures, rupture the hull and burst into psychological or physical violence—what Tina Fey's character calls "girl on girl crime" in *Mean Girls.*

Girl-on-girl crime or not, there was something in these on-screen relationships that I desperately wanted: the magnetic pull of a *best* friend, two people braided into a friendship so intense that only adolescents, buoyed by hope, could withstand its weight.

❧

I am not the target person for mentorship. I have always had a hard time asking for help; those who suffer from imposter syndrome likely understand the desire to hide inexperience for fear it reads as incompetency. I still cringe a little when I hear the word *mentor*; it feels too needy, as if having a mentor is acknowledging a weakness, I can't uproot that fear of being found out—*she doesn't belong here*, I constantly worry people will realize. Since I probably don't.

I know, of course, equating mentorship with weakness is not true. I am happy for my students of color and first-generation college students who mention their mentors. I know too well the difficult waters that these students will encounter in their institutions and future careers, and I hope mentorship can help them prepare and navigate future microaggressions and overt racism.

Though I have had many who helped me and continue to help me in my life, I have yet to have an official mentor–mentee relationship. I am sure I could have. I am old enough now to wonder what could have been had I asked for more help, and I wonder why I never built relationships with undergraduate professors or internship supervisors, often women or professors of color who likely would have been a mentor to me.

A younger version of me wrote: "I wanted to be Aphrodite, completely unto myself, born of seafoam and dreams." It's unclear when and how this long-held desire developed. Perhaps in growing up on this continent without an extended family, in being caught in the child-of-immigrants dilemma, perhaps in the solitude of feeling unmoored or the independence of being an older sibling. Like sea anemone polyps that float near the water's surface, I look down enviously at the polyps that have found a home, attached to a hard rock on the ocean floor as the waves move me around, neither here nor there, neither American nor not American.

Asian Americans, as with any demographic group, are not a monolith. In my life, I have experienced a privileged Asian Americanness through education, and I never questioned its proximity to whiteness despite always knowing this was a whiteness I couldn't achieve.

My high school friend group consisted mostly of East and Southeast Asian Americans, most the firstborn American children of immigrants, none of whom I am in contact with now. Our parents were highly educated and working in professional fields—the "right" type of immigrant, but this never protected them from US racism.

Looking for radical Asian American history in our education system is like wringing water from a rock. I don't think I learned anything about Asian Americans in my history classes, though I did read Maxine Hong Kingston's *Woman Warrior* in my AP English literature class, which is revealing in how we define Asianness. We don't celebrate the five-year Delano grape strike, where Filipino workers organized for better wages and conditions. Facing the potential of Mexican strikebreakers, Filipino leader Larry Itliong reached out to Cesar Chavez, brokering a cross-racial alliance that led to the United Farm Workers. We don't learn about May Chen and the 1982 strike of New York Chinatown garment workers.

Had I learned about these stories, maybe I would have found a past that matched the future I wanted.

In 2016, as Hillary Clinton and Bernie Sanders competed over the Democratic presidential nomination, former secretary of state Madeleine Albright spoke at a Clinton campaign event. Albright urged young women to support Clinton, arguing that Clinton had fought for women and reproductive rights her entire political career. Albright closed her speech, "There's a special place in hell for women who don't help each other!" (McCarthy).

Apparently, Albright had been saying that for years, but in 2016, she addressed young women who entered adulthood saddled with student debt into an anemic postrecession job market, young women who were less convinced by the pull of shared gender against growing inequality, unaffordable housing, unlivable wages, and racial injustice as evidenced in American domestic and foreign policy.

Albright, like others, found it perplexing that young women supported Sanders over Clinton, the potential first female US president. Here, I am less interested in debating the gender politics of the 2016 election; rather, I am interested in Albright's idea of women supporting women, integral to the conception of female mentorship.

If every girl friendship holds within itself the poison of a frenemy-ship, then mentorship is the grown woman's antidote. Albright's statement implies that women owe loyalty to each other *because* they are women, and the mere act of supporting women, then, becomes a feminist act.

Undoubtedly, capitalist patriarchy has rendered women's gatherings and relationships dangerous and unwanted. Silvia Federici, in *Witches, Witch-Hunting, and Women*, describes the evolution of the word *gossip* as an early example of capitalist patriarchy's capacity to co-opt language to demean, oppress, and marginalize groups of people. Gossip, as Federici writes, used to be "a term of strong attachment" between women (Federici). However, "by the sixteenth century . . . women's social position had begun to deteriorate, satire giving way to what without exaggeration can be described as a war on women, especially of the lower classes, reflected in the increasing number of attacks on women as 'scolds' and domineering wives and of witchcraft accusations. Along with this development, we begin to see a change in the meaning of gossip, increasingly designating a woman engaging in idle talk" (Federici). Against this history, there is radical potential in the act of being women together. But now, the act of "supporting women" has become a mechanism of capitalist control itself, and as Angela McRobbie wrote about, turns feminism into a commodity we can purchase.

Female mentorship ostensibly fills that gap caused by heteropatriarchy and institutional sexism, and this is an admirable goal. Yet, I wonder if it merely obscures existing institutional sexism and blocks the real means to combat this. If mentorship is not just a professional woman's version of #girlsquad, a way to mold women and people of color to fit an existing professional space without changing anything.

⁊⁊

In the movie *Don't Tell Mom the Babysitter's Dead*, recent high school graduate Sue Ellen (played by Christina Applegate) finds herself in charge of her four younger siblings after their mother leaves for a summer vacation with her new boyfriend and the hired babysitter dies of a heart attack. Sue Ellen fakes a résumé that lists her alma mater as Vassar and applies for a receptionist position at a fashion company. Her exemplary résumé lands her an executive assistant position instead—her new boss Rose is also a Vassar graduate and feels an affinity toward Sue Ellen. As Sue Ellen wears her mother's '80s power suits and finds herself overloaded with responsibilities beyond her skill set, an unknowing Rose confides in Sue Ellen and takes her under her wing. On her first day, Rose brings Sue Ellen the expectations of professional women helping each other out: "Whenever we're not alone or I'm on the phone and I ask you something, doesn't matter what it is, you always say: 'I'm right on top of that, Rose.'" Even after Sue Ellen is found out, Rose continues to help her, saying she could pull some strings to get Sue Ellen into Vassar.

This metaphor for mentorship, "under the wing," is a gendered metaphor of nurturing. A sweet image of a mama bird feeding weak hatchlings in a nest until the baby birds are ready to fly away and build their own nests. Most people would view mentorship as this: a more experienced (usually older) person takes a less experienced (younger) person under their wing, in hopes that the more experienced mentor can impart wisdom and guidance that benefits the less experienced mentee. The mentee can be assigned, or the mentor can make decisions on who they would like to mentor. With the latter, the mentor often chooses a mentee they recognize as similar to their younger selves. Mentorship, then, can reproduce structural biases, creating an "exclusive" model that leaves little space for women and people of color. Should you be a woman or person of color lucky enough to be invited into the room, you must quickly learn how to act and what to say, otherwise you may be told to leave (Wimmer).

In the spaces I travel, my possible mentors are almost always white women. In the nonprofit world and the arts, white women dominate the more powerful positions. Those in nonprofit and arts leadership roles must show comfort with moving in moneyed circles. One must feel—or fake—like they belong. As a stubbornly patriarchal, hierarchical space, academia remains very white. If the university is our center of knowledge production, its overwhelming whiteness conditions the ways we research, understand, and talk about the world.

In 2020, the AAUP released data snapshots on full-time faculty demographics pulled from 2018 data from the Integrated Postsecondary Education Data System (IPEDS) survey and additional research. White faculty represented over 70 percent of all full-time faculty (38 percent men and 34 percent women); Asian faculty make up about 10 percent (5 percent men and 4 percent women); and of the IPEDS's "underrepresented minority" category, Hispanic or Latino faculty make up 5.2 percent, Black or African American faculty make up 6 percent, Native American or Alaska Native make up 0.5 percent, Native Hawaiian or Other Pacific Islander make up 0.2 percent (roughly even gender split of 6 percent men and 6 percent women) ("Data Visualizations"). And this is a breakdown of just full-time faculty, which comprises only 51.5 percent of all faculty in 2019 in higher education (Lederman).

§.

These past decades of austerity and corporatization have heightened the academic's mean streak of individualism.

Mentorship belongs to a professional class of women. When we picture workplace mentorship, we don't think about retail or farm workers, telemarketers or Uber drivers, nannies or domestic workers. These working-class sites rarely populate our imagination of mentorship, which we associate with workplaces that have human resource directors and kitchenettes and monthly happy hours and company newsletters.

Midway through my PhD program, I attended a university-sponsored female mentoring event. Hosted off campus, the event included a seated dinner in a large, airy hall by the water. When I entered, I felt a buzz of anticipation in the room, possibly from the unexpected formality of the space or the excitement generated by the fact that so many female students felt lost, isolated, and uncertain about their academic career and finally, the university was acknowledging it. There was small talk, cloth napkins, a choice of protein that included salmon, and a basket of rolls on the table.

In retrospect, the event's gathering of "professional women"—I recall three white women—to impart career advice seems insulting to a room of mostly graduate students already instructors-of-record of their own classes, many working additional jobs because the stipend put us barely over the poverty line, and many returning to school after years of "professional" work. I should have known, and I should not have been surprised, at how the professional women's advice ignored our stark financial differences and assumed shared class backgrounds and career prospects. Their advice may have felt empowering to some women: don't be afraid to use nannies, hiring a cleaner can save a marriage. Yet there was never acknowledgment of *who* this help was.

And then, one of the older professional women finally said it: "You have it so much better than we did." The other women on the panel quickly nodded in agreement. I don't doubt the difficulties of navigating a professional space before sexual harassment policies and antidiscrimination laws were in place. But these statements were made by women sitting comfortably in their success to a room full of graduate students making under fifteen thousand dollars a year and a handful of undergraduate students who were considering graduate school without being told the realities of the collapsing job market.

Madeleine Albright's quotation claims that women sticking together is a political act that usurps policy change. We know women struggle in professional fields, but rather than upend the hierarchies on which these fields are built, we create women-supporting-women conferences, panels, and groups that so often feel like activity for the sake of activity. We tell women that they are the problem: change your individual behavior, we say, and you will succeed.

I still wonder about the handful of undergraduates in the room, who were easy to spot, the ones still bright with ambition and promise, still seemingly unbruised from being a professionalized woman in the professional world. I wonder what they thought of the evening.

&.

At its best, mentorship helps women move through spaces resistant to their success. In capitalist practice, mentorship often ends up functioning like concepts of female empowerment and empathy—abstract notions built on individual responsibility that displace the collective means to reconfigure structural biases. Believe in gender equality? Empower young women to negotiate for more money. Worried about racism? If only we felt more beholden to each other as humans, then maybe we could eradicate white supremacy. There is nothing inherently wrong with empowerment, empathy, or mentorship, but by shifting the responsibility solely onto the individual, institutions conveniently evade the structural changes that could actually lead to equity and justice.

Gender provides no protection from abuse of power. It is always easier to protect the status quo, and when mentorship becomes individualized, its success depends on the intentions of individuals. Every graduate student I know has stories of department faculty that closed ranks around emotional exploitation or sexual harassment of graduate students, female faculty being some of the abusers and even more of these protectors. Graduate students find themselves implicitly (or explicitly) perpetuating the cycle of abuse through their mere presence, and the institution rewards the students who look away and continue working with faculty regardless of what we all know is happening or has happened to fellow students.

The high-profile case of Avital Ronell exemplifies the abuse structurally sanctioned by university hierarchy. A well-known scholar and philosopher at New York University, Ronell was accused of sexual harassment by a former male graduate student. In the midst of #MeToo, the case attracted attention because of the flipped gender dynamics and the prominent feminist scholars who defended Ronell against accusations, some using the familiar parlance of queer and feminist studies (Greenberg).

However, as Andrea Long Chu astutely observes, Ronell's personal claim to be feminist should be contrasted with the nonfeminist nature of her academic work. It was easy to conflate a prominent female scholar with a feminist scholar (Chu). Chu writes, "It is simply no secret to anyone within a mile of the German or comp-lit departments at NYU that Avital is abusive. This is boring and socially agreed upon, like the weather." I was not a graduate student at NYU, and I have no firsthand knowledge or experience of Avital Ronell, but Ronell's alleged mentor–mentee relationship resonated uncomfortably with other relationships between tenure-track or tenured faculty and graduate students that I have witnessed and heard described.

Chu's essay identifies Ronell's feelings of persecution, and I heard this defense too, shared between graduate students across many different universities, after the two little words, "Yes, but." These two revealing words of tacit acknowledgment and resignation that can only replicate, not overturn, the system: "Yes, but she is really overworked as a junior faculty member." And, "Yes, but look at how the department treats female faculty of color." The clauses that follow the "yes, but"—I believe. Junior faculty are overworked. Faculty of color, especially women, are instrumentalized and mistreated.

What I don't believe are those two little words: "Yes, but."

&

It's unfair that women and women of color take an additional burden of mentorship, and this burden emerges due to the university's unwillingness to enact structural change that will make their hallways and classrooms more equitable (Vettese). Instead, administration creates deans of diversity and inclusion, colleges form committees, and overwhelmingly white departments brainstorm ways to "attract talent of color" that conflate scholars of color with a field of study. Even if a department successfully recruits a faculty member, retention is a different story.

Some institutions are notoriously allergic to granting tenure to early-career scholars, which seems to disproportionately impact scholars of color. These tend to be our most elite universities, the ones all other colleges and universities emulate. Harvard, for example, received outrage for denying Lorgia García-Peña, a prominent Latina scholar of Latinx studies, tenure (Aviles). Graduate students of color see this, which reminds them that they do not belong.

According to the American Academy of Arts and Sciences, of all doctorates awarded in the humanities in 2015, African Americans received 3.5 percent, Hispanics received 6.5 percent, and students of Asian or Pacific Islander descent received 3.9 percent. There is an even smaller percentage of Indigenous or Native students ("Racial and Ethnic Distribution"). According to the Council of Graduate Schools, "Despite growth in the past decade, the overall share of underrepresented minorities in total graduate enrollment among U.S. citizens and permanent residents remains disproportionately low" (Okahana and Zhou 17).

Instead, the university categorizes the work of "diversity" (slowly, universities are adding "equity" as corporations have done) as "service work," taken on usually by faculty of color. Job ads not so subtly imply that the department wants a new faculty member of color to take the lead in diversity and equity initiatives (Flaherty). And over and over, faculty of color note that this work is never recognized on par with publication in their tenure review (Matthew).

Then there are the mentoring initiatives that astonish but don't surprise, like Cambridge University's "reverse mentoring" program, which pairs "BAME" faculty (Black, Asian, and minority ethnic staff) with white senior faculty and administration (Batty). Someone, likely more than one someone, thought this might lead to institutional change. When I read about the program's likely termination, I couldn't help thinking that it would have been more equitable to pay contingent faculty more rather than spend money on this idea.

*

In the creative and knowledge production economies, there is work, and there is work, and there is "the work." I work, and I make money to pay for housing, bills, food, guilt-inducing amounts of face creams, and piles of multicolored Post-its, so many that, in all honesty, I can never use them up, but their mere accumulation brings me too much joy. I have my own intellectual and artistic work, the work that rarely pays me: the dissertation that will never be published, the novel manuscripts languishing on my hard drive, the art that always waits until next month or next summer or next year because right now, I have to do the work that pays.

There is also, for those committed to a more equitable world, the work of undoing. We must all "do the work" of antiracism, of feminism, of decolonizing, which involves self-reflection and critique, unearthing privileges, and dismantling hierarchies.

Mentorship is "work," but which of the three categories does it fall under? For some, perhaps mentorship is their paid work, part of their job description and responsibilities. For most, mentorship may be expected or gently encouraged by employers, but not compensated. Instead, we frame mentorship in the vague language of "support," an additional responsibility that women owe each other in the Madeleine Albright version of feminism.

In the context of academia, the only real work is intellectual work, not service work, and mentorship certainly does not count as intellectual work. More often than not, the university (or company) expects women or people of color to help young students and employees to navigate a toxic climate that is closed to them, to make the institutional space more accommodating, but there is little expectation that white faculty or employees change their behaviors or have a role or see it in their job description.

We want to believe that mentorship is the third type of work, but it rarely is. Mentorship is the hope for a different world. This hope can make manipulation feel like respect. Too often, professional mentorship replicates the logic of investment, not the logic of dismantling.

৯৯

Katy Perry used "redemption and forgiveness" to describe her rapprochement with Taylor Swift. In a friendship, that might be possible. In academia, we need self-critique and accountability. I don't know if professional mentorship will get us there.

As I completed this essay, we were at the beginning of a global pandemic. I was in New York City, where universities have shifted to remote teaching. Daily, it seemed, the administration made decisions, and I don't know whether they consulted faculty but faculty bore the brunt of the decisions: to adapt their class online, to integrate video conferencing, to assure anxious students, to accommodate the "unprecedented" pressures on students while being warned not to sacrifice academic expectations, to report excessively to the administration so the administration can assuage parents and students that they are getting their money's worth.

I was an adjunct working on four campuses. Before the COVID-19 crisis, graduate students were organizing against unfair wages in California. I watched professional academic women positioning themselves as for immigrant rights, for graduate student rights, for their undergraduate students, and some of these women are tenure-track and tenured professors who I know have taken advantage of their relationships with graduate students to extract free labor—menial, administrative, and affective. During this crisis, I, like so many other adjuncts and graduate students who are barely compensated for our work, have still not been compensated for the additional work of learning new online platforms and reconfiguring entire courses. Under the specter of financial crisis, university administration cut classes for adjuncts and terminated multiyear contracts.

We cannot begin a cycle of redemption and forgiveness if we cannot see the engine of exploitation and extraction, and our own complicity, that runs academia.

Angela Veronica Wong is an educator, writer, and artist living in New York City. She is the author of two books of poetry, including *Elsa: An Unauthorized Autobiography*. Her most recent publications include an essay on Mariah Carey, Hello Kitty, and public mourning. She is on the internet at www.angelaveronicawong.com or @avwusesherwords on Twitter.

Note

1. When you have some time to kill, gift yourself the imaginative Kaylor fan theories. Those who claim close reading is irrelevant have clearly never spent two weeks with the twelve- to eighteen-year-old set as they pore over celebrity photos, searching for sustenance.

Works Cited

Aviles, Gwen. "Uproar after Latina Professor at Harvard Denied tenure." *NBC News*, 4 Dec. 2019, nbcnews.com/news/latino/uproar-after-harvard-s-only-latina-professor-tenure-track-denied-n1095871. Accessed 19 Oct. 2021.

Batty, David. "Cambridge May Drop BAME Mentoring of White Academics." *The Guardian*, 14 Mar. 2020, theguardian.com/education/2020/mar/14/cambridge-may-drop-bame-mentoring-of-white-academics. Accessed 19 Oct. 2021.

Chu, Andrea Long. "I Worked with Avital Ronell. I Believe Her Accuser." *Chronicle of Higher Education*, 30 Aug. 2018, chronicle.com/article/i-worked-with-avital-ronell-i-believe-her-accuser/. Accessed 19 Oct. 2021.

"Data Visualizations of Full-Time Women Faculty and Faculty of Color." *American Association of University Professors*, aaup.org/data-visualizations-full-time-women-faculty-and-faculty-color. Accessed 19 Oct. 2021.

Don't Tell Mom the Babysitter's Dead. Directed by Stephen Herek, Outlaw Productions, 1991.

Federici, Silvia. "How the Demonization of "Gossip" Is Used to Break Women's Solidarity." *In These Times*, 31 Jan. 2019, inthesetimes.com/article/the-subversive-feminist-power-of-gossip. Accessed 19 Oct. 2021.

Flaherty, Colleen. "Separate and Not Equal." *Inside Higher Education*, 29 Nov. 2016, insidehighered.com/news/2016/11/29/book-argues-faculty-members-color-going-tenure-are-judged-different-standard-white. Accessed 19 Oct. 2021.

Greenberg, Zoe. "What Happens to #MeToo When a Feminist Is the Accused?" *New York Times*, 13 Aug. 2018, nytimes.com/2018/08/13/nyregion/sexual-harassment-nyu-female-professor.html. Accessed 19 Oct. 2021.

Lederman, Doug. "The Faculty Shrinks, but Tilts to Full-Time." *Inside Higher Education*, 27 Nov. 2019, insidehighered.com/news/2019/11/27/federal-data-show-proportion-instructors-who-work-full-time-rising. Accessed 19 Oct. 2021.

McCarthy, Tom. "Albright: 'Special Place in Hell' for Women Who Don't Support Clinton." *The Guardian*, 6 Feb. 2016, theguardian.com/us-news/2016/feb/06/madeleine-albright-campaigns-for-hillary-clinton. Accessed 19 Oct. 2021.

Matthew, Patricia A. "What Is Faculty Diversity Worth to a University?" *Atlantic*, 23 Nov. 2016, theatlantic.com/education/archive/2016/11/what-is-faculty-diversity-worth-to-a-university/508334/. Accessed 19 Oct. 2021.

Mizoguchi, Karen, and Eric Todisco. "Taylor Swift Felt 'So Much Lighter' about Her Life Once She and Katy Perry Reconciled." *People*, 18 June 2019, https://people.com/music/taylor-swift-katy-perry-reconciliation-felt-lighter/. Accessed 19 Oct. 2021.

Okahana, Hironao, and Enyu Zhou. *Graduate Enrollment and Degrees: 2007–2017.* Council of Graduate Schools, Oct. 2018, https://legacy.cgsnet.org/publication-pdf/5464/CGS_GED17_Report.pdf.

"Racial/Ethnic Distribution of Advanced Degrees in the Humanities." *American Academy of Arts and Sciences*, amacad.org/humanities-indicators/higher-education/racialethnic-distribution-advanced-degrees-humanities. Accessed 19 Oct. 2021.

Vettese, Troy. "Sexism in the Academy: Women's Narrowing Path to Tenure." *N+1*, no. 34, Spring 2019, nplusonemag.com/issue-34/essays/sexism-in-the-academy/. Accessed 19 Oct. 2021.

Wimmer, Rachel. "Mentoring Study Helps Redefine Success for Women in Academia." *UCF Today*, 28 Jan. 2019, ucf.edu/news/mentoring-study-helps-redefine-success-women-academia/. Accessed 19 Oct. 2021.